BEYOND
THE
MYTH

For my friend Arurima

With best wishes

Jayati Bhattacharya

18·8·2011·

The **Institute of Southeast Asian Studies (ISEAS)** was established as an autonomous organization in 1968. It is a regional research centre dedicated to the study of socio-political, security and economic trends and developments in Southeast Asia and its wider geostrategic and economic environment. The Institute's research programmes are the Regional Economic Studies (RES, including ASEAN and APEC), Regional Strategic and Political Studies (RSPS), and Regional Social and Cultural Studies (RSCS).

ISEAS Publishing, an established academic press, has issued more than 2,000 books and journals. It is the largest scholarly publisher of research about Southeast Asia from within the region. ISEAS Publishing works with many other academic and trade publishers and distributors to disseminate important research and analyses from and about Southeast Asia to the rest of the world.

BEYOND THE MYTH

INDIAN BUSINESS COMMUNITIES IN SINGAPORE

JAYATI BHATTACHARYA

INSTITUTE OF SOUTHEAST ASIAN STUDIES

Singapore

First published in Singapore in 2011 by ISEAS Publishing
Institute of Southeast Asian Studies
30 Heng Mui Keng Terrace
Pasir Panjang
Singapore 119614

E-mail: publish@iseas.edu.sg
Website: <http://bookshop.iseas.edu.sg>

The responsibility for facts and opinions in this publication rests exclusively with the author and her interpretations do not necessarily reflect the views or the policy of the publisher or its supporters.

ISEAS Library Cataloguing-in-Publication Data

Bhattacharya, Jayati.
    Beyond the myth : Indian business communities in Singapore.
    1. Indians (Asian people)—Singapore—Economic conditions.
    2. Businesspeople—Singapore.
    3. Business enterprises—Singapore.
    4. Trade associations—Singapore.
    I. Title.
DS610.25 I3B57   2011

ISBN 978-981-4311-36-6 (soft cover)
ISBN 978-981-4345-27-9 (hard cover)
ISBN 978-981-4311-37-3 (E-book PDF)

Cover photo (top right): Singapore River at present. Photo taken by the author, 2011.
Cover photo (bottom): Singapore River, 1960s. Photo from the Kouo Shang-Wei Collection. Reproduced with kind permission from the Family of Kouo Shang-Wei and the National Library Board.

Typeset by Superskill Graphics Pte Ltd
Printed in Singapore by Mainland Press Pte Ltd

Dedicated to My Family

CONTENTS

PART TWO

LIST OF MAP, TABLES AND FIGURES

MESSAGE

Dr Jayati Bhattacharya's book is a much-awaited work on the ethnic Indian business communities in Singapore. It analyses the subject comprehensively through different time periods and in different socio-political contexts. The book will make interesting reading beyond academia and the business world.

On behalf of the Singapore Indian Chamber of Commerce and Industry, I would like to congratulate Dr Bhattacharya. I wish her good luck in her future academic endeavours.

R. Narayanmohan
Chairman
Singapore Indian Chamber of Commerce
and Industry (SICCI)

FOREWORD

Since the pioneering work of Kernail Singh Sandhu and
S. Arasaratnam, studies of Indian communities in Singapore (and
Malaya/Malaysia) have grown significantly in scope and content.
Even before "Diaspora Studies" became topical, a spate of scholarly
and popular accounts, detailing the rich diversity and spread
of overseas Indians in Southeast Asia, published in the 1970s
and 1980s, has enriched our understanding of the movement
to, settlement in, and socialization of Indian communities in
their adopted homelands outside the Indian subcontinent. The
monumental trailblazer, *Indian Communities in Southeast* Asia,
edited by K.S. Sandhu and A. Mani (first published by the Institute
of Southeast Asian Studies in 1993, and reprinted in 2006) marked
a significant scholarly milestone in the development of the field
by bringing together, in one volume, in-depth analyses of Indian
communities settled in various parts of the region. This was
followed in 2006 by the publication of the *Encyclopedia of Indian
Diaspora,* produced by a group of scholars from the National
University of Singapore, which is, to date, still probably the most
comprehensive and authoritative account of the global South
Asian Diaspora. Close at its heels was the sequel to the earlier
book by ISEAS, *Rising India and Indian Communities in East Asia,*
edited by K. Kesavapany, A. Mani and P. Ramasamy (published in
2008), which provided scholarly perceptions of the changes and

transformations of Indians in East Asia with India's economic rise. Scholars in Singapore have, in many respects, provided an intellectual lead on research on the Indian Diaspora.

Continuing in that tradition, this volume is a useful addition to the expanding literature on the Indian community in Singapore and its major contribution lies in the fact that it is perhaps the first to focus exclusively on the local Indian business community. Taking a long view of the historical association of Indian business communities with the development of Singapore, the author explains the roles played by these communities in the country's modern economic history. Since its inception as a colonial port city, Singapore has attracted business and commercial classes to its shores. Among them were Indian trading communities, which already had their own long history of engagement with this part of the world. Setting up bases in Singapore, these commercial classes grew their businesses across the Indian Ocean through intricate and expanding trading networks, based mainly on family and kinship ties. The economic and social features of the commercial communities were, in the main, defined by the spaces and contexts of these transnational networks. This particular phenomenon is explained in this volume, which traces the evolution of the Indian business community and their commercial networks through a rich narrative of human and institutional accounts. Through these narratives, we have a well-told story of the manner in which business structures and practices have evolved in the changing contexts of Singapore's development, from colony to nation-state and global city. In the stories recounted in this study, the theme of adaptation features prominently. While staying true to their commercial calling, many enterprising business individuals and families were able to leverage on new opportunities, such as the economic rise of India, to grow and diversify their business portfolios. In this regard, the stories in this volume do not focus on the familiar themes of migration and settlement; rather, they reveal new and interesting dimensions on social change, network negotiations, organizational evolution and business strategies.

Writing business history is never a simple enterprise. The writer who needs to ground the account on sources and data will be frustrated by the inevitable dearth of useful sources in the public domain. Understandably, family businesses tend to guard their privacy, and will not readily divulge trade practices and business strategies for public scrutiny. This current study has obviously encountered some of these difficulties. Still, the writer should be commended for presenting a useful and interesting narrative, combining the histories of individuals, families and organizations in place of a "dry as bones" data-dominated economic history. Set in the contexts of Singapore's socio-economic development, this is a story of many parts: it is part social history; part business history; and part history of Singapore.

Tan Tai Yong
Professor of History
National University of Singapore

MESSAGE

In mid-2007, Dr Jayati Bhattacharya had approached me with this research proposal. It looked like a difficult proposition in view of the limited available sources on the subject. Gradually, as she began exploring different avenues for source materials, we had further discussions and the proposition looked feasible. What has been achieved is an analysis of the broad history of Indian business communities in Singapore spanning roughly over a century and a half. The book is the coordination and contextualization of the thoughts and ideas of the participating businessmen and entrepreneurs who have lived through different phases of Singapore's modern history. It is to Dr Bhattacharya's credit that she has ventured into an area that none had done so in the past. A book-length study of this kind has not been attempted before.

In recent decades, especially with the dawn of the new century, Singapore-India relations have attained new heights with an intensity of bilateral exchanges on the political, economic and social fronts. Against this background, a study of the different aspects of the multi-dimensional facets of Singapore-India relations could not have been more opportune. The signing of the Comprehensive Economic Cooperation Agreement (CECA) has further catapulted the volume of bilateral trade.

If Indian liberalization programmes in the 1990s has ushered immense opportunities of development for Indians, both on their home ground as well as abroad, Singapore has ably managed to attract a large pool of professional and entrepreneurial talent to enhance its status as a knowledge-based economy. Singapore has also served as a base for Indian companies to expand their venture into the Asia-Pacific region. As such, the complementary policy initiatives of both the states have been advantageous to business communities on both sides and have catalyzed and contributed to the "rising Asia" phenomenon. These changing paradigms of thought and action have been addressed in this research work. This book could pave the way for further research on lesser-known aspects of such linkages and connectivities in Southeast Asia.

ISEAS is happy to support this work by a young scholar from India now settled in Singapore with her family.

K. Kesavapany
Director
Institute of Southeast Asian Studies
Singapore

ACKNOWLEDGEMENTS

This research work has been a difficult and demanding journey, but, a fruitful and fulfilling one. There are innumerable people who have supported and helped me, directly and indirectly, to achieve this task. I express my heartfelt thanks to all of them and my sincere apologies for not being able to mention all the names individually.

I owe my deepest gratitude to ISEAS Director, Ambassador K. Kesavapany, without whose support and confidence, the book would not have seen the light of the day. He had given me the opportunity of joining ISEAS as a Visiting Research Fellow to work on this project and has been a constant source of encouragement throughout this academic journey. I shall remain ever thankful to the Institute and to Ambassador Kesavapany for nurturing my academic pursuits. I would also like to thank the Singapore Indian Chamber of Commerce and Industry (SICCI) for financially supporting this project and many of its members for sharing their time and valuable information. I would especially like to thank Mr Predeep Menon, former CEO and Executive Director of SICCI, for his patience and endurance during our various interactions and long meetings, and for sharing his insights into the Indian business community in Singapore. The present Chairman of SICCI, Mr Narayanmohan, has also helped me by sharing his long years of entrepreneurial experiences in Singapore and giving important inputs.

I owe my gratitude to all the members of the Indian business community who spared their most scarce resource, that is time, to enlighten me with their point of views on various aspects related to this research, without which this project could not have been completed. I would like to specially mention Mr Inderjeet Singh, Member of Parliament in Singapore and an established entrepreneur; Mr N.G. Chanrai, Director of Kewalram Group of Companies; Mr Sunny Vergese, CEO of Olam International Ltd. and Chairman of IE Singapore; Mr Vijay Iyengar, Director of Agrocorp and former Chairman of SICCI; Mr T. Chandroo, Director of MMI International; Mr Rajakumar Chandra, owner of JSFS in Little India and President of LISHA; Mr G. Shanmugam, owner of Gayatri Restaurant and President of IRA(S); Mr Haider Sithawalla, Director of KSP Group of Companies and Non-Resident High Commissioner to Mauritius and Zimbabwe; Mr J.M. Jumabhoy, former President of SICCI and retired entrepreneur, who in spite of his frail health, talked to me for a considerable length of time; and Mr George Abraham of GA Group Pte. Ltd. and former CEO of SICCI, for sharing their thoughts which enriched my research. Mrs Vivian Chandran, wife of late Robert Chandran, the founder of Chemoil had been very kind to send her comments and feedback after reading my case study on the organization. I am very thankful to her for that. My sincere thanks to Mr V. Vasudevan, Director of Delta Exports Pte. Ltd., who by his narratives introduced me to the Indian business scenario for the last few decades and helped me to formulate fresh perspectives in research at the very outset, and Mr Chhatru Vaswani for not only spending time with me for prolonged discussions and providing research materials on the Sindhi business community, but also translating many of the early Sindhi documents in English for my research.

The Indian High Commission in Singapore has been very supportive in providing me with various documents and allowing me to use its library. The conversations with HE Dr S. Jaishankar, former High Commissioner of India to Singapore, and Mr Rajesh Sachdeva, former Deputy High Commissioner of India to Singapore and Dr K.N. Raghavan, First Secretary (Commercial) have been extremely useful in influencing various aspects of this research. The staff at the National Archives of Singapore, the Asian Civilizations Museum (ACM) and the National Library Board (NLB) have been most cooperative in providing various documents, manuscripts and photographs which have gone into the making of this book. Special mention needs to be made of Dr Gauri Krishnan, Deputy Director, ACM, for her help and support. For the translations from various Tamil sources, Ms Valli Meyappan, currently a student at Nanyang Technological University, has ably assisted me as well as in transcribing interviews and other oral history sources.

My colleagues at ISEAS have been my relentless source of inspiration and strength. Dr Vijay Sakuja, former Senior Visiting Research Fellow at ISEAS, patiently bore the brunt of the initial sounding board of my ideas. Professor A. Mani, Dr Geoff Wade and Mr Asad-ul Iqbal Latif helped by proofreading and giving their comments of the different sections of the manuscript. I am also thankful to Dr Tansen Sen, Head of the Nalanda-Sriwijaya Centre at ISEAS, for his support and initiative in publishing the book in India as well. My heartfelt thanks to Mr Mustafa Izzuddin for sharing his inputs on the Bohra community and to Dr Jayani Bonnerjee for reading my manuscript. I also thank Ms Rinkoo Bhowmik for helping me with suggestions on the book cover. My colleagues at the Administration Unit and the ISEAS Library deserve special mention for their ever-willing-to-help gestures. A very special thanks to Mrs Triena Ong, Head of ISEAS Publications Unit, for her prompt, precise and professional way of handling the necessary details of publication, and to Ms Sheryl Sin, my copy editor, for her timely suggestions.

On a more personal note, I owe my special thanks to my mentor and teacher, Professor T.K. Roy Choudhury, who has always encouraged and guided me in my quest for knowledge and research, and instilled in me the confidence to surge forward. Above all, I will forever remain indebted to my family for their forbearance and constant support. My husband, Mr Prasenjit Bhattacharya, has been my biggest source of motivation. In spite of his hectic schedules and vigorous travelling for his corporate job, his timely suggestions and critiques were of invaluable help. I have also derived strength from my daughter, Noushka, who has patiently sacrificed many irreversible "mother-daughter moments" for my research work. I will ever be indebted to her for her understanding and composure, little expected from her kindergarten years. I hope that she grows up to believe that her sacrifices were all for a good cause.

I also wish to thank the anonymous reviewers, whose suggestions have helped me improve the manuscript. However, I am solely responsible for any errors and mistakes that might remain.

Jayati Bhattacharya

LIST OF ABBREVIATIONS

AIT	Approved International Trader
ASEAN	Association of Southeast Asian Nations
CECA	Comprehensive Economic Cooperation Agreement
CII	Confederation of Indian Industries
CUP	Cambridge University Press
EDB	Economic Development Board
EDC	Enterprise Development Centre
FASS	Faculty of Arts and Social Sciences
FDI	Foreign Direct Investment
FICCI	Federation of Indian Chambers of Commerce and Industry
FTA	Free Trade Agreement
GIBS	Global Indian Business Summit
GLC	Government Linked Company
HEB	Hindu Endowments Board
IBF	Indian Business Forum
ICT	Information and Communication Technology
IDA	Infocomm Development Authority of Singapore
IE	International Enterprise
IMA	Indian Merchants Association
INSEAD	Institut Européen d'Administration des Affaires (European Institute for Business Administration)
IPCS	Institute of Peace and Conflict Studies, New Delhi

IRAS	Indian Restaurant Association of Singapore
ISAS	Institute of South Asian Studies
ISEAS	Institute of Southeast Asian Studies
IT	Information Technology
JSFS	Jothi Stores and Flower Shop
JSG	Joint Study Group
LIRA	Little India Restaurants Association
LISHA	Little India Shopkeepers and Heritage Association
MOIA	Ministry of Overseas Indian Affairs, New Delhi
MOU	Memorandum of Understanding
MRA	Mutual Recognition Agreement
NAS	National Archives of Singapore
NLB	National Library Board
NRI	Non-Resident Indian
NUS	National University of Singapore
OUP	Oxford University Press
PBD	Pravasi Bharatiya Divas
PIO	People of Indian Origin
PNYI	Professional Network of Young Indians
QFB	Qualifying Full Bank
RAS	Restaurant Association of Singapore
RIS	Research and Information System for the Non-Aligned and other Developing Countries, New Delhi
SAAG	South Asia Analysis Group
SASP	South Asian Studies Programme
SBF	Singapore Business Federation
SCCCI	Singapore Chinese Chamber of Commerce and Industry
SEB	Small Enterprises Bureau
SFCCI	Singapore Federation of Chambers of Commerce and Industry
SIBA	Singapore Indian Business Association

SICC	Singapore International Chamber of Commerce
SICCI	Singapore Indian Chamber of Commerce and Industry
SIEA	Singapore Indian Entrepreneur Awards
SMCCI	Singapore Malaysian Chamber of Commerce and Industry
SME	Small and Medium Enterprises
STB	Singapore Tourism Board
TDB	Trade Development Board
URA	Urban Redevelopment Authority
VLCC	Very Large Crude Carrier
WGT	Working Group on Trade
WIN	Women's India Network

INTRODUCTION

Conventional historiography has had a tendency of associating the migration patterns of Indians to considerations of amelioration of their livelihood standards that was facilitated by the mechanisms of a hegemonic colonial economy and administration. Traditionally, attention has been generally focused on that largest segment of the minority ethnic groups of the region, a large social component of which comprised of migrant labour. Contrary to popular belief, large scale transnational flows of capital, goods and people were often well-organized into efficient systems of networks through different phases in history. In spite of intra-community differences in matters of castes or religion, these transnational connections were carefully bound by kinship ties and community networks that facilitated their global outreach much before the colonists had appeared on the scene.[1] Colonial intervention prompted them to reorganize and negotiate their business activities emerging out of opportunities and conveniences in the macroeconomic structure of colonial hegemony. Right from ancient times, Asia was in the throes of globalization that was demonstrated through the extensive trading systems within Asia, that is, China, Southeast Asia and India that extended as far as the trading systems of the Persian Gulf and the Mediterranean territories. Asian states expeditiously demonstrated their capacity and capability to harness the benefits of globalization prior to the arrival of the colonial rulers. In that context, it would be helpful to remember that even in the nineteenth century Asia contributed around one-third of the global economy.[2]

That the Indian business communities are a minority amongst a minority in the demographic structure of Southeast Asia cannot be contested, but their importance, both economically and socially, requires attention and consideration of greater analysis and research. For the people of the Indian subcontinent, the interregional spatial mobility had not been an introduction of the colonists — the traders, merchants, pilgrims and mariners were, in the words of Sugata Bose, tied to the world of the Indian Ocean "by webs of economic and cultural relationships" ... with "flexible internal and external boundaries".[3] This book makes an effort to draw a linear narrative of the ethnic Indian business community through the generations, particularly since the coming of Raffles to the island, dealing with its heterogeneities and complexities in matters linguistic, economic and cultural, and attempts to situate them in the larger framework of the multicultural background in the Singapore milieu.

The study of annals and movements of business communities is a digression from the conventional paradigms of sociological and anthropological narratives of the diaspora, though also closely associated with the peoples' movements in multifarious trajectories. It encompasses a broad organizational terrain of vertical and lateral networks[4] that serves as forms of incorporation and integration in the host country and their relationship with the complexities of economic networks. Almost all voluntary mobilities could be related to better economic opportunities and is articulated through the flows of people, capital and, now, knowledge. The traditional paradigm of the exchanges of labour and capital has been shifted to the contemporary transnational global networks connecting the home country with economic exchanges like remittances, commercial networks, investments or philanthropic sponsorships. In the circulation of population, money, goods and information, players have changed and global world of capital has shifted through generations.

I

Ancient Indian history is replete with numerous examples of explorers, traders and pilgrims between India and different parts of the world, almost since the age of Emperor Augustus in Rome (around 30 BC) when maritime trade flourished between Rome and India. The discovery of the Monsoons in AD 40[5] had encouraged and increased traffic of maritime commerce and political activities both in the Red Sea and the western coast of India as well as the Southeast Asia and the eastern coast. Ships sailed from the port of Tamralipti (a coastal area in modern West Bengal, India) to Suvarnabhumi (the land of gold; the Sanskrit name for modern Sumatra) through the Andaman Sea through the Ten Degree Channel in the winters to arrive in the west coast of Malaya.[6] From there they sailed through the Straits of Malacca to lower Sumatra and Borneo. The items of trade included silk, textiles, spices, jewels, medicinal drugs, incense, china and glass, which were carried further westwards to the Arabian and Greek merchants. This is not to reiterate the geopolitical theory of the subcontinent's hegemony from "Aden to Southeast Asia" in comparison to the later period of colonial suzerainty in a similar domain, used as a point of reference by some scholars to draw a similarity in ancient India[7] with the British supremacy in the Indian Ocean. It might, however, be regarded as rather a broader aspect of cultural influences and interactions culminating from continuous trade exchanges for generations with the Southeast Asian states. There had been sporadic political engagements, but the impact had been far more long-lasting and deep-rooted than any political invasions. Even in political dimensions, Indian rulers have, in certain cases carried out a policy of vassal states, granting autonomous power to the conquered both within the territorial borders of the subcontinent and elsewhere. The paradigm of comparative analysis between the much more politically belligerent and economically aggressive colonial rule with the approach of Indian influence rests on unsteady grounds.

Well-established trade routes, both through the land and the sea formed the major source of connectivity for economic, political and cultural exchanges for the Indian subcontinent throughout the world. Added to it was the political patronage and expansion from different regions and times. In the North, the Kushanas had a formidable influence in many parts of China that had helped to build extensive trade networks. Besides, the famous Silk route took back trade linkages to two millennia. The Cholas of South India had promoted a flourishing maritime trade with the Malaya archipelago[8] and thus encouraged economic and cultural exchanges. Their political pursuits took them as far as Sri Vijaya (modern day Indonesia) and beyond. The existence of merchant guilds and several edicts and inscriptions in South India depicting rules and norms laid down for foreign merchants[9] directly reveal the extent of trading facilities and practices enjoyed by the foreign merchants. The spread of Hinduism and Buddhism in ancient India to Southeast and East Asia and its consequent acculturation also played a significant role in the Indian influence over a large part of Asia. With a wide network of well-established trade routes, both by land and sea, it seems that the interaction and trading activities had never ceased, but the dimensions became different. With the onset of colonization from seventeenth and eighteenth century onwards, the nature and style of indigenous rules and norms gave way to a more imposed and westernized structural framework of operations. "Indian" and "Indianness" in the Asian perspective, suddenly changed its meaning to cater to the trends of modern colonization and imperialism.

In the circulation of populations across the Indian Ocean, there were constant efforts at integration and consolidation which resulted in unique manifestations, both in the economic and cultural dimensions. In the present context of the Indian business diaspora in Singapore, the complexities and overlapping interests of different groups of traders and businessmen form an interesting study in terms of the various aspects of these trading bodies, their methods of operation and their trade links, both within and outside Singapore and also their mobility and progress, both in terms of business and social status. This work is an attempt to bring forth certain aspects of the Indian linkages to Southeast Asia, particularly Singapore, deconstructing the acclimatized notion of earlier Indian presence, more simplistically put in the conventional history of Singapore solely as either convicts or indentured labour. As it has been generally believed, "Wherever the system exists, there the Indians are only known as coolies, no matter what their position might be."[10] While the presence of Indian labourers was an undeniable truth, it need not obliterate the constant presence in Singapore and other parts of Southeast Asia of traders and merchants from different regions of India. The symbolic story of Narayana Pillai (refer to Chapter 1 for further details) starts with the arrival of Raffles into the island nation. The establishment and development of a trading port here by the British undoubtedly facilitated the activities of the Indian merchants and traders, but this was only a part and process of continuity established long before in the region. Referring to the Indian Ocean economy involving the Indian and the Chinese participation in trade and finance, Rajat Kanta Ray, in one of his essays, argues that it formed "a distinct international system that never lost its identity in the larger dominant world system of the West."[11] The existence of this indigenous system of networks and business operation is further exemplified in Claude Markovits' work on the Sindhi merchant community.[12] Scholars like Rajeswary Ampalavanar Brown has also had considerable researches on Indian participation in the Asian business networks as well, both of them emphasizing on the indigenous connections and commercial links that was well synchronized and efficient.[13]

The present research forms an initial attempt to situate Indian business communities in Singapore in the course of their negotiation with the political, economic and social forces at different periods of time in the island nation, and thus makes an effort to contest the "myth" in the context of the composition of the Indian diaspora. It makes a modest beginning in terms of addressing the vast scope of scholarship that exists in the relatively unexploited terrain in the study of diasporic Indian business communities beyond the conventional constructed notions of the demographic structure in the gradual growth and development of the communities in different parts of Southeast Asia. There have been only a few researches which are devoted to the study of the Asian systems of trade networks through the lenses of a less Euro-centric vision. Takeshi Hamashita has rightly argued that the formation and functioning of the Asian trade networks had been propelled by forces emerging from within Asia and not essentially "formed" by the impact of Western hegemony, but rather "organized" and developed by them to an extent.[14] Chandra Jayawardena, while making a survey of the migratory Indians contends that the "development of colonial economies also created several commercial and petty industrial opportunities at those points where the Western capitalist economy articulated with the indigenous rural economy."[15] Both the Indians and the

Chinese commercial migrants had been able to tap these lucrative opportunities successfully and "provided the entrepreneurs who settled in the nooks and crannies of the colonial economies".[16]

Set in the paradigm of continuity and connectivity of the South Asian trade network with Southeast Asia and the world, this research work looks at the colonial and the post-independent phase in Singapore, recognizing the long-lasting presence of the Indians in the commercial world and the metamorphosis that it underwent at subsequent stages of nation-building and globalization. The chosen form of multiculturalism in the post-colonial phase, as in Singapore, promoted, as Clammer suggests, a "blending of differences and co-existence of alternatives within the same spatial contexts".[17] The Indian business communities then faced the challenges of restructuring themselves in the national framework of industrialization and technical innovations. It might be interesting to note how with all distinct and quite complex characteristics of the different ethnic bodies, they could apparently position themselves, parallel with other groups, within the larger framework of the Singaporean system.[18] The policy initiatives and the integrative approach of the Singaporean Government helped maintain the diasporic networks and retention of cultural roots, and at the same time fitting well with the multi-ethnicity propagated since the post-independence years. The present discussion on Indian business communities have, however, often been situated in the larger social and political context of the Indian communities to help provide a more comprehensive understanding of their changing rhetoric in geopolitical and sociocultural dimensions.

With the new waves of globalization, condensed geopolitical boundaries and increasing influence of consumer capitalism, there have been further challenges of negotiations in the circulatory movements of a mobile diaspora within Asia and beyond. The rise of post-colonial deconstruction and post-modern trends in Asian historiography and contemporary transnationalism has been notions that are well-accepted and deal with the mobile groups of people across fluid boundaries facilitated by the high technological innovations. Steven Vertovec has thus defined the present phenomenon:

> Transnationalism describes a condition in which, despite great distances and notwithstanding the presence of international borders (and all the laws, regulations and national narratives they present), certain kinds of relationships have been globally intensified and now take place paradoxically in a planet — spanning yet common — however virtual — arena of activity.[19]

Similar notions on issues of migration and territorial spaces associated with it have been in resonance with Robin Cohen who has pointed out that "transnational bonds no longer have to be cemented by migration or by exclusive territorial claims."[20] The concepts of "shared imagination" and common consciousness of the diasporic overtures have been complemented by global economic networks, the transnational corporations (TNCs) and the multinational corporations (MNCs) resulting in the new cultural dynamism.

The twenty-first century phenomenon, surfacing from the post-Cold War days, attempts to disseminate and diffuse commercial linkages beyond geographical boundaries with the emergence of the "knowledge economy".[21] The bulk of economic productivity and wealth in contemporary times has been generated by knowledge, which has transcended beyond political boundaries to capture the expansive world market and integrate production through means of global networks, almost defying "state surveillance".[22] Rather, the national policy initiatives of different emerging economies have been modified to circumvent this development and have encouraged a greater global integration. The Indian diaspora has come to be an active participant in this global phenomenon, which coincides well with the "Rise of Asia" and transmigrational mobility in the interplay of Asian market forces. This has generated a new growth trajectory in the plethora of commercial activities, which has little resemblance to the traditional position of the community in Singapore as well as in the rest of Southeast Asia. Building on the threads of historical connectivity and shifting through the various phases of market functions in Asian history, the growth trajectory of the Indian communities has gone much beyond the conventional diasporic thought processes and myth of shared homeland and spaces. The emerging diasporic consciousness is more about "multiplicity of histories, 'communities' and selves ..."[23] and the new "transnational imaginary".[24] The entrepreneurial fluidity across the boundaries and increasing global virtual connectivity has prompted it to be more a matter of conveniences than compulsions.

The Indian mercantile communities, even prior to the colonial times, had been a heterogeneous group representing a wide range of commercial activities from peddling to highly developed regional and international trading and finance operations. In spite of the heterogeneity, as Claude Markovits points out, there was a general pattern in the operational mechanisms where great importance was given to the family and there was a "predominant role of the *banias*",[25] the merchant caste of the Hindus and the Jains. One of the notable attributes of the existing system was the institution of guilds,[26] which were strong associations of ethnic merchants bonded with well-defined codes of conduct (this was much before the evolution of the Chambers of Commerce). There was also the unique system of *hundi*, the indigenous bills of exchange and the highly organized system of circulating credit facilities among the ethnic merchant bodies. These clearly reflected the existence of sophisticated and efficient regional mercantile entities as well as the successful functioning of the intra-ethnic networking of these communities. Some of these ethnic bodies like the Gujaratis, the Sindhis, the Chettiars and eventually the Punjabis (the Punjabis came much later than the others) looked beyond the seas from early times and became dominant trading and commercial groups in the Southeast Asian waters. The spread of British colonial wings in these waters facilitated the commercial exchanges with similar administrative structures, communication networks and infrastructural facilities on the one hand, but at the same time marginalizing the indigenous, self-sufficient networks with the over-looming economic and political hegemony on the other. The network of migratory Indian merchant bodies, according to some scholars, "operated outside the purview or interest of the colonial state".[27] However, it might be argued that they remained effective in the inland distribution system of manufactured goods, expanding the market for the colonialists in the hinterland trade, interacting with them at some nodal points and entrepot ports. While the Indians, pushed to the periphery, set to modify, recast and negotiate their entity with the needs of time, history was being re-written with Western notions gradually altering the established equations of the indigenous merchant diasporas and dynamic Oriental uniqueness, partly due to their inability to comprehend the complexities involved and partly ignoring them with hegemonic assertiveness.[28]

Set in the retrospect of colonialism, the history of Indians in Singapore is as old as the coming of Raffles to this island in 1819. Indian immigration mostly continued through import of Tamil labour to toil on public works, ports and plantations. Labourers continued to be a major element of the community and even in 1957 about 44 per cent of working Indians on the island were labourers.[29] However, there were other groups, one comprising of the English-educated middle class employed in clerical and technical positions, the other consisting of highly professional individuals earning high remunerations. Yet another group existed — the commercial sector, comprising of capitalists, entrepreneurs, middle-level traders as well as small hawkers and peddlers. The heterogeneity of their activities as well as their diverse ethno-linguistic genealogy has facilitated to portray the image of the group as "communities" rather than loosely generalizing it with an imposed homogeneity. Even in contemporary parlance, where one might argue about a homogeneous entrepreneurial zeal and considerable social mobility, there has been witnessed an inescapable divide in the mindset of the different generations of ethnic Indian business migrants in Singapore, and the existing contested beliefs and convictions within the community cannot be ignored. At the same time, there are certain elements of cohesion from the broader perspective of diasporic connectivity with the Indian subcontinent — the "unity in diversity" factor, which imparts an external homogeneity to ethnic Indian roots. With this duality and ambivalence, one is tempted to use the reference of both "the community" and "communities" as and when applicable.

II

Construction of the hypothesis has followed a pattern of a storyline with occasional vignettes of small details and mundane trade practices, which has been significant and helpful in the course of the narration. Kishore Mahbubani in his book writes, "Most people relate to human stories, not to statistics."[30] One could opine that narratives are sometimes more significant than mere statistical figures. However, the sparse statistical data within the study has not always been intentional. The dearth of adequate statistical information has made scholarship undertaken in this area of study a complex proposition, which has been well-accepted by historians and other researchers working in this area, motivating them to look for circumstantial evidences, oral history sources and other sources of information to support their hypothesis.

> Whereas European companies and countries contain rich sources amenable to statistical treatment, that is not the case for many economies in the Indian Ocean and the China Sea. That explains why many ...authors use biographical sources and anthropological research to fortify their cases. However, to dismiss their findings because of lack of statistical information would be a serious mistake.[31]

The methodology for the research has been based on relevant, though inadequate archival materials, several newspaper articles, oral history sources, related secondary sources and extensive conversations with the members of the business communities. The available sources at the British libraries and archives could not be used due to several constraints as also the exhaustive use of Tamil publications. However, Some Tamil and Sindhi primary and secondary sources have been translated and utilized in the hypothesis. About fifty interviews and short conversations have been conducted covering different sectors of trade as well as from different levels of economic strata. However, there were limitations regarding the interviewees' willingness to converse and their extremely guarded approach. The websites of the related business organizations have also been used quite liberally, especially for the case studies to obtain information regarding their enterprises. The names of a few individual entrepreneurs and their business concerns have been mentioned in the research work, sometimes with some details. These have been done indiscriminately with no deliberate attempt to highlight any particular firm or person, but to exemplify the hypothetical analysis and fit the narration into the thread of continuity of different generations of businessmen and enterprises. Besides, the mention of specific personal narratives also helped the study to be more informative on the entrepreneurial ventures of the community. However, this work does not serve as a directory of business names but rather analyses and theorises different perspectives on the community as a whole.

The term "Indian", used in the research had been initially applied to people from all over the subcontinent, not really conforming to the political distinctions and barriers. As regards the social construct in the colonial days, the affiliation and allegiance of community sentiments of the ethnic Indians was more linguistically based, as was often witnessed in the sub-community stratification of the enclave structure in the island nation. Thus, in this study, for earlier times, the term, "Indian" has been used in accommodating, on many occasions, the larger populace of the subcontinent. However, in the post-Partition era, that is, beyond 1947, identification of an Indian has been confined within the Indian political boundaries, lest it offends different national sentiments.

This book is divided into two parts. The first part deals with a connecting narrative of three different phases of time — colonial, post-independence and contemporary, which are dealt with in the first three chapters. Even though a rigid timeline has not been drawn, the period from the coming of Raffles to Singapore, that is, 1819 to the recent year of 2008 has mainly been in focus in the research. The first chapter deals with situating the Indian business migrants under colonial hegemony in their structural landscapes and their intra-ethnic networks as well as interaction with the colonial economy until 1963. However, while discussing several ethnic groups of trading and merchant bodies, references have also been made to the contemporary context of their situation, without which the discussion would have remained abrupt and irrelevant. Similarly, many of the enterprises that have been discussed in the second chapter had its genesis in the earlier period; however, the period of their progress and prominence had been the post-independence era. Thus, compartmentalizing the different periods along with the enterprises, in a very strict sense of the term, could not be followed. In the second chapter, the business migrants are shown to have had to re-negotiate their space under the new political and economic order in the post-independent period in Singapore, with rapid strides in industrialization, technological innovations and competition in a free market economy leading to subsequent diversification by traditional merchant bodies. In the third chapter, another phase begins with the end of the Cold War, which witnessed a re-shuffle in the economies and political affiliations in Asia as in the rest of the world. It also saw the phenomenal rise of two developing nations in Asia — China and, within a decade, India. These global changes brought about a reorientation of the geopolitical scenario in Asia thereby bringing about an enhancement of bilateral relations between Singapore and India, ushering in a new period of economic transition amongst the ethnic Indian business communities. There has been an influx of a number of Indian companies into Singapore, who are subsidiaries and arms of their Indian counterparts, but conform to Singapore's legal conditions, thus forming a part of the Indian business diaspora. The third chapter examines the transition both in terms of current economic progress and new trends in migration.

The second part of the book attempts to deal with various associations and enterprises that have evolved over the time period mentioned in the first section. It begins with Chapter 4, looking at the various ethnic Indian business organizations that have developed in Singapore to give voice to diverse interest groups. It engages with numerous associations and networking bodies established by the various regional groups at different periods of time, with Singapore Indian Chamber of Commerce and Industry (SICCI) eventually emerging as the most prominent one, but also examines the relations between them and their relevance to the bigger Singaporean community on the whole. Efforts have also been made to look at their interrelationships with similar organizations of other ethnic groups. The narrative brings the development of the Indian business communities into contemporary times in a macro-level study of interregional human interactions, which facilitates ascertaining their identities from the dynamics of the larger Singaporean community. The power relations that have developed have also helped to catalyse conciliation with resurgent political and economic forces of South Asia.

The second chapter in the second section, that is, Chapter 5 is based on three different case studies relating to the research hypothesis. They represent three different kinds of enterprises which characterize their uniqueness in different areas of business activity (this had further elaboration in Chapter 5) and signify the diversity of operations of the Indian business communities. The first case is based on the Kewalram Chanrai Group — one which has diversified and transformed their business from a traditional family-held organization to a globalized entity spanning a period of about a century and a half, and which has successfully embraced the style of professional management. The second study represents a popular name in the retail sector, Mustafa, which has been immensely successful and achieved a kind of popularity that has made it one of the prominent places of tourist interest in Singapore, and the third represents a new generation enterprise, Chemoil, a listed company in the Singapore SGX, which has been, perhaps, one of the important global front runners in their business sector. Sometimes, direct interviews and opinions could not be attained due to unavoidable circumstances. It was, however, not absolutely indispensable in the present context of research, though it would have certainly been helpful with additional information. The writing for the case studies has been mostly based on extensive materials available in the public domain and based on author's interpretation and understanding. What was more important in context was to track their growth trajectory under different circumstances and periods of time.

The Indian business communities have quite firmly disseminated and embedded themselves in the Southeast Asian region through generations of interactions, circular migration and cultural integration. States like Singapore have emerged out of immigrant communities with distinct cultural manifestations in spite of mosaic demography on the one hand, and new layers of transnational networks with shift in organizational paradigms and globalized policy initiatives of different nation-states, shifts in global capital and fluidity of national borders on the other. This has resulted in a new trajectory of growth and entrepreneurial initiatives in the economy across the boundaries both within Asia and outside its periphery. Within the framework of contemporary discourse, the "old" and the "new" migrants have to deal with "cooperation and incorporations", "resistances and rejections" or "exchanges and exclusions"[32] in the landscape of intra-diaspora interactions. The transition and the transnational connections present an interesting context in the study of the Indian business communities in the region.

Notes

1.   Makrand Mehta, "Gujarati Business Communities in East African Diaspora: Major Historical Trends", *Economic and Political Weekly* 36, no. 20 (19–25 May 2001): 1738–47.

2. Lee Kuan Yew, "Asia's Growing Role in Financial Markets", *Straits Times*, 3 March 2008. Singapore's Minister Mentor cited Klaus W. Wellershoff, chief economist, UBS Global Wealth Management & Business Banking, in saying that Asia had been one of the richest regions of the world accounting for about two-thirds of the world's economy in the eighteenth century. Post-Industrial Revolution, it had declined to less than one-third at the beginning of the nineteenth century, reaching a low of 15 per cent of global income by 1950.

3. Sugata Bose, *A Hundred Horizons: The Indian Ocean in the Age of Global Empire* (Cambridge, Massachusetts, London: Harvard University Press, 2006), p. 6.

4. For further discussion, refer to Stanley J. Tambiah, "Transnational Movements, Diaspora, and Multiple Modernities", *Daedalus* 129, no. 1 (Winter 2000): 163–94.

5. Evidence of the knowledge of the monsoon winds first appears from Hippalus (45–47 AD). Sila Tripati and L.N. Raut, "Monsoon Wind and Maritime Trade: A Case Study of Historical Evidence from Orissa, India", *Current Science* 90, no. 6 (25 March 2006): 864–71.

6. Walter F. Vella, ed., *The Indianized States of Southeast Asia by G. Coedes* (Honolulu: East West Centre Press, 1968), p. 28.

7. For readings on Indian influence, refer to R.C. Mazumdar, *Hindu Colonies in the Far East*, 2nd ed. (revised and enlarged) (Calcutta: Firma K.L. Mukhopadhya, 1973); R.C. Majumdar, *Ancient Indian Colonization in South-East Asia*, 3rd ed., Maharaja Sahajirao Gaekwad Honorarium Lecture, 1953–54 (Baroda: Maharaja Sahajirao University of Baroda Press, 1971); Alfred T. Mahan had argued that the rise and fall of nations rested on the command of the sea. In that context, the influence of the Indians and subsequently the British may be compared and contrasted. Besides a lot of writings by Mahan himself, an appraisal of Mahan's ideas may be read from William E. Livezey's work, *Mahan on Sea Power*, revised edition (Norman, Oklahama: University of Oklaham Press, 1981).

8. R.C. Mazumdar, *Hindu Colonies in the Far East*, 2nd ed. (revised and enlarged) (Calcutta: Firma K.L. Mukhopadhya, 1973).

9. For further details, see Noboru Karasimha, ed., In *Search of Chinese Ceramic: Sherds in South India and Sri Lanka* (Tokyo: Taisho University Press, 2004) and the edited volume by the same author, *Ancient and Medieval Commercial Activities in the Indian Ocean: Testimony of Inscriptions and Ceramic-sherds* (Tokyo: Taisho University, 2002).

10. Gopal Krishna Gokhale, one of the early nationalist leaders in India, said this in 1912 while protesting against the continuation of indentured labour. Cited from Marina Carter and Khal Torabully, *Coolitude: An Anthology of Indian Labour Diaspora* (London: Anthem Press, 2002), Chapter 2, p. 61.

11. Rajat Kanta Ray, "Asian Capital in the Age of European Domination: The Rise of the Bazaar, 1800–1914", *Modern Asian Studies* 29, no. 3 (1995): 553–54.

12. Claude Markovits, *The Global World of Indian Merchants, 1750–1947: Traders of Sind from Bukhara to Panama* (Cambridge: Cambridge University Press, 2000).

13 Rajeswary Ampalavanar Brown, *Capital and Entrepreneurship in South-East Asia* (Houndmills, Basingstoke, Hampshire and London: The Macmillan Press Ltd. and New York, St. Martin's Press, INC., 1994). While Brown talks about the extensive Chettiar networks and dominance of other Indian trading communities in the textile trade in her book, further research on the Sindhi networks has been done by Claude Markovits.

14. Takeshi Hamashita, "Rethinking Historical Network in Asia", in the workshop on "Asian Business Networks", organized by the Faculty of Arts and Social Science (FASS), National University of Singapore (NUS) and the Institute of Oriental Culture, Tokyo University, 31 March 1998–2 April 1998.

15. Chandra Jayawardena, "Migration and Social Change: A Survey of Indian Communities Overseas", *Geographical Review* 58, no. 3 (July 1968): 426–49.

16. Ibid.

17. John Clammer, *Diaspora and Identity: The Sociology of Culture*

in Southeast Asia (Subang Jaya, Selangor, Malaysia: Pelanduk Publications, 2002), p. 10.

18. The complexities of co-existence and areas of Indian enclaves has been very well discussed in the writings of Sharon Siddique and Nirmala Puru Shottam in *Singapore's Little India: Past, Present and Future* (Singapore: Institute of Southeast Asian Studies, 1982).

19. Steven Vertovec, "Conceiving and Researching Transnationalism", *Ethnic and Racial Studies* 22, no. 2 (March 1999): 447.

20. Robin Cohen, "Diasporas and the Nation-state: From Victims to Challengers", *International Affairs* 72, no. 3 (July 1996): 516.

21. This concept has been further discussed by Yin-wah Chu in his article, "Networking for Domination: The Interconnectivity among Business and Government Actors in the Formation Technology Industry of Hong Kong", in *Capital and Knowledge in Asia: Changing Power Relations*, edited by Heidi Dahles and Otto van den Muijzenberg (London and NY: RoutledgeCurzon, 2003), pp. 23–39.

22. D. Harvey deliberates on this in his work, *The Condition of Postmodernity* (Cambridge, MA: Blackwell, 1990).

23. Vertovec, op. cit., p. 451.

24. Rob Wilson and Wimal Dissanayake, "Introduction: Tracking the Global/Local", in *Global/Local: Cultural Production and Transnational Imaginary*, edited by Rob Wilson and Wimal Dissanayake (Durham, NC: Duke University Press, 1996), pp. 1–18.

25. Italics mine. Claude Markovits, "Major Indian Capitalists", in *Asian Merchants and Businessmen in the Indian Ocean and the China Sea*, edited by Denis Lombard and Jean Aubin (New Delhi: Oxford University Press, 2000), p. 310.

26. Indian guilds have been discussed in more detail in the fourth chapter.

27. Marina Carter, "Indians and the Colonial Diaspora", in *Rising India and Indian Communities in East Asia*, edited by K. Kesavapany et al. (Singapore: Institute of Southeast Asian Studies, 2008), p. 22.

28. Claude Markovits has also discussed this aspect in his book on the Sindhi network, *The Global World of Indian Merchants*, op. cit.

29. A. Mani, "Tamils in Singapore: Yesterday, Today and Tomorrow", in *Tamil in an International Arena 2002, First Step*, edited by Chitra Sankaran and S.P. Thinappan (Singapore: NUS Press, 2004).

30. Kishore Mahbubani, *The New Asian Hemisphere: The Irresistible Shift of Global Power to the East* (New York: Public Affairs, 2008), p. 22.

31. Denys Lombard and Jean Aubin, eds., *Asian Merchants and Businessmen in the Indian Ocean and the China Sea* (New Delhi: Oxford University Press, 2000).

32. Tambiah, "Transnational Movements, Diaspora, and Multiple Modernities", op. cit., p. 171.

PART ONE

Chapter 1

MAKING SINGAPORE THEIR HOMELAND: THE EARLY INDIAN MIGRANTS TO THE LION CITY

The geostrategic importance of the Indian Ocean has continued from ancient times and still flourishes as one of the pertinent theatres for complex maritime trading systems. Singapore, with its unique geopolitical entity, has gradually assumed centre stage in the historical evolution as a centre for commerce, trade, entrepot and other maritime and political activities. The Indian subcontinent, on the other hand, has also been successful in exploiting the favourable geographical location in the heart of the Indian Ocean for a much longer period of time. The Indian Ocean gradually came to be dominated by Western naval suitors in the seventeenth and eighteenth century onwards. The Portuguese extended their maritime expansion with state patronage and soon had to face other contenders in the British, French and Dutch naval powers. The reigning phase of colonialism leading to imperialism made the Western powers very ambitious and the Asian states more and more vulnerable, ultimately resulting in the extensive prowess of the former, especially the British.[1]

Centuries of maritime trade connectivities encouraged mobilization and migration of trading communities and others to different parts of Asia and beyond. As historian K.N. Chaudhuri writes, "There is every reason to believe that pre-historic movements and migrations of people took place both by sea and land."[2] Indian communities, being no exception to the rule, had travelled and migrated to different nooks and corners of Asia and beyond. The onset of British imperialism consolidated and facilitated greater movements of goods and people to cater to their administrative, military and commercial interests.

I. THE ADVENT OF COLONIALISM AND INDIAN MIGRATION

Stamford Raffles arrived in Singapore in January 1819 and opened the colonial chapter of a long established linkage, and globalization in Asia came to be redefined with a new rhetoric. Singapore became the key strategic location between Calcutta and Canton in the eastern trade routes of the British. It was an anchoring ground for a wide variety of sea vessels from the Chinese junks, Indian ships, Arab dhows and Portuguese battleships. Earlier trade was mainly seasonal, subject to the prevailing monsoon winds when the junks from China would arrive before Christmas and leave the following June for the ports of Amoy, Canton, Nanking and others. They also brought in a large number of impoverished people from southern China, who eventually settled on the island. Two-way traffic continued throughout the year between Singapore and Calcutta through the Malacca Straits with the East India Company as well as privately owned "country ships" bringing in Indian jute, cotton, wheat and opium to Singapore and sailing back with "pepper and spices, sago, tin and silver dollars".[3] The emergence of Singapore has been aptly described by G.S. Graham who writes, "... what was to be the greatest free port in the Indian Ocean emerged from the jungle, secured against all threats except piracy by the supremacy of the Navy".[4] The obvious strategic significance to protect their expanding empire as also to forestall any Dutch advance and the likely location to repair and feed their fleet could not be overlooked by the Imperial British visionaries.

When Raffles came to Singapore, he brought in his entourage 120 sepoys of the Bengal Native Infantry and a Bazaar Contingent of washermen, milkmen, tea-makers and domestic servants.[5] Since the Indians had strategically and culturally familiarized themselves in Southeast Asia from ancient times, migration to the Malaya Peninsula during the colonial period was not actually an innovation. This was the beginning of a new era of the Indian diaspora in Southeast Asia.

The common British colonial masters for both the Indian subcontinent and Singapore created a familiar base of administrative and political entity and also facilitated Indian migration to the island state. The island was under the East India Company's rule between 1826 and 1867 and was being administered from Calcutta. As Tan and Major write: "To a very large extent, Singapore's administrative and legal systems — a centralized administration in which civil power was supreme — were based on British-India lineage."[6] In fact, the Indian Penal Code, which came into effect in India in the 1860s, was adopted by Singapore in 1871 and "still leaves its imprint on the country's legal system".[7] Knowledge of English language and the similar administrative operational necessities made the English-educated Indians good candidates for the administrative services. English-educated migrant Indians from the states of Kerala, Tamil Nadu, Bengal and others catered exactly to the clerical efficiency that the British were looking for in the colonial subjects. They also fitted in the professions of lawyers, doctors and civil servants being familiar with the British colonial system for a much longer period of time. The Indians, thus, managed to develop good relations with the British and share a comfortable working relation with them over the other migrant settlers.

The presence of the early Indians in Melaka (Singapore was then a part of the Malayan Peninsula) dated as far back as 1413, and according to Samuel S. Dhoraisingam, numbered around 4,000 by 1510 comprising of Gujarati, Tamil and other Indian merchants.[8] Those Indian merchants who were domiciled in the area soon married into the "indigenous community which included Malays, Javanese and Bataks and some later into the wealthy Peranakan Chinese, the Nonyas"[9] and gradually severed relations with India as strict caste norms did not allow foreign wives in the society. The Peranakan Indians, that emerged, were Shaivites and were staunch Hindus in their beliefs. Most of them retained their religion in spite of being married to indigenous women. By the turn of the twentieth century, many of the educated Peranakan Indians came to settle in Singapore, and like other races of their times, began to reside in enclaves across the island. They had settlements on Waterloo Street, Dalhousie Lane, Kampong Kapor, Kinta Road, Chitty Road, Rowell Road, Serangoon Road, Bencoolen Street and Selgie Road.[10]

Another distinct local community that emerged from indigenous marriage alliances was the *Jawi-Peranakan*, the descendants of Indian Muslims and local women.[11] Also called the *Jawi-Pekan* (Indo-Malay) community, their descendants got assimilated into the "local-born" population.

There were distinct differences in characteristics of Indian contacts with Malaya in pre-modern and the colonial period. Arasaratnam has aptly pointed out to the fact that while in former times, these contacts were initiated by Indians themselves "for their own benefit and in response to their own needs", those in the later phase saw this exchange as "response to demands caused by external factors"[12] and serving interests of a third party. In the earlier phase, India received considerable benefits from Malaya in exchange of gold and spices. In the colonial phase, however, she was mostly supplying labour.[13] The scenario changed considerably in the post-colonial era, but the indelible imprints of the colonial legacy with its usual fallouts and predictable features has consumed quite an effort of the government to turn the tide in favour of mutual exchange of goods and services.

It is interesting to note that the maritime adventures and acquisitions in this island nation had commercial overtones rather than territorial and cultural expansions. When Raffles promoted it as an entrepot, he was initially making an effort to confront and contain the Dutch expansionist ambitions and also provide a safe and free passage for British ships through the Straits for their trade with China. In his own words, the purpose of establishing a colony in Singapore was "... not territory but trade; a great commercial emporium and fulcrum ..."[14] After three years, in 1822, he had remarked how Singapore was prospering with "at least 10,000 inhabitants of all nations, actively engaged in commercial pursuits, which afford to each and all a handsome livelihood and abundant profit".[15]

One of the first Indian civilians to come to Singapore was Narayana Pillai, who had been an associate of Raffles in Penang since 1804.[16] Raffles brought him to Singapore in 1819 to start brick kilns which would have been necessary for the construction work of the new settlement. Pillai is also believed to have worked in the Government treasury as a Tamil translator.[17] He became the first building contractor in Singapore and eventually also started a cotton goods shop in the Commercial Square area, thus becoming a wealthy merchant. He also built the first Hindu temple at South Bridge Road, the Sri Mariamman Temple in 1827.[18]

The British imperial enterprise provided a strong impetus to the Indians to migrate to the island as "free" commercial and labour migrants and also employees of the British administrative paraphernalia as has already been mentioned, but later on "forced" migration followed after the Anglo-Dutch Treaty in 1824 when Singapore was made into a British penal colony.

The process of migration was a continuous one, bringing along with it different facets of negotiations, interactions and also acculturation in social, cultural and economic dimensions. The process still continues, though at different levels, with succeeding generations of Indians in the demographic landscape of Singapore. There was an effort to preserve and nourish the characteristics, customs, habits and rituals of each ethnic group within the enclave structural pattern and linguistic familiarity initially, but gradually also to confront and assimilate the social and economic norms of the adopted country. This format of nurturing individual ethnic identity has been maintained by the independent Singapore Government later on to give more space and flexibility in the process of integration. This unique feature of Singapore has helped the Indian diaspora with individuality and a feeling of closeness to the homeland. However, this is more applicable to either the earlier migrants or the more recent ones rather than those born as Singaporeans, as the latter often finds little or no psychological attachment to the subcontinent.

The earliest known Indians who came along with Raffles after the formation of modern Singapore were the *sepoys* and soldiers of the East India Company, who stayed behind to guard British interests. They were accompanied by a contingent of civilians to help with daily chores as has already been mentioned. In due course of time, they laid out a well-established settlement structure on the island with a prominence that lasted for generations so much so that some names today like the Dhoby Ghaut denoting the workplace of washermen, still bear the legacy of those times. They also developed themselves into an organized occupational force, and though did not follow very traditional business norms, segments like milkmen, both from North and South India, made good money for themselves. So did the turbaned Sikh security guards, better known as the *jagas*, who became part-time moneylenders and later invested the accumulated wealth into business. Their moneylending business was, however, highly unorganized and sporadic in comparison with the Chettiars.

Another category of initial settlers were the convicts. Singapore served as a penal colony for Indian convicts for almost half a century from 1825. The convicts came from different regions and from diverse backgrounds. Convict labour was one of the most important sources of manpower on which Singapore was built. St. Andrews Cathedral (1862), Istana (1869) and other important colonial buildings were some of the outstanding contributions of Indian convict labour. A. Blundell had written in 1855 that "every bridge, all jetties, piers, canals, sea walls, and 150 miles of road were built by Indian convicts".[19] The participation of the convict labour in the growth and development of Singapore is a unique feature in its history. Eventually, with the end of the transportation of convicts from India, many were given "self-supporter" status and they settled down in these islands by marrying local women.[20] The fascinating structures built by them and their inevitable permanence has left indelible prints in the minds of the people of the convict labour contribution and forged links with the tale of Indian immigration in Singapore.

The practice of the indentured system of recruiting labour to work on sugar and rubber plantations in the Straits Settlements as well as work as domestic helpers was one of the first methods of importing labour from India. The indenture system fixed the tenure of work under an employer which could not be violated within the stipulated period and which was open to renewal or release at the end of that period. A parallel system of recruiting Indian labour, and the one more in practice in the Malayan Peninsula since the end of the nineteenth century was the *kangany* system. The *kangany*, an overseer or supervisor, got most of his labourers to work on the plantations. This was a system which supplied superior labour force and the Indian Immigration Committee appointed in 1907 legalized and regularized it as the most satisfactory system for the growing demand of labour in the plantations.[21]

Considering the conservatism of Indian religious and social practices and its growing complexities, it is remarkable that a huge exodus of migrant labourers arrived in the Malayan Peninsula within a few decades. However, it might not be surprising in the light of the fact that the traditional self-sufficient agrarian economy in India had broken down and the degeneration was further accelerated by "de-industrialization" triggered off by the imposition of the colonial rule. As a result, it failed to sustain the increasing number of population dependent on land as their source of income. Thus, the opportunity of income could not be ignored, especially from the point of view that the Malaya Peninsula was not an unfamiliar terrain to the coastal Indians, especially from the southern region of the subcontinent. It might be mentioned here that this inflow of labourers catered mostly to the needs of the plantation industry. It was the convict labour resource that was subsequently used to a large extent to develop the infrastructure of the city-state of Singapore.

Among the non-labouring migrants were the Sikhs, Bengalis, other Punjabis and North Indians, who came to the island as professionals, administrative and technical personnel, or recruitment in the police and other security services. At the same time came in the different categories of traders and merchants with various commercial interests. The North Indian business communities like the Sindhis, Marwaris, Gujaratis, Parsis and the Punjabis got involved with both the wholesale and the retail trade to provide for the different utilities and provisions to the migrant settlers. The Tamils (both Hindu and Muslims) and the Moplahs or the Malabar Muslims formed an important part of the business population from South India.

The commercial class of the Indian immigrants was best represented by the Chettiar community from Tamil Nadu, South India, who were mainly moneylenders. The Chettiars were the one business community from India who spread their wings in many places in Southeast Asia like Myanmar, Malayan Peninsula and Thailand but interestingly, maintained the strictures of the caste system and religious rites in a formidable manner. Further details of the lifestyle and occupational structures on the Chettiars shall be discussed subsequently.

The commercial migrants were attracted towards the lucrative trade that revolved around Singapore's emergence as an entrepot. A glimpse of the extent of trading activities that was carried out through this region may be seen from the Report of the Straits Settlements Trade Commision, 1933–34:

> ... this trade consists in the importation of cottons, cigarettes, machinery, milk, provisions, hardware and other manufactured goods from Europe, America, India and the Far East and their distribution to the Malay States, Siam, Borneo, Sumatra and other neighbouring parts of the Malayan archipelago and, on the other, in collecting general tropical produce from these countries and (after sorting, grading, conditioning and treatment) re-shipping it to the consuming markets of the world. The two sides of the trade

are complementary; the produce pays for the manufacturers, and the machinery of collection is closely interlocked with that of distribution. There is in addition a large import and export trade in rice, sugar and petroleum.[22]

Indian merchants and traders had a significant participation in the collection and distribution network, and often specialized in certain specific products like the textiles and the spices. In the following pages we shall see how the professions and the regional affiliations dictated the habitat cartography.

II. THE ENCLAVE STRUCTURE

At the beginning of Singapore's formative years, Raffles took the significant step of allocating distinct areas of residences and operations of the various ethnic communities in Singapore. In 1822, a Committee was appointed which marked out the "quarters or departments of the several classes of population".[23] The *Chulias* were given land up the Singapore river. The perimeters of different enclaves altered with time and generations, but "each group retained an unchallenged claim to defining the identity of various areas allotted to them".[24] Thus, the Indians spread out to the High Street area, Market Street, Arab Street area to some extent, the naval base in Sembawang, the Tanjong Pagar area, and of course, to Serangoon Road.[25] The areas of High Street, Market Street and Arab Street formed the part of the larger business district areas of Singapore also comprising of Collyer Quay, Cecil Street, Robinson Road and the adjacent areas. See Map 1.1.

Amidst the larger framework of Singaporean multi-ethnicity, the Indian business community has not only been a demographic minority, but also a heterogeneous entity. The Indians, almost as a natural tendency, first identified themselves with their "linguistic area and linguistic group", as A. Mani[26] points out

Map 1.1
The Indian Enclaves and Centres of Business Activities

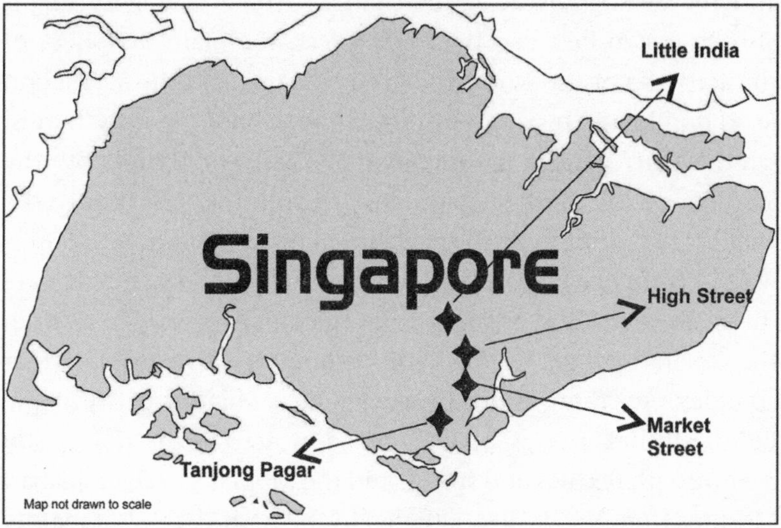

Source: Map from the Institute of Southeast Asian Studies (ISEAS).

before being identified as "Indians". While this has been true to a large extent, there are complexities involved which, if ignored, may easily mislead us to misconceptions and incorrect notions. Equally perilous would be to study the community only as entities of separate ethnic bodies and groups without reconciling them with the common "Indian" factor. However, broad distinctions may be necessary to bring out the characteristic features of each group for the convenience of study. Though the Indian migrants in Singapore came from various parts of the subcontinent and tended to form groups and associations of ethnic bodies with similar patterns of trade and commercial activities, any attempts to categorize them on the basis of region, religion, class or language is often fraught with tremendous difficulties. Following the legacy of Raffles' system of enclaves, we could attempt to sectorize them in the landscapes of the High Street, Market Street, Arab Street and the Serangoon Road merchants. A broad category might also be drawn between the High Street, the main periphery of the activities of the North Indian merchants and the Serangoon Road dominated by the South Indian merchants, mainly Tamils. On the other hand, a product-wise division would find both the Sindhis and the Tamils engaged in the textile business though the Tamils often dealt in retail trade, but in different enclaves. Tamils were also engaged in the dairy business in a big way, and so were the men from Bihar. Similarly, the spice traders were both from the Gujarati as well as the Tamil community. To consider other complexities, there could be a religious similarity between the Bohra Muslims from Gujarat,[27] based in Arab Street and mostly dealing with textiles and spices, and the Moplahs or the Malabari Muslims from Kerala, also situated in the Arab Street, but mainly catering to the food and the restaurant business. One of the earliest group of traders were the *Chulias* or the Tamil Muslims from the Coromandel Coast, who had established the Al-Abrar Mosque at South Bridge Road as early as around 1827.[28] The Kashmiri Muslims, on the other hand, who came much later, were mainly in the carpet business. Caste and sect also played a dominant role with some community like the Chettiar moneylenders from Tamil Nadu, who were quite conservatively caste based not only in matters of religion but also extending it to the functions of business. But they had little to do with their Sikh moneylending counterparts on the island. The conglomerates of the diverse business interests found manifestations in the formations of several regional associations like the Sindhi Association, the Gujarati Association, the Sikh Association and others.

The most obvious reason that accounted for the community groupings was the language factor. Serious linguistic differences between the majority Hindi speaking people from North India and mainly the Tamil speaking migrants from the southern part of the subcontinent created the major north-south divide. The people of these regions were as alien to each other as they were to the Chinese or the Malay community. It was not only the language but also the rites, customs and traditions that were quite different, which further helped to separate them in their own respective groups. Furthermore, the traders who came to look for new opportunities in Singapore depended a lot on the contacts in their homeland to mobilize the demand and supply chain of various commodities as well as finances to and from Singapore. Many of the early entrepreneurs started with trading and import and export business and gradually developed and diverted in search of greener pastures. Thus, regional affinity remained and progressed, much to the benefit of many.

The geographical location of the available commodities also played an important part in determining the components of trade. The spices of Indonesia had lured many Asians and the Westerners alike to the region for centuries. Similarly, European industrial revolution and imperialist designs had led to the flooding of English textiles and other Western manufactured products in the region and made it a formidable market for both the Europeans as well as the adventurous indigenous traders of Asia. For example, the monopolistic market of the English textiles soon faced competition from the competent textile manufactures of Japan, South Korea, Taiwan and even India. The colonial pattern of trade gave huge impetus to the traditional entrepreneurial communities in India like the Gujaratis and also the Sindhis, who inherited a legacy of participating in markets outside the subcontinent.

This chapter focuses on the divergent groups of Indian business communities briefly, their individual trading practices and how they gradually merged and correlated with the mainstream economy. The groupings were more marked in the colonial phase and gradually amalgamated after the independent government of Singapore took over in 1965. The regional group associations still exist, however, with the focus more on promoting cultural, religious and sometimes philanthropic activities among the different regional groups and communities. However, they should not be ignored for the legacy that they created and carried forward in the succeeding years.

Considering the small geographical extent of Singapore, it is indeed quite interesting to witness the coexistence of the varieties of complexities amongst one of the demographic minorities of the island nation. It is quite evident that the business migrants brought along with them the traditions of the mosaic coexistence and complexities of their homeland and nurtured it with different applications. The differences existed, but they have been successful to a great extent to integrate them in the collage of multi-ethnic coexistence of the Singaporean way of life. The diversity may be best clarified by some figures.

> About 64% are of Tamil origin .... There is also a sizeable Punjabi, mainly Sikh community (about 7%), most of whom initially arrived in Singapore as members of the British army and police. The other distinct Indian communities are the Malaylis (about 8%), Sindhis (about 6%) and the Gujaratis (about 2%). Indians are also the most religiously diverse of Singapore's ethnic categories; an estimated 50–60% are Hindus, 20–30% Muslims, 12% Christians, 7% Sikhs and 1% Buddhists.[29]

All the communities mentioned above comprised of businessmen, and there were those in other profession. P.P. Mishra, among many others, points out, "In spite of European dominance in inter-Asian trade in colonial period, traders from India acted in collaboration with trading organizations in Europe".[30] The Chettiars, Tamils, Gujaratis and the Sindhis became collaborators of the British trade at different centres throughout the empire. Facilitating the colonial trade also helped the individual communities to prosper at different locations.

Some white-collared workers and other categories of migrants took the bold step of venturing into individual business from employees, salespersons or managers under other organizations or businessmen. A large part of these people started off as petty traders. They were, at most times, satisfied with small time profits from retail trade, and more often than not, sent quite a big share of their income back to their families in India. Some business firms hired a few employees from the same region in their homeland, who were mostly single. After two or three years in service, they returned to India for a six-month break and probably got married. But they did not bring back their wives in most cases,[31] so the necessity and the willingness to send back money to India remained a priority. Most of these employees, after serving two or three terms in office were quite well versed with the technicalities of trade and soon started out on their own with or without the permission of their employers.[32] Many of them also had the urgent desire to go back to India on retirement or when they felt that they had accumulated satisfactory bank balance. This was one of the most serious hindrances in the growth and development of the Indian entrepreneurial community. Even many well-settled businessmen in Singapore continued with their philanthropic activities back in India. Having well established business activities not only in Singapore but also in other countries of Southeast Asia, they sometimes participated in religious and social welfare programmes back in their native homeland. This nature is in absolute contrast with the Chinese, who, for different reasons, did not get drawn back towards their homeland and tried to make the best of every possible opportunity in Singapore wholeheartedly.

North Indians

The North Indian business community developed wide trading networks in Southeast Asia, especially since colonial times and took advantage of the British promoting Singapore as a trading port and centre. This is applicable more to the Gujaratis and the Sindhis, who maintained and mobilized their communication links with the home country for manpower and logistic support. The lucrativeness of trading as a profession, the geostrategic position of Singapore as well as the relative underdevelopment of the manufacturing sector in the neighbouring Malaysia and Indonesia proved to be a big impetus to these communities to build up business centres in this region.

One of the pioneer Indian entrepreneurs in Singaporean history, Rajabali Jumabhoy, has given a very detailed picture of the High Street area and its surroundings. He said:

> High Street had almost all Indian merchants, and there were many Indian merchants also in North Bridge Road right up to Middle Road and Arab Street, Haji Lane, Bali Lane, Kandahar Street, Bussorah Street. The textile merchants and the sarong merchants were mostly in Arab Street, Beach Road, Kandahar Street and Bussorah and the surrounding areas; whilst North Bridge Road from Arab Street, right up to High Street, say about 30 per cent were Indians, dealing in consumer goods and textiles, shirts and so on …. High Street merchants were mostly from Karachi or West India.[33]

For most of the Indian businessmen, career started as employees in some firms or shops. Generally, as has been mentioned earlier, Indian firms in Malaysia and Singapore hired their employees from

India through personal contacts in the home country. This was the general pattern of migration apart from people who came to expand their already established business in India, or the ones who switched over from service to setting up a business. The process of sending young men overseas as employees or apprentices gained momentum with the rise of the national movement in the subcontinent during the twentieth century. Parents opted to send young boys abroad to be employed under a familiar kith or kin rather than exposing him to the wrath of British torture, imprisonment and the administrative turbulence that was brought about by participation in the freedom movement. In addition, it brought back substantial remittances at home. Girishchandra Kothari, a Gujarati textile merchant in later years, started his life on a two-year contract as an employee in a firm in Malaysia, P.S. Jamnadas and Co. in 1941 with a considerably good salary of Rs.1,200 a year.[34] There were others like Devji Gopaldas Shah, another Gujarati migrant, who had started with 400, 500 and 600 rupees per annum for the first three years of his career.[35] He started as a clerk and was then promoted half yearly as a godown clerk, bill collector, correspondent clerk and ultimately became a manager in two-and-a-half years.[36] Similarly, Bhagwan H. Melwani, a Sindhi businessman and the Managing Director of A.B. Melwani Pte. Ltd. later on, started his career as an employee in his uncle's shop from 1941 to 1947.[37] Food and lodging was provided by the employer. In most cases the office and residence was part of the same complex, with shops in the ground floor and residences on the second floor. Most of these employees were bachelors and were barely in their twenties. Only the manager was allowed to bring his family with him.[38] There was no existence of workers' rights (which came much later)[39] as such and the employers, almost on all occasions, made them work for seven days a week from eight in the morning to eight in the evening[40] with restricted social intermingling. A good and ambitious employee learnt the tricks of the trade quickly as well as accounting and bookkeeping and looked for opportunities to become a working partner and eventually start on his own. Experience was more important in starting up a business on one's own than raising the initial capital as initial investment to start independent business did not require a big sum of money and could be arranged with financiers of the same region and developing good relations with them.[41]

Gujaratis

Spices were another area where many of the Indian traders and merchants, especially the Gujaratis, participated in large numbers. They successfully managed to take forward the legacy of the pre-colonial days into the British times and continued even later on. However, with increase in participation and competition, it did not remain a monopoly with the Gujaratis. Spice traders were mainly situated in Malacca Street, Market Street and Chulia Street. The main sources of raw materials were Malacca and Indonesia and the exports from Singapore included the sago flour, betelnuts, gum-benzoin, copra, long pepper, nutmegs, maize, sago seeds, tapioca seeds and rattan, which were all sent mainly to India,[42] and chillies and turmeric powder were sent to Ceylon. These two were the primary markets for the Indian traders in the region. The raw materials were brought to Singapore and graded before being re-exported to other countries.[43] M/s Chandulal Co. was one of the biggest textile companies in the 1930s, one that could afford to own a car. The business was initially situated at shop no. 8, Malacca Street and later moved office to no. 9, Chulia Street in 1940. They also had offices in Jakarta and Makasar.[44] They were one of the leading exporters of sago flour, which was brought in from Sarawak, a commodity used up by the textile mills. Mr Chandulal, the boss, being situated in Ahmedabad, the hub of cotton textile mills in India, could easily book the orders for his company for Ahmedabad as well as Bombay and the material was then shipped through Singapore.[45]

Most of the Gujarati businessmen dealt with export in spices. There were also some imports from India which included cotton yarn and jute in large quantities which were sold directly to the Chinese merchants in Singapore. Some sort of lentils for the foodstuff and consumption of the Indians were also imported. Thus, the Gujaratis followed a very well organized business pattern, well set up with intra-ethnic networks, both in their home country and abroad making the best use of the location factors and geographical advantages. Added to it was the favourable factor of their entrepreneurial skills and mobility and access beyond the seas. The racial identity and the business links gradually induced them to organize themselves into their own associations and groups catering to the social and cultural necessities. The rapid improvement of communication facilities and modern nation-building process have blurred the effects of the concentric enclaves over the years and resulted in the diversification of their business interests, but the associations still exist, as with the other ethnic bodies, to enhance the bonding of diaspora and cultural congregations. A small excerpt from the website of the Singapore Gujarati Society reveals how the association evolved.

Written records around 1903 indicate that the early settlers used to gather for spiritual discourses in their homes and collected funds for the welfare of their community and newly arriving guests and merchants from India. The Kutchchi's featured prominently in this original effort. *The Parsis and Voras were also among the early settlers then.* One of the oldest known companies

that were present then was Ranchoddas Purushottamdas & Co.
Another was Waghji Laxmidas which started here in 1906. The
Hindu Paropkari Fund was established sometime around 1908.
In 1912, it was formalized and a property at 79 Waterloo Street
was purchased for the common use of the vegetarian Gujarati
community.[46]

There was another group of merchants, particularly from the
Gujarati community, who combined the business of the textiles
and spices, two of the most lucrative businesses at one point of
time. Such companies like that of Ranchoddas Purushottamdas
Limited[47] fared much better and sustained themselves for a
much longer period of time. They started out around 1905
and were continuing for three generations. They were also
into the transhipment business, bringing in rice from Bangkok
and shipping it to Zanzibar, getting cloves from Zanzibar and
shipping it to Indonesia or getting a consignment of sugar from
Indonesia and shipping it to India or the Middle East in large
quantities.[48] The different dimensions of their business interests
and successful handling of their operations in different parts of
South and Southeast Asia made them one of the most successful
trading enterprises in the region.

The trading transactions were carried out by the community
through intra-firm networks without the help of the banks. Credit
was given for about fifteen days to one month, or at the most
for two months, but after the War, the credit increased to four
or five months. D.G. Shah gives us an interesting account of the
system that was practised by their firm and, which was, perhaps
prevalent with most of the other firms that had links with the
subcontinent.

    ... in our case at least our office in Bombay would send the goods.
    They won't draw messenger, they will just send us a bill when

ready. They won't come to the bank. We don't want the bank
to earn anything from us. Those come here, we sell the goods,
money comes in. Then we got the money, we just transferred
it through some local broker or through the bank, so they get
the money we debited. Then again they go on sending goods.
It is competitive. Whatever we earn from premium of interest,
that was the tradition.[49]

The Gujarati community in Singapore may be broadly divided
into the Hindus, Jains and the Muslims, though the pattern
of trade and business remains identical for all the groups. The
discussion above has mainly focused on the Hindu and the
Jain section of the population. The similarity and overlapping
expressions of rites, ceremonies and festivals between the two not
only makes it extremely difficult to distinguish them, but is also
uncalled for and unwarranted in the present context. However,
the Muslims remained distinct from the others and a very closely
organized group amongst themselves. As early as the end of the
tenth century, Klang or Kalah was a thriving port in west Malaya
Peninsula inhabited by Muslims from Persia and India.[50] An
increased demand of spices in Europe gave a huge impetus to
the East-West trade and increased the Gujarati presence in the
Southeast Asian ports.[51] Among the Bohras, the Memons, the
Nizaris (Khojas), the Ithna-Asharis — the common sects of the
Gujarati Muslims, the Bohra mercantile community is arguably
the most established in the spice trade and the import and
export business and remains so till date. The Islamic merchant
networks across the Indian Ocean after the ninth century had
been quite vigorous and the Gujarati community, in keeping
with its seafaring and mercantile traits remained a constant
factor in the area. Dawoodi Bohra traders were engaged in the
barter trade in the east up to Indochina trading in cotton goods,
ghee, oil, leather, soap from India and returning with Chinese

silk, gold, spices and porcelain.[52] "Among the first families were Essabhai Motabhi, Abbasbhai Nakhoda, Sheikh Abdullahbhai, Esufallybhai Jafferbhai Motiwala and Tyebalibhai Sithawala."[53] In an approximate estimate, by the end of the nineteenth century, there were about twenty firms in Singapore employing around 100–150 people.[54] The firms of Angullia and Isabhai and Company came into operation around the middle of the nineteenth century.[55] Some other names mentioned by others were that of Hakimji Rajabhai, Muscatis, Motiwalla, Ismail and Ahmad Brothers, Mallal Das and Company, Nirmalla and Sons and Nomanbhoy among the old established firms,[56] most of whom continued to exist and prosper in the post-World War days and well into the 1960s and the 1970s too. The firms were spread out in Market Street and Arab Street area, and dealt with textiles, spices and import and export trading activities similar to their Hindu or Jain counterpart. They also maintained close ties with their kith and kin in India. Many Bohras profited from the post-war boom and later took advantage of the Korean and the Vietnam War in their trading activities and gradually spread all over the world in Africa, the Middle East, and America.

The Dawoodi Bohra community is a prominent sect in Singapore. One of the oldest families in Singapore were the Nomanbhoys, who hailed from Surat, one of the earliest of them arriving in Singapore in the 1890s as an employee of C.M. Mohammed Co. In 1914, they started the import-export trade of spices, a commodity that they had eventually specialized over generations to become a renown family business enterprise. Abdulkader Tyebally was another prominent name in the Bohra community, whose father had come to Singapore in 1910 and founded the Bombay Trading Company in 1917, the enterprise which had prospered in the twentieth century and also managed to make inroads into the monopoly of the rattan business by the Chinese merchants and later diversified into timber and tea businesses.[57] Both these companies, like many others, faced difficulties during the War and the Japanese aggression, but managed to tide over the crisis. Many in business eventually benefited from the post-war boom and the subsequent Korean War and prospered further.

The Bohras remain well-connected to their homeland as well as the mosque, which not only serves as a place of worship, but also as a place for congregation for socializing and networking as well. Their language of communication is an Arabicised form of Gujarati.[58] Quite naturally, the Malay and the Chinese Muslims, while welcome to pray in the mosque, frequent other mosques due to unfamiliarity with the language. That the Dawoodi Bohras maintain a strict rule of allegiance to the mosque[59] in which most major ceremonial functions take place has made them a very closely-knit ethno-religious organization. However, the younger generations have generally tended to do away with the religious strictness and are also less attached to their ancestral home, gradually imbibing more Singaporean characteristics. Thus small groupings within the community like the *Shebab*, prominent in the 1970s, had gone into a long hiatus because it had outlived its usefulness concomitant with its declining membership. The Shebab was later revived and revitalized in the year 2000 to form the present-day Shababul-Eidiz-Zahabi with the dual aim of maintaining the community's identity while also catering to the aspirations of the young Dawoodi Bohras in Singapore.[60]

The history of the Singaporean business community would remain incomplete without the mention of the very dynamic Muslim Gujarati businessman, Mr Rajabali Jumabhoy, who was not only a successful entrepreneur, but was also intimately involved in the building up of modern Singapore.

Rajabali Jumabhoy hailed from a family of Khoja Muslims merchants in the Kutch region of Gujarat.[61] His grandfather, Kassim,[62] who had businesses in Arabia, in places like Aden, Makalla and Hodeda retired to India in about 1890.[63] The house

of the Jumabhoys was founded in Singapore in 1915. The firm
bearing his name, R. Jumabhoy was set up at 9, Market Street in
partnership with his elder brother. However, the brothers split
soon after and Rajabali set up his own business in January 1922 at
103-A Market Street, just opposite to the older firm.[64] The initial
business of the company was mainly as import merchants and
commission agents. He used to export coffee to Muscat, Dubai,
Bahrain, Basra and other Persian Gulf ports. He was, perhaps, the
biggest exporter of sago flour to Bombay. "Other exports were
gumbenjamin, rattan, gambier, tin ingots, canned pines and other
produce."[65] The Hong Kong office, which was opened in 1924,
exported "Cassia and greenpeas to Singapore, Colombo, Aden and
Sudan; fire crackers to Madras; batteries to Calcutta and Hosiery
to Aden and Africa."[66] The Sourabaya office in Java, which was set
up in 1925, used to export coffee, sugar and grains to Colombo
and parts in South India, and coffee, especially to the ports in
the Persian Gulf. There were also imports of consignments of
dates from Muscat, Bahrain and Basra, Onions from Port Said
(between 1923 and 1930) as well as gunny bags from Calcutta,
all business transacted on commission basis.[67]

From 1924, Rajabali added his business of property
development.[68] In 1930, he also became the chief agent for the
Bombay Life Assurance Company Limited in Singapore,[69] thus
getting involved with the insurance business too. Between 1924
and 1935, Jumabhoy managed all his offices from the Singapore
Head Office. The Bombay office helped in the indenting process
as well as in settling disputes, which was common especially
when the prices fell.

Thus, Rajabali Jumabhoy managed to optimize his ancestral
knack of entrepreneurial skills and spread his businesses in
different directions. However, it was not a smooth sail all the way.
He had to deal with severe financial difficulties at various points
of his life when his speculations failed or prices in commodities

fell and was most badly hit during the slump years. He, however, did not give up, and each time started afresh with renewed vigour giving a new lease of life to his business and learning from his experiences. Situations began to improve post-1936 and the World War years, but with the Japanese occupation, he fled to India for fear of retribution from the aggressors as he was very well connected with the British administration. After the War, he was mainly dealing with cloves from Zanzibar between 1946 and 1949, selling it on a 2 per cent commission basis.[70] In this way, he earned a good amount of money.

Sindhis

The Sindhi merchants had a similar beginning in business as his Gujarati counterpart in the more recent colonial history of Singapore. As has been seen earlier, most of them started out as a humble employee and later made the best use of the opportunities to strike big. Like the Gujaratis, they were a merchant community hereditarily and had also made good use of the opportunity of European penetration in different parts of Asia and Africa, but with a difference. There were mainly two groups of Sindhi merchants who had established their links and networks abroad, the Shikarpuris and the Hyderabadis.[71] The Shikarpuri bankers took to Indo-Central Asian trade from 1840 onwards "to rebuild an active network based on the financing of the caravan trade and on close links with the Uzbek khanates of Central Asia".[72] The Hyderabadis, on the other hand, took advantage of the British rule and "the strengthening of commercial links between Sindh and Bombay to embark upon a completely new venture, which was the sale of local craft productions to a European clientele".[73] The latter, also known as the "Sindworkies", was a sea-based network on a worldwide scale, a direct product of the political and economic changes of colonialism.[74] They made good use of the benefits of being British Indian subjects and the consequent mobility that they enjoyed throughout the globe, especially over the Chinese and Japanese merchants, who faced political obstacles for travelling abroad, and managed to become "global middlemen" between Far East and India.[75] The first known Sindhi firm in Singapore was Wassiamall Assomull, which opened its branches in 1873 along with one in Surabaya about the same time.[76] The Dutch East Indies was a popular destination for the Sindhi merchants and another firm, Jhamatmal Gurbamall, which continued over generations, was established in the 1880s by Jhamatmal Gurbamal Melwani who went to Medan from Singapore and made a large fortune in the textile business.[77] Mention may also be made of the company owned by the Chortimal family, Chortimal and Company which opened its branch in Singapore in 1882 and spread to different parts (Seoul in 1966, Madrid in 1967, Bangkok in 1968 and Taipei in 1971, to mention a few of their offices around the globe) of the world.[78]

"The high noon of imperialism", that is, the second half of the nineteenth century, as John Mackenzie puts it,[79] witnessed a growing interest and appreciation in Oriental products, especially silk and curios from India, China and Japan. It might be borne in mind that the Indian textiles were already in high demand much prior to the colonial age. The Sindhis, especially the Hyderabadi Sindwork merchants lost no labour to grab the opportunity to become links between India and the Far East and to the west of the Arabian Sea, eventually to different corners of the globe to meet the growing demand of European consumers for Asian products.[80] This pattern of trade practised by the Sindhis eventually characterized them as catering to the European interests and demand throughout the globe. This was also a point of difference with their Gujarati counterpart, but only initially so, as both the communities tried to capitalize on similar opportunities and interests and similar trade networking pattern, quite obvious in the commodities that they participated in like the textiles as we have already seen at the beginning of the chapter. As Markovits pointed out, "The Sindhi merchants' privileged connections with the big Japanese firms allowed them to steal a march on their competitors in the 1930s and to start emerging as a community of particular importance."[81] They were facilitated by the Chinese merchants' boycott of Japanese goods after the Sino-Japanese War. The Japanese extended easy credit facilities to the next available Indian merchant group, who were very well-connected with the trading networks in the Indian subcontinent as well as well-versed in the nuances of the British demand-supply management. Singapore presented additional advantages of entrepot location as an important linkage between the Far East and other parts of Asia as well as the Western trade networks.

The number of Sindhi merchants who initially came and settled on the island may be difficult to account for, but interesting information has emerged from the study of Markovits, who has studied the details of the number of applicants (preserved in the India Office Library, U.K.) who applied for permission to travel abroad for trade related activities. The number of applicants for the Straits Settlements in 1915–16 was seventy-nine.[82] Some of the firms who had settled down in Singapore by the Second World War were those of J. Kimatrai, Khemchand Sons, J.T. Chanrai, D.R. Binwani, B.H.T. Daulatram Jubilee Silk Store (Dalamals), N. Ramchand (Nihalchand), U. Gulabra, Crown Silk Store, Modern Silk Store, Taj Mahal Silk Store, Singapore Silk Store, Parmanand Bros., M. Odarmal and others.[83] The structure of their shophouses was similar to that of other communities in High Street. They had shops on the ground floor and residences on the first floor. Food was served from a common kitchen and employees tried to save from their meagre earnings to send back to Sind.[84]

Sindhi entrepreneurs like Chanrais, Chellarams, Jashanmals have made their fortune in Hong Kong, Singapore, Dubai,

London, Africa, etc. One of the most successful names in Singapore
is that of the Chanrais. Kewalram Chanrai Group, headed by the
83-year-old Murli Kewalram Chanrai, is one of five companies
spun off from 150-year-old Chanrai family empire with business
interests in textiles, commodities, and real estate.[85] It has ranked
seventh among forty of the richest Singaporeans listed by Forbes
magazine with a net worth of $880 million. One of the five
companies in the Chanrai Group, Olam International as "the
world's largest trader of cashews and second-largest trader of
cocoa" has been enlisted in the Singapore stock exchange.[86] A
detailed study is outlined in the case study section (Chapter 5)
of the book.

Punjabis

Punjabis have been a constant factor in Singapore ever since the
British set up their administration on the island, especially the
more visible, tall, bearded and the turbaned Sikhs, who formed
a part of the regular contingent of armed forces and security
personnel. Unlike most of their South Indian counterparts, they
were free migrants who were either employed in the service of
the colonial government or came to try their luck on their own.
Under the British rule they were employed as part of the police
and paramilitary forces in colonial administration, purveyors of
fresh milk as dairy farmers, security staff sometimes also drivers
and owners of bullock and own-carts, or retail traders and also
moneylenders. It might be mentioned here that amongst the
Punjabis, it was the mainly the Sikhs who made a mark in the
business circles apart from a few Punjabi Hindus and Muslims.
So, it might not be totally incorrect to address the business group
as the Sikh business community. The Sikhs had also served in
allied roles — "as railway policemen, veterinary policemen,

government security guards at public buildings and at quarantine stations at the ports to prevent the spread of disease; prison warders; and also residency and palace guards".[87] The Chinese, who both feared and disliked them, referred to them as *Mungkali Kwai*.[88] The Chinese entrepreneur as well the British authorities endorsed them to guard their plantations and other places of their business interests.

A group of Sikhs also belonged to the moneylending community though they combined it with other occupations. The Sikh moneylending class was a rather unorganized group in comparison to their Chettiar counterparts. They gave loans on smaller sums than the Chettiars, which could range from $5 to $100. This was an easy business with high returns[89] and the usual rate of interest on small loans was "ten cents in the dollar per month without, as a rule, security. The Sikhs' almost only luxury is litigation."[90] The dispute and pressures of paying loan sometimes also ended with loss of lives. The interest charged could be flexible and was sometimes too high, "as high as 200 to 500 percent",[91] and working class borrowers like clerks, *tambis* and peons were engulfed in the vicious circle of impending debts. The Sikh moneylenders made a handsome earning on the interests and it was but logical that they would invest the accumulated wealth in business.

The Sikhs faced a similar dilemma as the Sindhis with the Partition of 1947 in the Indian subcontinent and many lost their ancestral homes to Pakistan and were left with little options except to migrate to other countries in search of a new abode. Singapore provided them with familial grounds as the Sikhs had been a part of the early migration process. But unlike the Sindhis, who were inherently occupied with merchant activities, the Sikhs devoted their time and money in entrepreneurial activities in the post-Partition era on a much larger scale than before, and having being blessed with hardworking skills and industrious nature, soon made a mark as a prominent business community in the entire Southeast Asian region and in many parts of the world.

The Sikhs had come to Singapore after India's Partition with different backgrounds. Some of them had been businessmen earlier, while others were forced to try their hands at any and everything, from peddling and hawking, slowly rising up the ladder of progress in making a livelihood. Some of them had, perhaps come earlier to Singapore, and thrived as big names like Gian Singh Co., Bajaj Brothers and Hardial Singh Company, all of whom were departmental stores at the Raffles Place area, on both sides of Change Alley.[92] They also participated in the textile business. Gian Singh was a group of companies that was originally started in the early twentieth century in Kuala Lumpur as a provision shop, and later expanded to departmental store. Hardial Singh and Balwant Singh, belonging to the same family started Gian Singh Company in Singapore around 1935/36.[93] They also dealt with "Japanese cotton goods, Indian cotton piece-goods and Indian cambric".[94] Hardial Singh also headed the Indian Chamber of Commerce in 1949.[95] Little information, however, can be obtained about them, except from the word of mouth of the older generations, who had lived in those times and some oral history records. They were in direct competition with the British departmental store, "Whiteway Laidlaw", situated not far from them in Battery Road, where the building of the Bank of China stands at present.[96]

Parsis

The Parsis were a minority community of Zoroastrians who had settled in India for many centuries. Though Bombay was their principal region for settlement, they were spread extensively across India and beyond, and were mostly involved in trade and commerce. The largest numbers of Parsis, according to the NLB Singapore inforpedia,[97] are in Singapore, followed by other countries in Southeast Asia such as Malaysia, Indonesia, Thailand and Brunei. The Parsi Lodge Charity was set up in 1829 to "furnish a burial ground for Parsis"[98] which proved the presence of Parsis in Singapore at the beginning of nineteenth century. The Parsi Road in the Tanjong Pagar area was one of the locales of their earlier settlements. The Mistri Road, near the Parsi Road in the Central Business District area, has been named after one of the prominent businessman N.R. Mistri. Parsis were active participants in the Eastern Triangular Trade between India, East Asia and Europe, and a number of Parsis lived in Tientsin, Shanghai and Hong Kong, and several other places in the Far East, many of whom relocated to Singapore, especially during the Communist Revolution in China.[99]

Two of the most prominent Parsi businessmen in Singapore were N.R. Mistri of Phoenix Aerated Water Works and P.M. Framroz of Framroz and Company. Both were in similar business of aerated water works and made huge amount of money.[100] Mistri was a philanthropist and built the Mistri Wing of the Singapore General Hospital at a cost of nearly a million dollars.[101] Framroz, who had come to Singapore in 1904, was the first President of the Parsi Association that was formed in 1954.[102] Another prominent Parsi businessman of the next generation was B. Ratanshaw Vakil, who not only served the Association as a Secretary and Vice-President, but was also elected as the Vice-President of the Indian Chamber of Commerce in the late 1970s, thus also serving in the Federated Chambers of Commerce that was actively promoting trade with ASEAN countries at that point of time. He was also a member of the Board of Governors of the Singapore Polytechnic.[103]

Over the years, the enterprising zeal of majority in the community has given away to more options in professional services, as has been the case with many other business communities. Not much can be learnt about their communities due to scarcity of sources except that they have remained as active participants of the Inter-Religious Organisation of Singapore.

South Indians

The ethnic South Indian community has been present in the Malayan Peninsula since very early times. While a large part of them came as labourers during the colonial period, there was quite a substantial presence of economic migrants too. They settled down in the areas along the western fringe of the central business area of Singapore in the Market Street and the Chulia Street area and comprised of a population of "Chettiars and Tamil Muslim traders, financiers, money-changers, petty shopkeepers, and boatmen and other kinds of quay-side workers".[104] The "South Indian" group was a diverse community among themselves comprising of different religious and regional groups. While the *Chettiars* represented dominant Hindu presence in the area, South Indian Muslim merchants, generally known as the *Chulias* also came to settle down in good numbers. The *nanaks*, *mamaks*, or *tulikans* are terms applied to South Indian Muslims from the Coromandel Coast, whereas the Malayalee Muslims from the Malabar Coast are known as the *moplahs* or the *kakaks*.[105] There were also the *Mudaliars* and *Thirupathur Vellalars* among the participants in business. These people were engaged in merchandising and commercial activities ranging from "the smallest level of peddling, hawking, and vending of edibles in small kiosks to the running of the grocery shops, textile marts, and other retail business, jewellery making, pawn-broking, money-lending and incipient banking".[106]

The earliest Indian Settlements were concentrated in and around the Market Street or the Chulia Street area, an area of petty shopkeepers, moneylenders, bankers, lawyers and watchmen.[107] This area was mostly characterized by the *kittingis* or the moneylenders' shophouses, from where the moneylenders, or more famously, the Chettiars conducted their business. The Chettiars as a commercial community have been discussed in the later section of this chapter.

"Little India", commonly known today among Singaporeans and foreigners alike, is synonymous with the ethnicity of the area. However, this is comparatively a newly coined termed for the Serangoon Road area, the name which resonated with the South Indian settlements in earlier times. Soon after Raffles came to this island nation, the Serangoon Road area had been marked on the map laid out by Lieutenant Jackson in 1828.[108] The Serangoon area was attractive to early settlers for the abundance of grass and water supply, and as has been true of any early settlement, the option of agriculture was tried out with gambier, nutmegs and coconuts. However, these attempts had failed and were substituted by cattle rearing. The cows and buffaloes were reared for dairy trade, bulls and buffaloes were kept for means of transportation, and cattle were also reared for the slaughter houses, which the Tamil Muslims had been engaged in. There were also pineapple merchants in the area and pineapple skins along with sesame and wheat husks became fodder for the cattle in the area.[109] Kader Sultan was one of the wealthiest of the cattle owners in the region who also owned a lot of properties. Gradually the Serangoon Road area along with the Farrer Road began to accommodate new migrants who came as dock or railway workers or small and petty shopkeepers catering to Indian necessities. K.S. Sandhu has objectively summarized the growth of this area in the following words:

> Lack of space to organize a homogenous community within the central core, coupled with the opportunities in the new area

to pursue such uniquely Indian economic activities as dairying and tanning, led the Indians to establish a ribbon development along Serangoon Road. This was later intensified and confirmed as a dominantly Indian area through the government's siting of labour lines there for a predominantly Tamil labour force and the overflow of shopkeepers and traders from the central core.[110]

The Serangoon area was the centre for Indian migration, especially Tamil and Malaylee workers, in the first decades of the twentieth century with the opening of the Naval Base, Seletar and the Changi Air Bases. During the 1930s, it was eventually transformed into a residential cum commercial area for migrant Indians. Lines of shophouses cropped up in the area, typically housing shops in the ground floor and residential dormitories for the employees in the upper storey. Similar commercial cum residential structures were also found in the High Street area, though the ethnicity and the business structure was widely different.

The business structure in the Serangoon area was, as is evident from above, dominated by the ethnic South Indian community. Unlike the High Street business, they were mostly catering to the everyday necessities of the social and religious life of the Indian community as provision stores' businessmen, clothes merchants, garland-makers and florists, goldsmiths, restaurant owners and other sundry commercial activities. They were mostly into retail trade with very few participating in wholesale activities or any "outward bound" business operations outside Singapore.[111] The language used was, almost obviously, of South Indian origin and one could well do without any knowledge of English, the main language of the nation since colonial times. In fact, Tamil language has played a significant role in bonding the South Indian communities irrespective of regional or religious dissimilarities. There has been a unique essence of self-sufficiency for Indian necessities in the area generated by the multifarious activities of the shops, big and small, successfully operating with gusto of loud popular music and the effervescence of incense sticks blending it in an air of antiquated modernity.

Two famous names in Tamil business during the formative years of Singapore were that of Ramasamy Nadar and Govindasamy Pillai. Nadar had a good business in the Serangoon Road area and also owned a number of shophouses. However, his business declined after the Second World War.[112] Nadar was one of the wealthiest men among Indians in pre-war Singapore, who had accumulated wealth by supplying provisions to the estates all over Malaya. He had also invested in properties and made money either by selling or renting them. He resided in Buffalo Road where he had built a row of double storied houses for his family and close relatives. This was the place where Tekka market was located, now in the midst of renovation. He had left for India just before the Japanese arrived and died there in 1953. Unfortunately, his business could not be sustained by future generations. It succumbed to the changes in the structural conditions and lack of efficient stewardship to override those conditions. Some of his descendants still reside in Singapore in the HDB housing complexes.[113]

P. Govindasamy Pillai, popularly known as PGP, was born in 1890 in Kaaraikaal in India. He came to Singapore in 1903 at the age of thirteen and started his career as an assistant in a provision shop. In 1908, he became an employee in N. Ramasamy's sari shop at Selegei Road.[114] He soon branched out on his own and eventually came to own a number of shops in the Serangoon Road area, selling provisions, medicine, canned items, etc. The main office was located at 48–50 Serangoon Road.[115] He also had a textile and a grocery shop. One of the biggest properties consisting of a stretch of houses in Buffalo Road belonged to him.[116]

Govindasamy Pillai was strict in business discipline and maintaining accounts. He followed a strict code of conduct, but at the same time helped the diligent workers financially. The business usually started early around 7 a.m. in the morning and closed for lunch break for two hours and then continued again till 9 p.m. and the workers were provided with residence in his house. There were people under him working for more than three or four decades. Some names of such employees were Jayaram, Sababathy, and Adaikalam Pillai.[117] PGP was also a philanthropist having taken part in the building of the Perumal Temple and the Krishan Temple. He also built wedding halls for the convenience of the people. He also carried out similar work in India.[118]

PGP made his fortune by "trading in textiles and spices to shoes and canned goods" and his "sundry goods and textiles shop"[119] in the Serangoon Road area was visited by one and all. His son, G. Ramachandran, further developed a branch of the business in wholesale trade in spices. Govindasamy Pillai was involved in building up the Indian Chamber of Commerce as well. He was the founder member of the Indian Chamber of Commerce, being one of the few South Indian merchants to take interest in building up a chamber of commerce for the Indian community.

There were also a number of rich Indian landed property owners across the island. One such name was that of H. Somappa, who owned large properties in areas which is at present known as Changi, Simei and Upper Serangoon Road.[120] There were also roads named after them, according to one of the descendants, Naidu Parangsam, which were renamed at the time of the urban redevelopment.[121] Less visible but quite old areas of ethnic South Indian settlements were the Naval Base area and Tanjong Pagar. They were not essentially commercial areas, but some utility shops which became quite popular later on.[122] Arab Street also had a number of Tamil Muslim merchants. But more famous for South Indian commerce was Market Street for the dominant existence of the moneylending class — the Chettiars. A brief look at both the communities reveals their importance and involvement in the daily financial and business transactions in Singapore.

Tamil Muslims

The Chulias were among the earliest of the Indian traders and merchants who had come to the island and some prospered as wealthy merchants in the Southeast Asian region. There were prominent players in the development of "Indo-Southeast Asian trade from the 1660s",[123] particularly in the Coromandel Coast of South India, and carried on trading activities in textiles, tin and other commodities with important trading centres in Southeast Asia like Perak, Kedah, Bantam, Johore, Acheh, Macassar, Pegu and Arakan, to mention a few.[124] Chulia Street in the Chinatown area of Singapore has been named after them. During a later period, a lot of Muslim plantation workers and labourers also came from villages in Tamil Nadu when they were forced to seek their livelihood when a severe famine struck. A large number of them were the *Kadayanullar* Muslims and the *Tenkasi* Muslims named after their respective villages. There were also a substantial number of petty traders, hawkers, small shop owners and money-changers who were Tamil Muslims. They also owned shops selling textiles, stationery and sundry goods. The cigarette shop owners in the alleys were Muslims from Athikadai in Tanjore district. However, the Prata stall owners or the push-cart hawkers selling foodstuffs like *thosai* and *appom* were mainly Malabar Muslim immigrants from Edna village in Kerala.[125]

The moneychangers formed an important component of the Tamil Muslim community in Singapore. For several decades now, they have been prominently involved in the business of changing money other than the banks. Interestingly, most of the moneychangers had imbibed this acumen through practice and apprenticeship in Singapore, and did not possess the business traits hereditarily from India. Yet, they had made an important mark for themselves in the moneylending business, passing the acumen to the succeeding generations. An expert in the business had to be well informed on the circulation of foreign currencies, and distinguish genuine ones from the fake. They were mostly located at the Collyer Quay, Raffles Place, Market Street, Change Alley, Chulia Street or Changi International Airport.[126] They have prospered with the booming of the tourism industry in Singapore and are usually located in places of tourist mobility. They have also benefited from the increasing prospects of Singapore as facilitating node in the business networks in the whole region, thus attracting many businessmen on short visits or possibilities of networking in transit *en route* to other parts of Southeast Asia. At present, they are also found to be operating in the East Coast area or Lucky Plaza and other places in the Orchard Road area besides a number of them being located in and around Raffles Place business district area. Interestingly, the Tamil Muslim moneychangers do not have any formal organization of their own,[127] but have maintained a very closed knit intra-community network among themselves.

Chettiars

A pivotal role in the development of early commerce of Singapore was played by the Chettiars, the dominant group of moneylenders from Chettinadu area in Tamil Nadu, South India,[128] which comprised of twenty-six villages of Chettiars. With a long history of financing and business acumen, they appeared to "have provided credit to sultans, nobles and Malay peasants".[129] They lent money both with and without security. Obviously in the latter case, the rate of interest was much higher. They were quite well settled by the 1930s and also ventured into investments in landed property, both in rubber plantations and urban land. Acting as intermediaries between the Western banks and the small Chinese and Indian traders, they formed an important part of the Southeast Asian diaspora from very early times. The Nattukottai Chettiars were the chief Indian merchant-banking group in Singapore. They were in fact the largest banking group compared to Jews, Armenians and others and can be argued as the only group that could transact business in all the British territories in Southeast Asia apart from the Madras Presidency (and Bengal Presidency of which Burma was a part till 1905). They were a religio-centric business community, and one would easily mistake them with the Brahmin caste as they often adopted similar physical appearances and the insignia of the priestly class though the occupational structure and hierarchical stature were so different. R.N. Walling describes Chettiars thus:

> ... priestly figures in white shirts, robes and sandals, with shaved heads, chalked foreheads ... towels over their shoulders, rings on their fingers, and an official looking document in their hands ...[130]

The Chettiars established their business across Market Street in unique structures known as *kittangis* or *kittingis*,[131] which were long buildings with no partitions, each *kittangi* housing around twenty-five business firms. Each moneylender was assigned a definite area, where he sat on the floor with a wooden cashier's box (*peti*) for conducting business. At the end of the day, this box was kept aside in the cabinet and the space used for sleeping at night, thus operating in simplest of structures with minimal establishment costs. This business mechanism is very similar to the Marwari businessmen in North India, who however, left for home after a day's work. Most of the Chettiars or their employees did not bring their families from India, so residence at the same place did not pose any problem. The *kittingis* were usually three-storey large buildings, where the first two storeys were used for business-cum-residence purposes and the third storey for residential and worshipping deities.[132]

The *kittingis* on the Market Street were surrounded by spices and other sundry goods merchants with whom the Chettiars had good business relations. The Chettiars lent out money to the big and the sundry business alike. Loans were drawn against the issue of promissory notes, which mentioned the principle sum of money borrowed, the amount of interest, which was usually 24 per cent, the stamp and the signature or their mark.[133] They also gave loans to people on mortgage and through personal guarantor. They charged high interest but also gave loans to those with a weak credit standing. Eventually, they became venture capitalists pouring the money earned in the tin and rubber investments in the early twentieth century. Many of them invested in properties too. When the moneylending business boomed, it attracted more members in the community and *kittingis* were also established on Clemenceau Avenue, Cantonment Road. Names of roads like Arnasalam Chetty Road, Vulthuraman Chetty Road, Narayanan Chetty Road and Muthuraman Chetty Road, Annamalai Avenue and Meyyappa Chettiar Road are indicative of the financial dominance of the Chettiars in the Singaporean socio-economic structure. In fact, Market Street, which had the maximum number of *kittingis*, was known as *Chetty Theruvu* or "Chetty's Street" by the Tamils. A.R. Annamalai Chettiar, after whom one of the roads is named, had also founded the Chettiar *Varthega* (trading) Club in Tank Road in the 1920s.[134]

The life and business of a Chettiar have revolved around the institution of the temple. Chettiars followed the practice of building temples dedicated to Lord Muruga wherever they settled in different parts of Asia — in Burma, Thailand, Vietnam, Malaya, Sri Lanka and Singapore. In the austere and frugal lifestyle of a Chettiar, the temple was the only place other than his business where he spent his time and money. The Arulmigu Sri Thandayuthapani Temple, more popularly known as the Subramaniam Temple by the non-Chettiars was built in Tank Road as early as 1859. The present complex has been built in 1983 and more recently in 1996 and has been listed in the Singapore Tourism Board as a place of attraction. This temple and another one, the Sithi Vinayagar Temple at Keong Saik Road (since 1925) are managed and run by the Nattukottai Chettiars.[135]

The Thandayuthapani Temple is the oldest Murugan temple managed by a board of representatives of the various *kittangis* headed by a Trustee, the position which is annually rotated among the *kittangis*. Important decisions in the Chettiar community as well as temple related matters are taken at the Chettiar community gathering, the *Nagara Koottam*.[136] The Tank Road temple also houses the Nattukottai Chamber of Commerce, which was officially opened by Mr Bradly, then Municipal President on 8 May 1931.[137]

Religion and business was very closely related to the functioning of the Chettiar firms. Every Chettiar firm voluntarily contributed to the temple to raise the temple funds. Each member contributed annually a certain percentage of their capital invested in business, which was usually half of 1 per cent of the capital.[138] The temple also formed the sleeping partner of many in business, where a share of profit was given to the temple, but in case of a loss, it was totally faced by the active partner.[139] Many of the *kittingis* were also owned by the temple. The Chettiars had the unique feature of sharing the business profits with the temple fund. Schrader has interpreted this as the "traders' dilemma-hypothesis", "the dilemma of a commercial or a financial agent in a moral economy to accumulate capital and hold a capital stock that is indispensible for business",[140] which required redistribution of individual wealth. The corporate and collective nature of the temple funds, which were used for entrepreneurial activity and formation of business networks "circumvented the individual trader's dilemma within the moral economy".[141] The collective responsibilities create a pattern of trust and reliability in the lending and borrowing policy.

The legislative bills to regulate moneylending activities between 1930 and 1940 were the first major blow to the thriving and lucrative business of the Chettiars. Then came the Japanese aggression and the Second World War. The Chettiars lost a lot of investments in the plantations and also accumulated properties from the defaulters' mortgages, but were unable to reap the gains due to the prevailing economic conditions. Many of them fled to India and came back only after the British regained their lost ground.

III. THE GREAT DEPRESSION, SECOND WORLD WAR AND AFTER

During the 1930s, the Indian subcontinent was involved in trade with the Malayan Peninsula in a big way. It was exporting about 20,000 tons of coal to Malaya in 1936, about 1,400 tons of coriander seeds, 9,000 tons of onions, a considerably good amount of cotton yarn and a monopoly supply of gunnies.[142] It is, however, not certain as to what extent of this trade was carried out by the Indians, but the mention of these products in the Reports of the Indian Chamber shows that the participation must have been fairly prominent except products like coal that was mostly carried out by the British. In the piece-goods trade, the Textile Quota System was started in 1934 to help the British

Empire trade,[143] where only fixed quantity was allowed to import from foreign countries and the rest were to be imported from the United Kingdom. Some traders gained in the process whereas others were deprived, and looked for other channels to conduct their business. The Indian cotton and cotton/art silk mixed sarongs were in great demand in the Dutch East Indies — 70 per cent of the Indian imports were intended for them. However, the quotas restricted the quantity of these imports and the profits of the traders. Trade was also affected when the shipping conferences continued to maintain high freight tariffs. Traders involved in importing goods from Siam or Saigon and re-exporting them to different parts of Asia and Africa were hit hard and the entrepot trade was considerably reduced.[144] Thus, Indian merchants in Singapore were faced with a double-edged sword in the 1930s — discrimination and the Depression.

The steady migration of Indians to the Malayan Peninsula received a setback in the late 1920s and 1930s with onset of the Great Depression. Usually some of the Indian immigrants would return to the homeland after seven to eight years of work in Malaya, while some of them chose not to return. With the *kangany* system in vogue, the percentage of labourers amongst the Indians was quite large. In 1937, of the 375,000 Indians employed in Malaya, 244,000 were employed on rubber estates while about 40,000 were traders.[145] However, during the lean years of the slump, many labourers were repatriated to India. Protests were made by the nationalists against the discriminatory attitude towards the Indians to which the Government of India yielded and banned the shipping of the unskilled labour from India in 1938.[146] Thus, the percentage of unskilled labour among the Indian population steadily declined in the coming years.

The recession also dealt a blow to the moneylending business. The Chettiars as well as some of the Sikh moneylenders tried to forcibly extract money from their debtors when money became scarce in 1942–43 and considerably embittered the Indo-Malay relations. According to one view, the Chettiars contended that "unable to meet the Azad Hind Government demands for contribution, their agents had been forced by circumstances to press the debtors for re-payment".[147] Whatever the truth of the allegation might be, the Chettiars were badly hit by the World War and the Japanese aggression. Many of them lost their money in the plantations due to the financial depression and also because they were cut off from Malaysian plantations during the Japanese occupation. Their agents, even if they recovered the money from the debtors, did not pass it to the Chettiar, and the latter could do nothing about it. Many Chettiar moneylenders were also repatriated to India on suspicion that they were financing rebellious elements. The Chettiar community was so badly struck they could never bring back the glorious days of the past.

The recession, the Japanese occupation and the destructions of the Second World War were a major setback to the inflow of Indian migrants in the modern history of Singapore. Indians were faced with a peculiar situation here. Though many went back to India and returned only when the British re-occupied the city-state, the ones who stayed on, faced a dilemma. On the one hand, there was violence, torture, starvation and economic collapse with the coming of the Japanese, on the other was the emergence of Subhas Chandra Bose, the hero of the Indian national movement and one of the most charismatic leaders that the world had ever known, who forged an alliance with the Japanese to set up a provisional government in Singapore to oust the British from the Indian subcontinent. The ethnic Indians in the Malayan Peninsula got the opportunity to participate in the fight for India's freedom from the colonial clutches, and moved by the ideology and the magnetic personality of Bose, joined the Indian National Army in large numbers.[148] The Indian business community also lend their helping hand in their own possible ways. It is known that a Sindhi businessman, named Khiamal of M/s L. Khiamal, Saigon (V.K. Lal Co.) had given a donation of more than two lakh dollars to the Azad Hind Fauj in 1943–44, and was one of the very few businessmen who had close contacts with Bose at his Katong bungalow in Singapore.[149]

Many critics were of the opinion that Indians joined Bose in such large numbers to evade Japanese brutality, since the Indians had the option to escape the wrath of the aggressors and they conceded willingly or unwillingly to join Bose in exceptionally large numbers. However, the situation was much more complex and the outcome of Bose's assimilating of Indian manpower had the effect of enlightening the Indian settlers in Malaya in a manner that had a very deep impact in their self-awakening and mobilizing their collective spirit in future years to come.

The 1940s was an eventful decade in the history of Singapore. In the first half of it, the Singaporeans were reeling under the wrath of the Japanese occupation. For Indian community too, there was a lot of suffering in store. When the British armed forces withdrew with Japanese aggression, the government personnel as well as the foreigners employed in the private sector were also evacuated, thus leaving the entire plantations without proper management and their entire operations were dislocated. Indians being employed in the plantations in large numbers felt the entire brunt of the mismanagement and went without wages or other amenities provided to them by the plantation authorities. Sanitation and health facilities deteriorated as well as regular supplies were interrupted. Production and efficiency of the Malayan rubber also suffered internationally and the labourers were left in dire condition. The Japanese tried to revive the functioning, but succeeded marginally. Also added to the hunger and malnutrition was the special conscription of labourers by the Japanese to work in projects like the Siam Railway in most inhuman conditions, the stories of which still evoke spine chilling memories of a fateful generation.[150] Thus, the 14 per cent Indian population in Malaya in 1940 dropped down to 10 per cent by 1947.[151]

People of Malaya were relieved to welcome back the British rule in 1945 with the defeat of the Japanese and the Axis Powers in the Second World War. From 1948, Singapore became a separate political entity. Some of the people who had been repatriated to India, including some businessmen, decided to come back and start afresh. The Jumabhoys were one such business group who flourished in the later years.[152] In the post-war days, he was recalled by the British to help in the rehabilitation work and he started his business again. He managed to make good money in trading with sago flour, tin and tea.[153] In January 1948, he converted his firm into a private limited concern and named it R. Jumabhoy and Sons Ltd. In the same year, he bought a number of properties on Scott Road and elsewhere and again invested in a field that had resulted in huge losses during the slump years. However, properties were picking up in the post-war days, and prices were soaring up, especially the vacant land and the bungalows and Jumaboy made good use of the situation. They also obtained the Indian Government's shipping agency from 1950 through Mr Sarabhai Haji from Scindhia Steam Navigation Co. Ltd. However, Rajabali retired from active business from 1952 and was taken over by his son, Ameerali.

Trade resumed after the War with regular flow of textiles from Hong Kong, America, Italy, U.K. and India, however, with lower prices. The competition from Japanese supplies was an important factor in further lowering the prices. Indians had already been handicapped by the unfair export policy of the colonial government, which allowed some goods to be exported to certain countries but were banned for export to India. Copra, coconut oil and some other products could be exported to other countries, but not to India. In another case, virtual monopoly of tin export had been given to a British concern. In addition, there was shortage of shipping exporters.[154] On another front, the Government did not settle many claims under the War Risk Insurance locking the money of many of the traders and merchants creating added difficulties. Interestingly, there was no representation on the Board in spite of the members of the Indian Chamber transacting over 90 per cent of the import and export trade between India and Malaya.[155] The Indian Chamber tried to voice its protest, but little could be achieved easily. The Indian businessmen were a heterogeneous group of people with individualistic interests, minority in numbers and had learnt to adapt to the discriminatory policies of the colonialists with experiences of two centuries in the subcontinent.

The decade of the 1940s was very significant for the Indian subcontinent too. On the one hand, India received the much awaited and cherished independence in 1947 and the ensuing challenges of re-building the country after two centuries of colonial rule; on the other hand, it was conjointly battered with the heavily-bloodied Partition wrecking havoc to millions, the price that the Indians had to pay for its freedom from the British rule. Singapore, more than any other countries in Southeast Asia, was affected by the impending situation in the subcontinent. Post-1947 saw the second wave of Indian immigration to Singapore, the veritable ground of opportunity in commerce and trade. Though there has been no general consensus on the immigration figures,[156] there was supposed to be a big influx from across the causeway[157] and other immigrating Indians came to Singapore in large numbers. Most of them were the dislocated and the uprooted Sikhs, Sindhis and others who came in search for a safer haven and a lucrative business atmosphere in Singapore and other Southeast Asian countries. Also in the 1950s, opportunities for jobs expanded after the price of rubber rose, thus many Indians sought to exploit the opportunities. However, in 1953, visa was introduced to control the migration figures and only the well educated could enter Singapore.

Singapore witnessed an exodus of Sindhi migrants in the post-Partition era when they, majority of whom were Hindus, were uprooted from Sindh, their homeland that formed a part of modern Pakistan. Suddenly, all the links were severed and return to the ancestral homeland became a thing of the nostalgic past. "The enterprising Sindhi businessmen had almost flocked to Singapore just before 1950s."[158] Their business aptitudes and industrious nature helped them to find footholds and establishments in new homes in spite of the psychological tensions and dilemma, and they soon emerged as one of the most affluent communities. They soon diversified from the traditional business of textiles and tailoring into trade, manufacturing, real estate, tourism and hotel industry in the nation-building phase in Singapore.[159] Before the War, there were around 150 persons with 6 settled families and 17 firms that increased in number to 5,000 persons, 600 families and 450 prominent firms in 1988.[160] In the 1950s and 1960s the Sindhi community witnessed a dramatic expansion in terms of the number of settlers as well as an increase in the business firms.[161] Similar circumstances were also created for the Punjabis, as we shall see later on, however, with the exception that the business lineage and the trade linkages were not as extensive, hereditary or precipitous as the former.

The Sikhs faced the similar dilemma as the Sindhis with the Partition of 1947 in the Indian subcontinent and many lost their ancestral homes to Pakistan and were left with little options except to migrate to other countries in search of a new abode. Singapore provided them with familial grounds as the Sikhs had been a part of the early migration process. The Sikhs devoted their time and money in entrepreneurial activities in the post-Partition era on a much larger scale than before, and being hardworking and of industrious nature, soon made a mark as a prominent business community in the entire Southeast Asian region and in many parts of the world.

The names of Sikh entrepreneurs have been prominent in textiles and garments and later on in electronics and sports goods sector. The Katong Gurdwara (registered in 1953) formed a place for congregation for many Sikh businessmen in Singapore. Though very strongly bonded with elements of religiosity and ethnicity, the business network did not extend much beyond family kinship ties and there were little evidences of cross funding of business ventures among different families. It was almost in all cases a family business affair with rudiments of paternalistic norms. Also, penetrating in areas of established trade and businesses, as the post-Partition migrants had to do, required capitalizing on sectors with low barriers and low level of capital outlay to enter into the market. R. Singh, in his thesis on Sikh entrepreneurship states that, "The peddling, sports, textiles and sundry trades these men occupied needed very little technical knowledge, training, capital and labour expertise."[162] Mostly a family-oriented set-up, it was preferred that the younger generations apprenticed with hands-on experiences rather than earning University degrees. They also had an affinity towards making rich assets in properties and gold, which had enabled them to tide over any financial crisis and change and sustain the continuity of the "family business" legacy.

IV. CONCLUSION

The pattern of the new migration in the 1940s and the 1950s was different. Unlike the prior cases where traders, businessmen or labourers came to the Malay region from South India mainly, the new wave witnessed quite a large number of North Indians making inroads into the country amidst political upheaval in the subcontinent. They were mostly professionals or businessmen, educated and politically conscious. Enthused by the contemporary national movement in India and elsewhere and anti-colonial upsurge and sentiment in the world environment and also influenced by the rise of communism, the ethnic Indians were ready to participate in the trade union movement and other political parties. In the 1950s and 1960s, we find a number of Indian names who were active in Singapore political scene.

In the 1950s, Singapore authorities passed restrictive ordinances to halt migration but about 50,000 Indians[163] crossed over from Malaya to escape the uncertainties arising out of the emergency there. From the 1960s onwards, immigration came down to an insignificant number on account of especially the government rules and regulations, where they decided, as the Report of the High Level Committee on the Indian diaspora mentions "to recruit most semi-skilled and unskilled labour from 'traditional' sources of recruitment, wherein India did not figure".[164] Relaxation of these rules and the changing bilateral relations during more recent years had its effects on the new or the third wave of migration where the new settlers were either highly educated and skilled professionals in the upper strata of the society or the unskilled labourers and domestic help serving under the temporary work permit. Various factors came into play with increasing globalization and changes in the political economies of the Asian countries. More of the prospects and consequences shall be discussed in detail in the forthcoming chapters.

As has been seen above, the generation of Indian businessmen who flourished in colonial Singapore dominated mainly in the traditional areas of textiles and spices in a big way. This was in spite of the various discriminatory policies that they had to face from the British colonialists. In fact, the wholesale Asian textile trade for the post-war years was controlled by the Indians in Singapore, especially the North Indians.[165] This was the result of a continuous maintenance of extensive intra-ethnic networks among these communities spreading from the subcontinent through the entire regions of Southeast Asia. The recruitment of manpower, logistic support, financing networks and many a times, manufacturing bases (for example, sports goods manufactured in Sialkot or special cotton yarns from Pakistan were traded by the Punjabi Sikhs in different parts of Southeast Asia) were all centred around the subcontinent and functioned on community-based lines. Either the head office was in India or the credit system was dependent on the Indian indigenous finance system. "Rarely did capitalists themselves leave India for long periods", points out Markovits,[166] with few exceptions and "of the occasional big trader who transferred his activities to a location outside India to be in a better position to exploit certain specific kinds of market opportunities".[167] The strong threads of trade networks helped to maintain the bonds of ethnicity successfully outside the subcontinent too. The efficient maintenance of the supply chain resulted in the overwhelming success of the trade in textiles and spices. It also helped to maintain an almost parallel system of smart and self-sufficient functioning of their operations with little dependence on the colonial economic paraphernalia. The Indians and also the Japanese had developed strong interwoven network with their trading houses. In the words of R.A. Brown, "The intricate and often tangled network of distribution which emerged after World War One underlies British failure, and Japanese and Indian successes in the interwar years."[168]

Among the South Indian communities, the Chettiars were the most organized, hereditary business group with well formulated structure of intra-ethnic network having large investments in plantations and to some extent real estate properties. In their strictly laid out financial norms, they created room for business relations with the English banks as well. What apparently appeared to be acutely simple structure of a red coloured accounts' book, a *peti*, and a cabinet, was actually an intricately woven organization with strictures of overlapping socio-economic norms and temple-centric efficacies. However, the efficiency was only manifested within the ethnic organizational arrangement involving external agencies only in the periphery. Neither did it believe in imbibing modernization techniques or operational methods, thus drastically reducing its visibility in a progressive economy.

Another aspect of business operations was the inter-ethnic networking and interdependence among the traders and merchants in Singapore. The *bazaar* language was Malay and most of the Indian and Chinese businessmen learnt it for communicating with each other.[169] The Chinese, apart from being their clientele in the market, also provided with the logistic support to the Indian export-import firms in the form of the labour contractors or the *kapalas*. There was a *kapala* attached to each firm. Rajabali Jumabhoy had given a vivid description of the *kapalas* in his oral history recordings. He said: "There were about two main (or head) *kapalas* and these main *kapalas* had their sub-heads sitting in different offices of their clients along with a few *coolies*."[170] According to the agreed rate of contract the merchants were tied to them and they were paid per package or bale. Interestingly, the *kapala* could change or take over other new merchants, but that liberty was not given to the merchants.[171] The *kapalas* with their *coolies* were in charge of weighing the goods and getting them delivered to the buyer's weighing scale, from where the *coolies* of the buyer took on. Remarkably, this system continued without any major conflicts between the Chinese *kapala* and the Indian merchant portraying a peaceful negotiation of their space and they were successful in setting up economic equations and ascertaining well balanced indigenous commercial system which was exclusive of the establishments of the colonial regime. The system survived till taken over by the norms of the f.o.b. (free on board) or c.i.f. (cost, insurance and freight) prices of the much up-to-date and efficient logistic support companies.

The tale of the downfall of many of the first generation of businessmen has been attributed to a number of factors inherent within the community apart from the political and the economic changes in the Southeast Asian scenario which is briefly discussed below.

Indian firms were, more often than not, family-oriented affairs with the father remaining at the helm of affairs and decision-making till his dying day. The business would then automatically come into the hands of the eldest son of the family, irrespective of his aptitude, knowledge or expertise in the field as the prevalent Indian social practice, unless the father willed otherwise. Thus, the management and control of such business firms lacked professionalism, and in several cases, family feuds ensued between successors. Thus, consolidation and progress of business concerns did not remain in the priorities of the entrepreneurs as they could have been.

For the migrant Indian community, post-1947 posed dilemma not only with the wrath of the Partition but also with the indifference on the part of the Indian Government. Neither the Indian Government, nor Jawaharlal Nehru personally, had been advocates of dual citizenship. Nehru was rather of the opinion that Indians had to choose between the countries of domicile or Indian nationality. Many of the domiciled Indians were disillusioned; especially those who had advocated and participated in the nationalist cause and always looked homeward for at least a comfortable retired life. The new situation prompted many to take up citizenship of the countries they were residing in. Besides, there were the traumatized Sindhis and Punjabis, the victims of Partition, who were looking forward to carving out a niche for themselves in their new homeland. The South Indians, on the other hand, were reeling under the influence of the breakup of the Madras Presidency along linguistic lines into Kerala, Tamilnadu, Andhra Pradesh and Karnataka. The fissiparous tendencies of the post-independence period in India[172] had a direct impact on the ethnic Indian population in Singapore. Some sense of re-unity was re-instilled with the Sino-Indian War of 1962. However, no remarkable manifestation was witnessed in Singapore, given the existence of the majority Chinese population here.

Cohesive mentality was also missing for the Indians. Thus, a well united entrepreneurial group never actually emerged at any point of time in history. Part of this was because of the difference in languages of the mixed migratory population. A part was also played by the traditional caste structure in the social hierarchical order on Indians, which they followed with considerable rigidity even outside the country. There was also the divisive factor of the differences in religion. Added to it were the separate traits of business acumen of the High Street merchants and the Serangoon Road ones, each of them generally dealing with different segments of business. The identifications, both in social and economic perspectives were so distinct from each other that any attempt to consolidate it under one canopy did not meet with much success. The efforts undertaken in this respect, especially by the Indian Chamber would be discussed in a succeeding chapter.

Indian business concerns also generally faced the drawback of restricting themselves to the traditional methods of operations and technical know-how and maintaining modest economic standards. They also enjoyed the opportunity of going back to their native land after a few decades of reasonable earnings or as a retirement option. Staying back was not a necessity, but settling down with their respective families would have contributed to better consolidation of the diasporic community. As we have already discussed, the profit accrued in Singapore was remitted to India for family support and sometimes for philanthropic activities there. Thus, they were also wary of taking up Singaporean citizenship when there was easy opportunity in the 1960s, having planned their retirement in India. The post-independence migration laws, restricting the migration mobility put the Indians into new throes of adjustments and negotiations. The Indian Government, after its independence, had already shown ample indifference to its overseas population issues. This was quite unlike the Chinese migrants, who had little choice of looking homeward, settled here permanently without any dilemma. The wave of communism brought different political repercussions, which forms a separate context of study. For the Indian residents in the island nation, it had to be a choice between Singapore and India. Those who stayed back continued to struggle in the wave of modernization, and attempted to recast and adapt themselves to a large extent. Many established businesses and enterprises lost out in the process of structural modifications, while new ones emerged. While the older generation were living with the nostalgia of the past, the new age group worked out an identity that was rooted in the Indian culture, but essentially Singaporean in the mindset and ways of living.

Notes

1. For further details, refer to K.M. Panikkar, *India and the Indian Ocean: An Essay on the Influence of Sea Power on Indian History*, 1st reprint (Bombay: George Allen & Unwin (India) Private Limited, 1971).

2. K.N. Chaudhuri, *Trade and Civilisation in the Indian Ocean: An*

Economic History from the Rise of Islam to 1750 (Cambridge: Cambridge University Press, 1985), p. 15.

3. Roderick Maclean, *A Pattern of Change: The Singapore International Chamber of Commerce from 1837* (Singapore: Singapore International Chamber of Commerce, 2000), p. 14.

4. G.S. Graham, *Great Britain in the Indian Ocean: A Study of Maritime Enterprise, 1810–1850* (Oxford: Clarendon Press, 1967), p. 342.

5. Locally known as *Bengalees* possibly for their association with the Bengal Native Infantry, some left the garrison to become civilian migrants in the new land. Brij V. Lal et al., eds., *The Encyclopedia of the Indian Diaspora* (Singapore: Editions Didier Millet in association with the National University of Singapore, 2006), p. 176. Most of the migrants from Punjab, Uttar Pradesh, Bihar and any other places of North India became the victims of mistaken identity for the same cause.

6. Tan Tai Wong and Andrew Major, "India and Indians in the Making of Singapore", in *Singapore-India Relations: A Primer*, edited by Yong Mun Cheong and V.V. Bhanoji Rao (Singapore: Centre for Advanced Studies/Singapore University Press, 1995), p. 5.

7. Ibid.

8. Samuel S. Dhoraisingam, *Peranakan Indians of Singapore and Melaka: Indian Babas and Nonyas — Chitty Melaka* (Singapore: Institute of Southeast Asian Studies, 2006), p. 4.

9. Ibid.

10. Ibid., pp. 17–18.

11. George Abraham, "Indians in South-East Asia and the Singapore Experience", a paper presented at the International Conference on "Contribution by People of Indian Origin (PIO) in the Development of the Countries of their Adoption", Indian Council for International Cooperation, New Delhi, 12–13 February 2000.

12. Sinnappah Arasaratnam, *Indians in Malaya and Singapore* (London: Institute of Race Relations, Oxford University Press, 1970), pp. 1–2.

13. Ibid.

14. Colin Anderson et al., eds., *Singapore 30: A Portfolio of Singapore's Leading Companies* (Singapore: Springham Anderson Design Pte. Ltd., 1995), p. 7.

15. Ibid., p. 8; Walter Makepeace et al., *One Hundred Years of Singapore* (Singapore, Oxford, New York: Oxford University Press, 1991), p. 344.

16. Robert Godfrey and Samuel Dhoraisingam, eds., *Passage of Indians, 1923–2003* (Singapore: Singapore Indian Association, 2003), p. 8.

17. M. Sangaralingam, "The Role of Tamils in the Development of Singapore", in *Our History in Singapore* (in Tamil), edited by A. Veeramani, Tenth Singapore Tamil Youth Conference Proceedings (Singapore: The Tamil Youth's Club, 1999).

18. Godfrey and Dhoraisingham, op. cit., pp. 8–9.

19. Quoted from Godfrey and Dhoraisingam, op. cit., p. 13.

20. *The Encyclopedia of the Indian Diaspora*, op. cit., pp. 45–46.

21. Arasaratnam, op. cit., pp. 12–20; C. Kondapi, *Indians Overseas* (New Delhi: Oxford University Press, 1951), pp. 29–52.

22. Straits Settlements, Trade Commission, *Report of the Commission appointed by His Excellency the Governor of the Straits Settlements to enquire into and report on the Trade of the Colony, 1933–1934*, Part-II (Singapore: Government Printing Office, 1934), Chapter 6, p. 41.

23. Makepeace et al., op. cit., p. 345. See *Journal of the Indian Archipelago*, V (1851), VIII (1854) for further details.

24. Sharon Siddique and Nirmala Puru Shotam, *Singapore's Little India: Past, Present and Future* (Singapore: Institute of Southeast Asian Studies, 1982), p. 7.

25. Ibid.

26. A. Mani, "Indians in Singapore Society", in *Indian Communities in Southeast Asia*, 2nd ed., edited by K.S. Sandhu and A. Mani (Singapore: Institute of Southeast Asian Studies, 2006).

27. The "Bohras", "Khojas" and the "Memons" formed the three most common sects of the Gujarati Muslim migrants, of whom "Bohras" perhaps, were the largest in number.

28. "Al-Abrar" was also known as "Koochoo Pally", which meant a

small mosque in Tamil. Originally a thatched hut, a mosque made of brick was built in 1850–55. The mosque has been gazetted as a national monument in 1974. For further reference, see Norman Edwards and Peter Keys, *Singapore: A Guide to Buildings, Streets, Places* (Singapore: Times Books International, 1988).

29. *Report of the High Level Committee on the Indian Diaspora*, Chapter 20-South East Asia (New Delhi, India: Indian Council of World Affairs, Ministry of External Affairs, December 2001), p. 264.

30. Patit Paban Mishra, "India-Southeast Asian Relations: An Overview", in *Teaching South Asia: An Internet Journal of Pedagogy* 1, no. 1 (Winter 2001): 105–15.

31. Rajabali Jumabhoy, Oral History Recordings, Accession no. 000074, Reel no. 4, National Archives of Singapore.

32. Ibid.

33. Jumabhoy, op. cit., Reel no. 8.

34. Girishchandra Kothari, Oral History Recordings, Accession no. A000549, Reel nos. 7 and 8, National Archives of Singapore.

35. Devji Gopaldas Shah, Oral History Recordings, Accession no. A000796, Reel no. 1, National Archives of Singapore.

36. Ibid.

37. Bhagwan H. Melwani, Oral History Recordings, Accession no. 000146, Reel no. 1, National Archives of Singapore.

38. D.G. Shah, op. cit.

39. It might be mentioned here that the Sindhi Merchants Association that was established in 1924, declared in its rules that shops had to be closed for one day in a week. Any exception required prior permission of the Association. Refer to Chapter 4 for further details.

40. G. Kothari, op. cit., Reel no. 15.

41. Ibid., Reel no. 13.

42. Kantilal Jamnadas Shah, Oral History Recordings, Accession no. 000094, Reel no. 2, National Archives of Singapore.

43. Ibid.

44. Ibid., Reel nos. 2 and 3.

45. Ibid., Reel no. 2.

46. "Singapore Gujarati Society", <http://sgs.org.sg//history.htm> (accessed 29 April 2009).

47. D.G. Shah, Oral History Recordings, op. cit., Reel no. 1. Later on it was known as R.P. & Sons Pte. Ltd. The name of this company is also mentioned in the Gujarati website as one of the oldest companies in Singapore, <http://sgs.org.sg//history.htm> (accessed 29 April 2009).

48. D.G. Shah, ibid.

49. Ibid. Rajabali Jumabhoy also talks on similar lines saying that the British importers would sell their goods either for cash or for three months' credit. The buyers would then sell to the smaller distributors on similar credit. R. Jumabhoy, *Multiracial Singapore: On to the Nineties*, revised ed. (Singapore: Chopman Publishers, 1990), p. 51.

50. Syed Farid Alatas, *Notes on Various Theories Regarding the Islamization of the Malay Indonesia Archipelago* (Kuala Lumpur: Dewan Bahasa and Pustaka, 1969), p. 163.

51. Sinnapan Arasaratnam, *Islamic Merchant Communities of the Indian Sub-continent in Southeast Asia* (Kuala Lumpur: University of Malaya, 1989), pp. 5–6.

52. "About Us — History", <http://www.singjamaat.org/index.php?option=com_content&view=article&id=53&Itemid=88> (accessed 29 April 2009).

53. Ibid.

54. Moez Nomanbhoy, Oral History Recordings, Accession no. 000823, Reel no. 3, National Archives of Singapore. The figures mentioned are given by the interviewee.

55. D.G. Shah, op. cit., Reel no. 2.

56. Ibid.

57. The information is based on a collection of interviews conducted by Mustafa Izzuddin in 2002. The author is indebted to Mustafa for permitting the use of information for present research. Mustafa Izzuddin, "A Muslim Gujarati Community in Singapore: Dawoodi

Bohras", National University of Singapore University Scholars Programme, unpublished paper, 5 November 2002.

58. Nomanbhoy, op. cit., Reel no. 3.

59. Ibid.

60. Ibid. "Shebab" was a small group within the community comprising only of men in the age group of fourteen to forty to discuss what had been going on in the community. The women folk had a similar group organization too. Both groups have been revived to form the Shababul-Eidiz-Zahabi for the young men, see <http://www.singjamaat.org/index.php?option=com_content&view=article&id=57&Itemid=93> (accessed 11 January 2011) and the Talebaat-il-Kuliyaat-il-Moominat for the young women, see <http://www.singjamaat.org/index.php?option=com_content&view=article&id=63&Itemid=96> (accessed 11 January 2011).

61. Kutch is a peninsular region in the state of Gujarat in India surrounded by the Arabian Sea and the Thar Desert. The industrious and enterprising Kutchees had been famous as merchants, businessmen and skilled mariners travelling far and wide both in the Persian Gulf and Africa in the west as well as to the Southeast Asia and the Far East.

62. Kassim was a Muslim convert, whose Hindu name was Sakar. He had sailed to the Persian Gulf region around 1830 and must have been an accomplished name there to have a seaport, Bundar Kassim or Cassim, in Somali Coast named after him. See Jumabhoy, *Multiracial Singapore*, op. cit., p. 13.

63. Jumabhoy, op. cit., Reel no. 4.

64. Jumabhoy, *Multiracial Singapore*, op. cit., p. 38; Michael Mukunthan, "Rajabali Jumabhoy", National Library Board, <http://infopedia.nl.sg/articles/SIP_859_2004-12-27.htm>.

65. Jumabhoy, *Multiracial Singapore*, op. cit., p. 40.

66. Ibid.

67. Ibid.

68. Mukunthan, op. cit.

69. Jumabhoy, *Multiracial Singapore*, op. cit., p. 40.

70. Ibid., p. 46.

71. These are names of two towns in the Sindh province of the Indian subcontinent, presently in modern Pakistan.

72. Claude Markovits, *The Global World of Indian Merchants, 1750–1947: Traders of Sindh from Bukhara to Panama* (Cambridge: Cambridge University Press, 2000), p. 30.

73. Ibid.

74. Ibid.

75. Ibid., p. 120.

76. A. Mani, "Indians in Jakarta", in *Indian Communities in Southeast Asia*, edited by K.S. Sandhu and A. Mani (Singapore: Institute of Southeast Asian Studies, 1993), pp. 98–130.

77. P. Bharadwaj, *Sindhis Through the Ages* (Hong Kong: World Wide Publishing Company, 1988), p. 367.

78. Ibid., p. 269.

79. J.M. Mackenzie, *Orientalism, History, Theory and the Arts* (Manchester: Manchester University Press, 1995), p. 107. Some protagonists of the same theory were Christopher Dresser, Owen Jones and others.

80. Markovits discussed this phenomenon in details in his book. Markovits, op. cit., pp. 117–24.

81. Ibid., p. 149.

82. Ibid., Table 4.1, p. 127.

83. <http://www.sindhitrade.com/nri/singapore.asp> (accessed 31 January 2008). The names of Assomull, Gurbamal (Melwani) and Chotirmull have already been mentioned earlier.

84. Ibid.

85. <http://www.forbes.com/lists/2006/79/06singapore_Murli-Kewalram-Chanrai_BXGD.html> (accessed 8 June 2008).

86. Ibid.

87. Ibid. Kaur also mentions this in her Masters thesis, "North Indians in Malaya: A Study of their Economic, Social and Political Activities, 1870–1940s" (Unpublished Masters thesis, University of Malaya, 1973–74).

88. Brij V. Lal et al., ed., *The Encyclopedia of the Indian Diaspora*

(Singapore: Editions Didier Millet in association with the National University of Singapore, 2006), p. 176.

89. Exhibition panels, *Cash, Credit and Collateral, Money-lending in Singapore, 1820–1930s: Some Perspectives from the Koh Seow Chuan Collection*, Level 10, Lee Kong Chian Reference Library (Donor's Collection), National Library, Singapore, 7 May to 7 August 2007.

90. "Treatise on Asiatic Life in Malay Peninsula", in *Directory on Malaya*, Singapore, 1927.

91. Cheng Gin Low, Oral History Interview, Accession no. 287, Reel no. 17, National Archives of Singapore.

92. Jaswant Singh Bajaj, Oral History Recordings, Accession no. 000167, Reel nos. 1 and 3, National Archives of Singapore. This information was also given by Chhatru Vaswani, then Honorary Treasurer of the Sindhi Association in conversation with the author on 14 May 2009.

93. Jaswant Singh Bajaj, ibid.

94. Rajeswary Ampalavanar Brown, *Capital and Entrepreneurship in South-East Asia* (Houndmills, Basingstoke, Hampshire and London: The Macmillan Press Ltd. and New York, St. Martin's Press, INC., 1994), p. 209.

95. Singapore Indian Chamber of Commerce, *Fortieth Anniversary Souvenir Programme*, 17 November 1977, p. 10.

96. Conversation with Vaswani, op. cit.

97. "Parsi Association", <http://infopedia.nl.sg/articles/SIP_668_2005-01-04.htm> (accessed 18 March 2010).

98. "Parsi Lodge Charity", <http://infopedia.nl.sg/articles/SIP_250_2005-01-04.htm> (accessed 18 March 2010).

99. Behramgore Ratanshaw Vakil was one of the Parsis who came to Singapore from Tientsin, China, where as he mentioned, there were a number of Parsis who were engaged in business. B. Ratanshaw Vakil, Oral History Recordings, Accession no. 000297, Reel no. 10, National Archives of Singapore.

100. Rutton Patel, Oral History Recordings, Accession no. 000302, Reel no. 4, National Archives of Singapore.

101. Ibid.

102. Ibid.

103. B. Ratanshaw Vakil, op. cit., Reel nos. 11 and 19.

104. K.S. Sandhu, "Indian Immigration and Settlement in Singapore", in *Indian Communities in Southeast Asia*, edited by K.S. Sandhu and A. Mani (Singapore: Institute of Southeast Asian Studies and Times Academic Press, 1993), p. 778.

105. Sharon Siddique and Nirmala Puru Shotam, *Singapore's Little India: Past, Present and Future* (Singapore: Institute of Southeast Asian Studies, 1982), p. 8.

106. A. Mani, "Tamils in Singapore: Yesterday, Today and Tomorrow", in *Tamil in an International Arena 2002: First Step*, edited by Chitra Sankaran and S.P. Thinappan (Singapore: NUS Press, 2004).

107. Siddique and Shotam, op. cit.

108. <http://www.streetdirectory.com/travel_guide/singapore/facts_old_singapore/331/history_of_old_little> (accessed 11 June 2008).

109. Ibid.

110. Sandhu, op. cit., p. 778.

111. It is only very recently that businessmen like Mustafa and Haniffa Textile owners have opened branches outside Singapore.

112. Muthiahpillai Paramanayagam, Oral History Recordings (in Tamil), Accession no. B001285, Reel no. 4, National Archives of Singapore. Muthiahpillai was an employee of Govindasamy Pillai.

113. For the information on Ramasamy Nadar, I am indebted to Prof. A. Mani, currently Professor at the Graduate School of Asia Pacific Studies, Ritsumeikan Asia Pacific University, Japan.

114. Pugalenthi Sr., *Indian Pioneers of Singapore* (Singapore: VJ Times International Pte. Ltd., 1998), p. 68.

115. Arumuga Muthuvellu, Oral History Recordings (in Tamil), Accession no. A001175/04, Reel no. 3, National Archives of Singapore. He claims that there were about eighty workers in his shop.

116. Paramanayagam, op. cit.; Pugalenthi Sr., op. cit.

117. Muthuvellu, op. cit. Arumuga also worked under him for a number of years.

118. Ibid.

119. Suzanne Ooi, "Changing Face of Indian Business", *Sunday Times*, 25 November 1985.

120. Naidu Parangsam, Oral History Recordings, Accession no. A001179, Reel no. 4, National Archives of Singapore. Parangsam was the descendant of H. Somappa and he talks about the early Indian property owners and contractors.

121. Ibid. According to Parangsam, the large piece of land that was recorded as "Somappa" is the present district of Simei. He further says that there were roads like "Lorong Bersapa" and "Veera Ragu Close" in the Upper Serangoon Road which do not exist anymore.

122. S.T. Murthi, Kambalan and Gopalan Nair had popular tailoring business and "Manimekhalai" was a popular restaurant set up by Thamba Pillai in the Naval Base area. Karunakaran Nair, Oral History Recordings (in Tamil), Accession no. 001177, Reel no. 11, National Archives of Singapore.

123. S. Arasaratnam, *Maritime Trade, Society and European Influence in Southern Asia, 1600–1800*, Collected Studies Series (Hampshire, Vermont, Variorium: Ashgate Publishing Limited, 1995), Chapter XIII. This article was published earlier in *Moyen Orient et Ocean Indien, IV, Paris*, 1987, p. 128.

124. Ibid., pp. 132–37.

125. For a large part of the information on Tamil Muslims, I have referred to the research by Zehra Jumabhoy, *Indian Muslim Community in Singapore*, research conducted for the Asian Civilisations Museum, Singapore, 3 June to 10 July 2002.

126. Syed Mohamed Baquir bin Md. Ibrahim, *The Tamil Muslim Community in Singapore*, Academic Exercise, Department of Social Work, University of Singapore, December 1973, p. 117.

127. Interviews with moneychangers and other Tamil Muslims conducted by Zehra Jumabhoy in June–July 2002, op. cit.

128. There might be some confusion between the terms "Chettiar", "Chitty" and "Chetty". While Chettiar has been interchangeably used with Chetty, Chettiar happens to be a more dignified term.

Chitty, meaning a merchant, also refers to the Chitty Melakas or the Peranakan Indians who have evolved from the mixed marriages between the South Indian merchants and the local Malay women from the fifteenth century. When they migrated to Singapore in the nineteenth century, they too settled around the Serangoon Road area, Selegie Road, Race Course Road and the Chitty Road.

129. Arasaratnam, *Indians in Malaya and Singapore*, op. cit., p. 37. To learn more about the Chettiar heritage and their homeland, refer to S. Muthiah et al., ed., *The Chettiar Heritage* (Chennai: Madras Editorial Services, 2006).

130. R.N. Walling, *Singapura Sorrows* (Singapore: Malaya Publishing House, 1931), p. 84.

131. "Kittangis" in Tamil means warehouses or godowns.

132. Conversation with Dr S.P. Thinappan, Fellow, South Asian Studies Programme, National University of Singapore (NUS) on 16 May 2008.

133. Exhibition panels, *Cash, Credit and Collateral, Money-lending in Singapore, 1820s–1930s*, op. cit.

134. Ibid.

135. S.P. Thinappan, "Nattukottai Chettiars", in *Singapore: The Encyclopedia* (Singapore, Kuala Lumpur, Paris: Edition Didier Millet in association with National Heritage Board, Singapore, 2006), p. 377.

136. A. Palaniappan, "Arulmigu Thandayuthapani Temple, Singapore", a publication of Sri Thendayuthapani Temple on the occasion of *Maha Kumbabishegam* (bilingual — Tamil and English), 29 November 1996.

137. Thinappan, op. cit.

138. Somalay alias S.M.L. Lakshmanan Chettiar, "Chettiars and Hinduism in Southeast Asia", a seminar paper published by Somalay, Madras, 1973.

139. Conversation with Thinappan, op. cit.

140. H.D. Evers and H. Schrader, eds., *The Moral Economy of Trade: Ethnicity and Developing Markets* (London, New York: Routledge,

1994); Heiko Schrader, "A Comprehensive Analysis of Chettiar Finance in Colonial Asia", Working Paper no. 208, Faculty of Sociology, University of Bielefeld, 1994.

141. Schrader, ibid.

142. Singapore Indian Chamber of Commerce, *Report for the Year 1936* (Singapore: SICC, 1936), pp. 24–25.

143. Ibid., p. 25.

144. Ibid., pp. 13–14.

145. Sudhansu Bimal Mookherji, *Southeast Asia: A Study of Socio-Economic, Political and Cultural Problems and Prospects* (Calcutta: Post-Graduate Book Mart, 1966), p. 62.

146. Ibid., p. 54.

147. Ibid., p. 62.

148. For further discussions on Subhas Chandra Bose and his activities in Singapore, see Joyce C. Lebra, *Jungle Alliance: Japan and the Indian National Army* (Singapore: Donald Moore for Asia Pacific Press, 1971); Lebra, *Japanese Trained Armies in Southeast Asia: Independence and Volunteer Forces in World War-II* (Hong Kong: Heinemann, 1977); Subbier Appadurai Ayer, *Unto Him a Witness: The Story of Netaji Subhas Chandra Bose in East Asia* (Bombay: Thacker, 1951); Sisir K. Bose and Sugata Bose, eds., *Chalo Delhi: Writings and Speeches, 1943–1945/Subhas Chandra Bose* (Calcutta: Netaji Research Bureau, Delhi, Permanent Black, 2007).

149. "Sindhis in Singapore", <http://www.sindhitrade.com/nri/singapore. asp> (accessed 31 January 2008). The information has been corroborated by an elderly member of the Sindhi Association.

150. Arasaratnam, *Indians in Malaya and Singapore*, op. cit., pp. 110–11.

151. Ibid., p. 111.

152. R. Jumabhoy, Oral History Recordings, op. cit.; Jumabhoy, *Multiracial Singapore*, op. cit.

153. Jumabhoy, *Multiracial Singapore*, op. cit.

154. The Indian Chamber of Commerce, *Report for the Year 1946*, pp. 16–17.

155. Ibid., pp. 18–19.

156. K.S. Sandhu, *Indians in Malaya: Some Aspects of their Immigration and Settlement (1786–1957)* (London: Cambridge University Press, 1969), pp. 16–18.

157. K.S. Sandhu, "Indian Immigration and Settlement in Singapore", in *Indian Communities in Southeast Asia*, edited by K.S. Sandhu and A. Mani (Singapore: Institute of Southeast Asian Studies and Times Academic Press, 1993), p. 776.

158. Singapore Sindhi Association, <http://www.singaporesindhi.com.sg/aboutus.php> (accessed 31 January 2008).

159. This was true not only in Singapore but also in other places of Sindhi business hubs such as Hong Kong. The changes coincided with the emerging trends of new demand and supply equations as a part of the economic transition of the nation-building era.

160. <http://www.sindhitrade.com/nri/singapore.asp> (accessed 31 January 2008).

161. Refer to Figure 2.1 in Chapter 2 for the increase in ethnic Indian population in the post-Partition decades.

162. Ravinder Singh, "Migrants to Merchants: Dynamics of Sikh Entrepreneurship in Singapore" (Unpublished thesis, Department of Sociology, National University of Singapore, 1998/99), p. 53.

163. *Report of the High Level Committee on the Indian Diaspora*, op. cit.

164. Ibid.

165. Sandhu, "Indian Immigration and Settlement in Singapore", op. cit., p. 781.

166. Markovits, op. cit., p. 18.

167. Ibid.

168. Brown, op. cit., p. 197.

169. The Malay language remained the communication link among the Indian and Chinese traders and businessmen well into the 1970s and the 1980s.

170. Jumabhoy, Oral History Recordings, op. cit., Reel no. 8.

171. Ibid. In Jumabhoy's own words: "There was seldom any quarrel between the *kapala* and the merchant. If the cost went high, they

sat down amicably and worked out their charges and settled the matter among themselves. ... our firm had a small *kapala* who used to have allegiance to another chief *kapala*. We could not change him from 1915 all through till after the war even. The *kapala* used to sit in the office for our import/export trade. He used to take an advance for his work and every three or six months adjust the account."

172. A. Mani, "Indians in Singapore Society", op. cit., pp. 795–96.

Chapter 2

THE POST-INDEPENDENCE PERIOD: CHANGING DYNAMICS AND THE SHIFT IN BUSINESS ACTIVITIES

In the different phases of Singapore's economic progression, the Indian business communities, like any other community, had been trying to negotiate its space and identity through fissions and fusions, inclusion and exclusion, and working out the nuances of religious, regional and ethno-cultural issues. In the continuous process of changing dynamics, the economic factors had been intimately related to other circumstantial elements. The Indian business communities in Singapore as in most of the other Southeast Asian states, evolved and restructured themselves in the post-colonial phase, and again in more recent trends of globalization. In the various stages of negotiation and evolution, enterprises went through their highs and lows, business changed hands and the character of the goods and commodities of trade altered. The ethnic Indian business groups, broadly categorized as North and South Indians, as we have seen in the previous chapter, gradually disseminated from the visible spatial architecture into the larger framework of the multiracial identity in the country. This chapter will focus on some of the challenges faced and diversification efforts of the different Indian business groups and individuals and their negotiations with the new vistas of modernization.

I. CHANGES AND CHALLENGES

Nation building and restructuring an independent Singapore had been a daunting task that the Singaporean leaders had undertaken in 1965 and accomplished with consummate success. The new trajectory was based on making the best of its geopolitical advantages, the foundations of which was already laid down by the colonial rulers; and at the same time implementing different facets of modernization in economic, social and political perspectives. Thus, on the one hand, Singapore became the busiest port of the Commonwealth by 1969, the container transhipment centre for Southeast Asia by 1972 and claimed to be the third important port in the world by 1975 only after Rotterdam and New York;[1] on the other hand, Singapore invested in building up a modern armed force to protect itself and in development expenditure on infrastructure, building HDB estates for residences, improvising communication facilities and setting up of manufacturing units. Jurong was set up as an industrial estate and by the end of 1970 she had 264 factories with 32,000 workers which were in production and another 106 factories under construction.[2]

Singapore had little choice but to opt for a free market economy, thus hailing the influx of foreign capital investments and expertise either as multinationals or joint collaborations which set the pace for the rapid development and progress in the small island nation. However, the challenges of an open economy made Singapore very vulnerable to world fluctuations. She also had to guard her interests against the political and economic differences of her neighbours. She made the most out of the advantages of the geographical location, but did not have any natural resources to capitalize on. Above all, she had to protect herself from the ensuing Cold War tremors that were so vigorously felt in different parts of Southeast Asia. However, Singapore not only survived, but excelled in propelling the country to an exemplary level of economic success, especially in the areas of trade, tourism and transport.

With the colonial powers withdrawing their clutches from Southeast Asia, there was a natural urge for the nation states to develop their own manufacturing industries and also deal directly with the countries from which raw material had to be procured, thus undermining the well-established colonial trading networks and activities in Singapore. To survive and succeed, it was necessary to embark on a process of industrialization given the limited possibilities of extensive agricultural activities and a rapidly growing population (at 4 per cent per annum)[3] to be taken care of. However, the strategic location of Singapore in one of the most historically important traditional sea route between India and China remained significant enough to modernize and develop its port facilities and maintain and upgrade itself in trading activities, and its importance as a commercial and financial centre has been well developed by the government to create an incredible success story in Asia.

The industrialization process that the government embarked on in the 1960s was that of import substitution, which solved the unemployment problem by the 1970s and expanded the trading activities of the island nation. But by late 1970s and early 1980s, it was changed to that of export oriented industrialization with a great impetus to the modernized growth of the manufacturing sector. With a higher wage policy and a switch over to less labour intensive methods, encouragement was given "to mechanize, automate and computerize".[4] This had the apparent necessity of attracting modern technology and foreign expertise to help Singapore carve out a niche in the extremely competitive foreign markets thus paving the way for a turning point in the economic restructuring with the participation of "skills, expertise and connections of multinational enterprises".[5] This was not a difficult proposition given the legacy of Singapore's foreign driven development during the colonial period.

Involving the multinational enterprises (MNEs) in the country's development would ensure inflow of advanced technology and managerial expertise as a part of their integrated industrial structure and also facilitate "asystemic power balancing operations"[6] between Singapore and the other nations leading to increased prospects of coalition between them. The assimilation and integration of the acquired foreign know-how also enabled Singapore to apply these innovations to the traditional sectors for greater levels of efficiency and eventual prosperity. For the MNEs, it was not only a matter of "better communication between the headquarters and the subsidiary, and between management and other local employees" as Choy has suggested[7] but also the advantage of administrative and logistic cost effectiveness and less expenditure on cheaper human capital as well as making inroads into the virgin markets with tremendous scope and potential. This marriage of convenience served the intentions of both sides extremely well and led to volumes of foreign investments.[8]

With the emergence of independent Singapore in 1965 came in a new political order where the fundamental principles were that of equal status and opportunities for all. Educated Indians, who were proficient in English, came to occupy a number of important positions in the political field as well as the civil service in the 1960s and 1970s. However, the business communities faced various challenges in the process to survive. The MNCs were encouraged to come to Singapore with tax and other benefits. At the same time, the Government-Linked Companies (GLCs) like INTRACO, Jurong Town Corporation (JTC) and the DBS were set up in wide range of economic activities.[9] The GLCs were formed in the 1960s and 1970s to boost up economic development in some sectors, where some shares were held by the government (in the 1980s and the 1990s they were formed from corporatization of the government bodies and departments). They posed serious challenges to the traditional business communities, whether Chinese or Indian as the latter were left to survive on their own without any government incentives. The rapid introduction of modern methods and technology and competing with the multinational companies created quite a test for the family-oriented business patterns and constraints of capital for the ethnic Indians and many were unable to keep up with the pace of modernization and gradually waned out. The Urban Land (Ceiling and Regulation) Act as well as the Control of Rent Act of the new government also turned the tide against the fortunes of many propertied Indian businessmen as well as wealthy landowners[10] and they were unable to sustain themselves in the face of the changing tide.

As an inevitable part of the Singaporean system, the ethnic Indians were under the same government rules and regulations in matters of education, health care, housing facilities or job opportunities. However, being a minority race in Singapore left them somewhat anxious and insecure about the opportunities, demands and desires and initially, they remained quite sensitive in relation to the Chinese majority.[11] One reason for a very high rate of unemployment which prevailed just after Singapore's independence was perhaps due to the military withdrawal.

Figure 2.1

The Ethnic Indian Population in Singapore over the Years

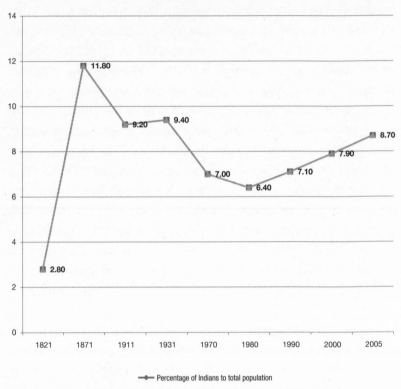

Percentage of Indians to total population

Sources: K.S. Sandhu and A. Mani, eds., *Indian Communities in Southeast Asia*, 2nd ed. (Singapore: Institute of Southeast Asian Studies, 2006); Leow Bee Geok, *Census of Population 2000: Demographic Characteristics, Statistical Release 1* (Singapore: Department of Statistics, Ministry of Trade and Industry, 2001); *General Household Survey 2005, Socio-demographic and Economic Characteristics* (Singapore: Department of Statistics, 2006).

However, the non-technical mindset also accounted for the difficulties. "The profile of the unemployed Indian reveals an affinity for non-technical jobs. A disproportionate number were looking for clerical and service occupations; the non-preference was due to a genuine lack of technical skills among the job seekers."[12] This tendency dissipated in the later years with increasing number of Indians joining the field of computer sciences and information technology, business, engineering, medicine and other physical sciences, with some professionals eventually diverting to entrepreneurship in the service sector.

Right from the time of Singapore's independence in 1965, PAP leader Lee Kuan Yew's commitment to multiracialism made him become an "unswerving protector of Singapore's minorities".[13] The general pattern of Indian occupation did not change dramatically in the post-1965 years. Apart from being involved in business and trading, big and small, quite a number of them made a mark as civil servants and lawyers, union leaders and doctors. Names like foreign minister, S. Rajaratnam; labour leader, Deven Nair; and head of Singapore Airlines, J.Y.M. Pillay appear as significant players during the formative years of modern day Singapore.

The Singapore Indian Chamber of Commerce had taken some initiatives to encourage traditional Indian trading community to venture into industry. The new President in 1970, Roop Vaswani, in an interview with the *Malay Mail* talked about members investing about $10 million in a holding company which would be aimed at creating more employment and more export products.[14] The company was to be known as "Lion City Holding Company", which would be investing in profitable industrial ventures.[15] The attempt, however, did not prove to be much fruitful, and Indians continued with their trading activities, but diversifying to different products. In spite of the rapid industrialization process undertaken by the government, trade still continued to contribute the largest share in the country's GDP, until very recently, when it has been substituted by the service industry. As far as the holding company of the Chamber is concerned, it took up a similar investment venture directed towards India with the establishment of the Parameswara Holdings, more about which has been discussed in Chapter 4.

II. LANDSCAPE OF THE INDIAN BUSINESS GROUPS

Ethnic Indians in Singapore, generally speaking, maintained an inconspicuous, but inevitable presence in different spheres of life at a time when Singapore was taking giant strides towards technological modernization and globalization in the 1970s and 1980s. A number of reasons accounted for this. A majority of them were from middle and lower level income groups with not very high educational qualifications or professional skills. A look at the occupational structure exemplifies this rationally.[16] This had much to do with the status of the migratory labour population of their forefathers which formed the bulk of the Indian population on the island. As regards the diverse business groups, they found themselves shaken from their own small niches that they had built within the margins of the imperial economic periphery.

From a structural point of view, the High Street shops still remained the same during the immediate years following independence, that is, in the 1960s and 1970s. From an account of the High Street shop, we come to know that in the two-floor shop buildings in the area, the ground floor housed all the retail shops and upstairs had rooms doing wholesale as well as import-export business. There were around fifty to sixty shops doing retail as well as wholesale business and another 500 of them were textile wholesalers.[17] The numbers had dwindled down to hardly fifty or sixty shops doing textiles around 1985.[18] Even if these numbers appear somewhat exaggerated, they are successful enough in impressing us with the magnitude of the business prosperity in textiles. The Gujaratis, the Sindhis and the Punjabis participated in the business in a big way.

Textiles were both a popular and a lucrative business for the Indians till the 1960s and 1970s. G. Kothari talks of the printed cotton fabric, *tobralco* from England which was very popular with the Chinese, and especially catered to the better-off customers.[19] Wholesale business generated comfortable profit margins, around 7–10 per cent[20] and neighbouring Indonesia and Malaysia provided ready markets for merchants who were re-exporting Japanese products first and later on from South Korea and Taiwan with the increase in competition.

Singapore served as the centre for entrepot trade in textiles, or "the warehouse for the whole area", as one textile merchant points out,[21] from the post-Second World War days into the 1950s. Goods came to the island from Italy, America and India mostly during this phase and catered to almost the whole of South and Southeast Asian countries like Sri Lanka, Burma, Thailand, Vietnam and Cambodia. However, from the early 1970s, the decolonization and nation-building process in Southeast Asia began to be visible with the nations embarking on their indigenous development of the manufacturing industries and infrastructural facilities and promoting their own trade and commerce. This in turn had a backlash on the colonial patterns of trade practices which the Indians were familiar with. Besides participating in the entrepot trade, they were actively involved with the network of inland distribution system as well.[22] However, there were some who confined their activities to trading only. The monopolistic tendencies of exports and re-exports began to decline in its profit margins and merchants were left with little choice but to diversify. Many players in the High Street area did just that. For others, business volumes came down and they soon petered out. A case which fits in the latter explanation is that of Girishchandra

Kothari, a first generation Gujarati businessman in textiles. It might be interesting to look into his story, which had similarities with many others who experienced the same fate.

After having encountered some difficulties in the Indonesian markets, Kothari diversified to semi-wholesale business to cater to Arab Street, Serangoon Road, Tanjong Pagar as well as Malayasian markets. He travelled to different parts of Malaysia to sell to Chinese and Indian customers. He started off at 91, High Street with three people in his office — a salesman and a *tambi* (a peon) besides himself. With the increase in competition, margins of profit went down and the dimensions of market changed with fewer people doing big volumes of trade for different territories like Bangladesh, Colombo, Nigeria and the risk factor was also much greater. On the other hand, in the 1970s, Malaysia had started developing direct business and taxes were imposed to restrict imports. Indonesia had also done the same, but the problem there assumed a more political colour than only encouraging indigenous national interests. All these factors contributed in accumulating lots of bad debts, less sales and delayed credits apart from mounting expenses. This was especially true in the trade with Indonesia where merchants transacted business with one month's credit and eventually increased the time span only to suffer huge losses in the end. In the case of Kothari, from 1974 onwards he was barely able to maintain himself. He first did away with the salesman and then with the tambi, and worked single-handedly till he retired from business altogether.[23]

Kothari forms a classic example of the study of the aspirations of the first generation businessman, who was unable to sustain himself with changing political and economic circumstances or diversify, manage and invest a bigger amount of capital when necessary. Most of them had started off as employees in other firms and had been lured by the profitability in trade, experience and training gained in employment of other firms as well as useful contacts made during the course of his employment.[24] It happened with most of the ambitious and enterprising young employees, who had the opportunity to start with small capital and enjoy good profit margins. But, when political circumstances changed, both internally and externally, it required a change in the economic structure too. On the one hand, there was the nationalist drive of industrialization, as has been mentioned earlier, which was a setback for the textile trade, which most of the Indian merchants were engaged in. Added to it was the political problem of *Confrontasi* propagated by Indonesia, thus almost severing trade links with Singapore. On the other hand, the changes in government policies internally brought about by new migration and employment laws, moneylending strictures, laws regarding land management system and the Control of Rent Acts, and also the huge competition from the MNEs and the GLCs, all of which acted against the survival of that thriving generation of ethnic Indian businessmen. Many of them were unable to cope with the situation due to dearth of capital needed to sustain and progress. As a result, numerous mushrooming businessmen in the heydays of the 1950s and the 1960s made an inglorious exit and sometimes went back bankrupt. This was true to a large extent for the High Street merchants, who were mostly engaged in trade and wholesale business, but was also applicable for some of the Serangoon Road businessmen as well, who were mainly in the retail business and general provisions, but also in wholesale business of textiles and spices. Some of the popular earlier retail shops in the area were that of Sithi Vinayagar and V.K. Kalyanasundaram Stores, the first generation businessmen, who had started from scratch and rose to be popular names in the area.

Kalyanasundaram had a lot of shops in the area. There were two shops on Buffalo Road while the rest were situated on Dunlop Street and Serangoon Road. These sold textiles, cosmetics, electronic goods, and many other consumer goods. A large number of people were employed under him. Like other businessmen, he provided food and residence to his employees and was considered a good employer.[25] Business was good till the 1980s when it had to face tough competition from the other emerging giant in the area, Mustafa. Kalyanasundaram faced huge losses, and unable to cope with the changing situation, soon lost his business. Similar fate befell another retail business outlet, MRP K. Vandayar & Sons.[26] Unable to adapt to the changing situation and modernization and restricting themselves to the small domestic market, which could be easily saturated, these enterprises eventually went bankrupt.

The business of the popular Govindasamy Pillai was taken over by his son, G. Ramachandran, who diversified his father's textile and the sundry goods business into wholesale trade in spices, petroleum business, where he lost a lot of money and properties.[27] Spices proved to be most lucrative for him, and, between 1968 and 1972, his business expanded to annual sales of $50,000 to net profits of $750,000.[28] With losses in other business, this provided him with the financial support.

The Chettiar community also received a big jolt financially in the post-independence era. This was the second big blow after the Japanese aggression and the financial depression of the 1930s when a large part of their investments were lost. They faced stricter immigration rules and employment policies, legal sanctions and restrictions on moneylending activities, and stiff competition from banks and other financial institutions. They were also displaced from their *kittingis* in the Market Street area as it was required for the urban renewal process in the 1970s which made them concentrate in the remaining few *kittingis* in Tank Road. They eventually diversified into professional activities and took up jobs in the banking, civil service, educational centres and the private sector. Thus from 108 registered Chettiar moneylenders in 1966, the number dwindled to a mere seven by 1981.[29] Moreover, younger generations, who had received education in Singapore, and later went abroad for higher studies and jobs began to feel less connected with the rigid, socio-religious structures of the past and opted for other professions. To the future generations, the traditional but lucrative business of the Chettiars was lost forever. Naturally, the older members of the community, who usually passed on their method of accounting to succeeding generations, met with the setback of finding suitable successors to their firms.

The Chettiar community still exists as a close-knit structure, not exclusively as moneylenders that they did in the past, but as a small part of the larger Singaporean mosaic. The strong allegiance to the temple still remains, mostly for religious and sociological reasons. A few *kittingis* have survived near the Tank Road Temple with sparing business activities, but their business structure, both physically and operationally, has remained the same. The Nattukottai Chamber of Commerce has remained a close-knit, introvert, caste-based association and continues with the intra-community regulations, both in social and economic matters, while the others, who are the non-moneylenders or professionals "still comply with those in the traditional occupation".[30] The strong religious element in their business structure is a unique phenomenon, which has already been studied in different researches.

It is interesting to note that the colour and vibrancy of the Serangoon Road merchants have continued over the generations with their involvement in diverse activities, albeit, mostly on a smaller scale with very few exceptions. Goldsmiths and their glitterati remains a striking feature of Little India with a number of shops, Chinese and Indian, displaying a variety of designs and filigree work. However, in the 1950s and 1960s the picture was quite different. According to Ramachandra, the founder of Jothi Stores, there were hardly two/three Indian Muslim gold shops and one/two Chinese shops in the area.[31] However, a much larger number of Indian goldsmiths thronged the area, who were associated with the shops and had developed individual clientele. Rethnavelu Suppiah, the name usually associated with Ani Mani Porchalai, a famous gold shop in the area, started out by helping his elder brother, who had a similar small business in the area. They were inspired by their father who had gems and stones' business in India.[32] He claims that there were only three Indian gold shops, no Chinese shops in that area when they started out in 1947/48.[33] The jewellery designs were typically Indian made for Indian clientele. However, they did not get them from India but got it made locally by employing goldsmiths. They had about ten goldsmiths working for them, who used to go to India once in a while but would return back. The specialized techniques were handed down hereditarily.[34] However, Rethnavelu asserted that there are no more goldsmiths who emigrate from India.[35] The gold jewellery is supplied by the Chinese workers, who surprisingly, keeping the market necessities and choices in view, supplies jewelleries with Indian designs to minute details. At present, there are also many Chinese jewellery shops in the area showcasing and selling the same kind of products to especially, the Indian clientele. Batu Pahat, owned by Mr Lam, started in 1969,[36] and is perhaps one of the oldest of the Chinese shops in the string of jewellery shops in the area. The large number of shops that sprang up subsequently indicates lucrativeness of the trade. It is interesting to find an increasing number of glittering Chinese shops in the area selling jewellery which are typically designed for the Indian clientele. It helped them to take advantage of the Indian traditions where gold is not only regarded auspicious, but extremely relevant in social interactions, both for the rich and the not-so-rich people. Shops like the Jewels of Palace and others have been in the business for around fifteen to twenty years. However, increase of shops also meant increase in competition over the years.

The gold shops in Little India are unique in the sense that they bring out elements of strong inter-ethnic networks, that too in a place which has an overarching presence of Indian characteristics, rightfully highlighting the essence of the Singaporean muticulturism and multi-ethnicity. However, restrictive employment laws have been a setback to bring in employees specialized in the craft of making intricate designs since the 1970s. Thus, many Indians have opted to close down, diversify or sell their business and return to India. The vacuum created had been taken over skilfully by the Chinese in this business.

Serangoon Road area has essentially been the heart of the ethnic South Indian business community with a recent trend of increased participation of North Indian businessmen, mainly in retail goods and electronics and other consumerables and also the food sector to capitalize on the booming tourism industry in the country and the inevitable attraction that Little India holds to all. One famous North Indian name that appeared in business in the area long before the recent medley of shop owners appeared was that of Mustafa, a retail outlet that has managed to create a global recognition for itself almost synonymous with other places of tourist interest in Singapore. Hailing from a Muslim family in Uttar Pradesh in India, Mustafa created a revolution in the retail market of the area and has become synonymous with the attraction of the Serangoon Road area. We shall learn more about his business ventures in Chapter 5.

The picture of the Serangoon Road area remains incomplete without the mention of the Indian restaurants. "Komala Vilas" (established in 1947), "Ananda Bhavan" and "Saravana Vilas" were some of the older names mainly catering to the strictly vegetarian South Indian clientele with a very modest get-up. From the 1980s, there has developed an interest in various Indian cuisines among the non-Indian community as well and entrepreneurs were quick to exploit the fondness for spicy food, Singaporean and foreign. The Race Course Road area became synonymous with the Indian restaurants serving North Indian, South Indian and also Chinese and Singaporean food. The later names that appeared were that of "Banana Leaf", "Muthu's Curry", "Gayatri", more recently "Anjapaar" (2004)[37] and several others with newer business still being started. A lot of restaurants serving North Indian cuisines have also added up to the aroma of the Race Course Road, one of the most popular names being that of Gurucharan Singh of "Jaggi's".[38] It might be mentioned that new names in North Indian cuisines have also appeared in restaurants in Clarke Quay, Boat Quay, Holland Village and other upmarket areas. The restaurant owners are both from North and South Indian backgrounds and have a much more professional and attractive get-up in comparison to the older generations. Very few of the earlier restaurant owners made any efforts to change and continued business in their traditional garb. In fact, the Komala Vilas ownership got divided among the brothers and each shareholder opened a new branch, the most progressive appearing to be the "Komalas", vegetarian, but including a number of fast food items in their menu. The original restaurant, however, continues its business with a traditional structure.

Serangoon Road has changed its appearance from the unimpressive row of obscure looking shophouses of the 1960s and early 1970s to a vibrant, colourful and aromatic commercial area teeming with people, mostly South Asians, but also others like Malays and Chinese, especially on weekends. The initial residential areas of Dunlop Street, Campbell Lane, Buffalo Road, Kerbau Road have all been included in the commercial commotion of Little India now. Many people also flock to the area with the mindset of bargaining and lesser price options. The pulsating Little India has made it an important tourist attraction, and also encouraged the government to retain a number of shophouses in the area as heritage sites. The thriving mix of old and new is something that neither the residents nor the tourists can let go amiss.

One of the characteristic difference between the North and the South Indian merchants in general has been in their nature of business. Whereas the South Indian community catered to the retail sector and were more inward looking accruing to the daily needs of the ethnic Indians in Singapore, the North Indian businessmen were more outward bound with their wholesale and retail businesses aiming to attract a clientele both in and outside Singapore. More flamboyant and cosmopolitan in nature, they were also more dependent and affected by the market dynamics of Asia and the world. Whereas most of the North Indians who initially came to Singapore in search of fortunes were involved in business and trading, it was not the case with the South Indians. They depended on small accumulated savings from other jobs and also on moneylenders to start a business for the first generation and gradually expand if the going was good. Unlike the former, they were few from business oriented castes or ethnic groups, except the Chettiars. The Singapore Indian Chamber of Commerce and Industry (SICCI) has traditionally been identified with big business and international market, which soon received the common social interpretation as the representative body of the North Indians, since the group were a majority who were venturing abroad. Talking about his South Indian counterparts, Rajakumar, President of LISHA and owner of JSFS, says:

Unlike the north Indian businessmen, I would say we are very
conservative ... they are risk takers. ... they don't do much of
retail business. They have a lot of family members all over the
world whom they work with and that way they do big business.
Whereas the small businesses run by the South Indians who
are very conservative, very cautious about the money they have
and what they spend, very, very careful until today — that's
the way.[39]

However, the commercial viability of the Serangoon Road
area has been thriving well and physically more appealing as
a neighbourhood space of Indians, especially with the recent
government incentives to create heritage sites in the area. The
preservation of the traditional physical structure has helped to
accommodate and sustain many small-level businessmen, though
dealing with the problem of rising rent has remained a matter of
serious concern for many. The combination of culture and market
has been explicitly defined in ethos and spirit much more than
what can be visible in the High Street area, which unlike Little
India, portray a more amalgamated business structure in the larger
multicultural picture of the Singaporean system. Of late, however,
there have been efforts made to refurbish structures in Little India
into a more contemporary image than what has been existing
in the area. "The Verge", comparatively new shopping mall in
the area, was built with a more contemporary look in its new
mix of shops and restaurants which would be less Indian related
and more a generous mix of the larger shopping architecture of
Singapore.[40] This effort, perhaps, reveals an attempt to shed off
the typical characteristics of the location and identify with the
structural planning of the bigger canvass of the Singaporean
system. The changes also reveal the mindset and outlook of
the new generations who would be inspired by the beckoning
of contemporary trends rather than remain confined to the
peripheries of the "subcontinent nostalgia".

III. DIVERSIFICATION OF BUSINESS INTERESTS AND NEW PARTICIPATION

The disturbance of the balance established by the participants in the colonial economy in the process of decolonization and nation building facilitated in ushering in remarkable changes in the functioning of the Indian business communities. A number of ethnic Indian enterprises could stand the test of time and embark on the path of progress, diversification and modernization, gradually severing the homeward bound connections. There were also others who started in the 1970s with more forward-looking approaches, diversified products and a global vision. They excelled in the field of electronics, chemicals, sports goods, tourism and commodities. Trading still remained lucrative with commodities and spices, and the ones with the desire to expand and look beyond the national borders not only set up offices elsewhere but also made efforts to establish overseas manufacturing bases. We have seen the examples of companies investing in Africa, Australia, Estonia and other places in Southeast Asia. In fact, ethnic Indians have excelled in trading to places far and near and were the first to grab opportunities in the Middle East and Africa in a manner not generally witnessed among other communities. The transition continued well into the era of globalization with enterprises adjusting and readjusting into the dynamics of the global economy.

Thus, post-1965 changes in the political situation resulted in the three different categories of businessmen.

- Those who did not manage to survive and petered out.
- Those who not only survived but also progressed.
- New enterprises that emerged and flourished.

Examples of entrepreneurs who did not manage to carry on with their business activities, has already been discussed to some extent. A considerable number of Sindhi and Gujarati firms that had opened up during the colonial days accounted for this category. Many of them survived through the 1960s and 1970s with diminishing popularity and profit and finally closed down, or shifted base elsewhere. Big companies of the Chhotirmal family shifted their business to Hong Kong and closed down the Singapore office. This was in spite doing very well financially. The primary reason for this was that once the entrepot trade of Singapore diminished with the changed circumstances, it was less lucrative to run the show without further improvisation and value-addition and the support of a domestic market. Hong Kong provided that support of the mainland Chinese market, and at the same time, the opportunities of looking outwards into the Asia Pacific or other regions.

Among the big business families that thrived and progressed were the Kewalram Chanrai Group, the Tolarams, the Jumabhoys, the Thakrals, Pars Ram Brothers or the Royal Brothers Group to name just a few. Almost all the successful business enterprises ventured out of the periphery of the domestic Singapore market and established their market operations or manufacturing units in other parts of Asia, Australia, Africa or Eastern Europe.

The Jumabhoys were a very important name in the formative years of Singapore. Rajabali had played a significant role in spearheading the formation of the Indian Association (1923), Indian Merchants Association (1924) and subsequently the Singapore Indian Chamber of Commerce (1935). He was the only Indian representative in the Trade Commission (1932–34) appointed by the Governor of the Straits Settlement to advise on dealing with the economic slump. Apart from other representations, he was elected into the Legislative Council in 1955 in the first General Elections of Singapore. It is unfortunate that the reputation thus earned was diminished in the face of family feuds and conflicts.

This had, however, been a general pattern of many of the declining ethnic Indian firms and enterprises, which we shall eventually see in many cases in our research. In 1975, the family residence at Scotts Road was developed into a commercial area with the Scotts Shopping Centre and the Ascot serviced apartments and in 1991, the Scott Holdings decided to go public. However, family feuds ensued soon after and led to the decline of the fame and the name of the Jumabhoys. In October 1995, Rajabali initiated legal action against his son, Ameerali concerning the management of their family business, the Scott Holdings[41] and division in the family dealt a severe blow to their reputation.

Another name which had made a remarkable mark in the business world of Singapore during this period is that of the Royal Brothers Group. Started by Naraindas in 1947 as a small silk garments trading firm in Singapore, it ventured into Africa in the 1950s and 1960s and successfully capitalized on the opportunities. In the 1970s the firm passed on to the second generation of the family — Mr Raj Kumar and Mr Ashok Kumar, who brought about significant strategic changes within the company and made a foray into the property business in the region.[42] They form an example of successful attempts of the traditional first generation textile merchants transforming and diversifying themselves into the second generation of property businessmen and other opportune ventures. By the 1980s, they had acquired significant number of shop units in the major commercial centres of Singapore like Lucky Plaza, Peninsula Plaza, Queensway Shopping Centre and other important places. In the 1990s they diversified into the hospitality business and managed to acquire a number of important hotels in and outside Singapore. The "Royal Brothers Building", which was purchased in early years of the present century, is located at Raffles Place, the financial centre of Singapore.[43]

The Tolaram Group is another important name in the world of ethnic Indian business. Their success story began in 1948 with a modest textile shop in Malang, Indonesia known as Toko Vaswani. The first overseas office in Singapore was established in 1965, which forms the Group's headquarters now.[44] The Tolarams set up their first green field textile manufacturing plant in Indonesia in 1973. They stepped into the African market way back in 1976. "Today it has emerged as a manufacturer and distributor of electronics and household consumer goods, paper, instant noodles, chemicals and dyestuffs, floor coverings, fishing nets and textiles in the African continent."[45] The Tolaram Group ventured into Estonia in 1995, the first Singaporean company to do so after the end of the Cold War. The present Chairman, Mohan K. Vaswani and the Vice-Chairman, Vishamkar T. Adnani have successfully steered the enterprise towards rapid progress and expansion and have also diversified its operations in many parts of the world under capable professionals. The Group presently employs over 8,000 people of different nationalities making it a multinational organization.

Among its new initiatives in business, the Tolarams are looking forward to building up of a petrochemical project and a world class multipurpose facilities' port in Nigeria. They have also launched a brand of soya bean beverage, whose main market would be Nigeria and Iran.[46] The main focus of the Tolaram Group remains the markets in Nigeria and Estonia. They have also been involved in many social and community related activities. In their own words, "We focus on education, sports, community development and childcare — areas that mean something to our business and where we can make a positive impact."[47]

In spite of its widespread business activities both in terms of products and markets, the Tolaram Group, like many ethnic Indian corporate bodies, remains a family-owned structure with some subsidiaries and minority shareholders.[48] While it is indeed remarkable to have a close-knit family owned structure of an enterprise with such diversified interests, one cannot rule out the challenges of upholding the essence of solidarity for the future generations to come.

One of the biggest names in the Singapore business community has been that of the Thakrals, who form an example of business and entrepreneurship that forayed into Singapore from outside in the region. Starting with the modest "Punjab Store" in Bangkok, Sohan Singh Thakral laid the foundation of the multi-billionaire empire which gradually spread out to the world spanning two dozen countries and employing about 8,000 people[49] in about two generations' time. The Singapore office was started by Kartar Singh, the family patriarch, in 1952. The "Thakral Brothers" started as a corner textile store situated in High Street, the place where Kartar Singh started his business career in Singapore.[50] His business grew by leaps and bounds and eventually became a limited company in 1973. Talking about his business ventures, Kartar reminisces, "It has gone beyond what I had imagined .... we believed in modern management and started modernizing in the mid 1970s."[51] They diverted into the electronics business from 1973, and this sector eventually accounted for most of their profits. Over the years, the Thakral Group has ventured successfully into the field of consumer electronics, investment and financial services, hotel management and tourism-based services.[52]

Kartar established contacts with China as early as the 1960s. Taking advantage of the reforms starting in 1979, the Thakral Group set up its first office there in 1984 and began selling electronics products. This was so successful that it began to market VCRs under its own label and had managed to assimilate a customer base of about 1,500 dealers, distributors and retailers in seventy-five of its major cities.[53] The success story was spearheaded by Kartar's son, Inder Bethal. Major Japanese companies like Panasonic, Sharp and Sony had anointed Thakral to be their main wholesale dealer in the section of audio-visual products.[54] Despite success in trading, the Thakrals also ventured into warehouses, property and hotel business as well as manufacturing. The Thakral Group had established the Chengdu plant in China for the manufacture of television sets in 1993 and joined with the Chinese to set up the electronics park in Wujiang in 1995.[55] The company has been listed on the Singapore Stock Exchange since December 1995.[56] Talking about his achievements in China, Kartar Singh demonstrates, "Our race is Indian, but our brains are Singaporean. I don't find a difference between Chinese and Indians doing business. Business is business."[57] He further adds, "The Chinese trust Singaporeans. They find Singaporeans to be straightforward people."[58]

The Thakral Group has spread far and wide spanning different corners of the globe from Australia, Middle East to Europe and Africa. China, however, remained their biggest revenue source.[59] Besides, Thakrals had also established business links with India, their ancestral homeland. In the early 1980s, Thakrals brought in Japanese television sets into the Indian market. Of late, it has put in its stakes a garments factory in joint collaboration with Marzotto of Italy, joined with Natsteel of Singapore to launch a ship-breaking operation and has been involved in developing the Gurgaon Technology Park near New Delhi along with other partners.[60]

Like most traditional Sikh family-oriented entrepreneurs, Kartar Singh did not believe in acquiring formal higher education. None of his sons received university education. In his opinion, "if you wish to be a trader no Harvard MBA is going to help you. The key is to find each person's talent."[61] Kartar's convictions, entrepreneurial skills, foresight, shrewdness and a flair for taking up the challenges of a promising market have contributed to making of the famous and enviable business entity that he is at present. However, the Thakrals faced difficulties during the Asian Financial Crisis in 1997. They faced huge losses and the company tried to cope with the crisis by restructuring themselves and reducing debts by 2002–03 until their share prices arose again. In the words of their own chairman, "The problems of competitive pressures and component supply issues" affected their core business divisions.[62] For the financial year ending 31 March 2005, the consolidated revenue was S$522.3 million which fell to S$391.7 million for the financial year ending 31 March 2006. The organization has been taking "firm measures and made several internal changes", as the Chairman pointed out in his Statement in the Annual Report, "to deal with macro factors like changing trends and dynamics in the Chinese market".[63] The giant corporate has been restructuring itself to face the new challenges of the twenty-first century.

The big names like Thakrals were few, but there was a consistent existence of small and middle-level businessmen in the High Street area. Amrik Singh, who set up the business of wholesale garments in 1966, is one of them. His business reached its peak in the 1970s and he converted it into a limited company in 1980.[64] What was remarkable was that in spite of tough competition and the usual diversification of business that ensued in the years that followed Singh remained hooked to his garment business only changing the style and makeover in the garments as the market demanded. He has managed to retain some old and loyal customers and, according to him, continues to make reasonable profit.[65] His sons have, however, taken up products like watches and electronics, and his grandsons are in the field of higher education, so the fate of his garment business remains quite uncertain.

Among the non-Sikh Punjabi entrepreneurs, two names stand out in the business circles of Singapore, the Pars Ram Brothers (Pte.) Ltd. and Khattar Holdings. For the former, it was a journey from being export merchants to improvising themselves to global traders in commodities and also establishing factories in different countries. The foundation of the Pars Ram Brothers in Singapore goes back to 1937 when the family moved to Singapore and set up their business.[66] However, their history of migrating in this region goes much earlier. The grandfather of Kirpa Ram Sharma, the present Managing Director of the Company, migrated with his brothers from Beas, near Amritsar in India in 1901 to Ipoh, Penang and Kuala Nerang in Malaya to begin as a money trader. After Sharma's father, Ishwar Dass Sharma joined them later, they moved to Singapore.[67] They have been a global trader in spices, dealing with around 130 varieties of Southeast Asian products, and pepper making, yielding the major share of the revenue.[68] They became a private limited company in 1973.[69] The company has been trading in "authentic natural spices (both in whole and grounded form) like cloves, cumin seeds, fennel seeds, fenugreek seeds, ginger, mustard seeds, nutmegs, pepper as well as processed spices like crushed chillies and different recipes of curry powders and seasonings",[70] besides different nuts and other agricultural commodities. They ventured into Australia and established themselves as a private company in 1977. Preferred to be known as "'global trader in commodities and produce",[71] the family business is at present headed by Kirpa Ram Sharma in the capacity of the Managing Director of the Company.

Another area where the North Indians, especially the Punjabi Sikhs made their mark was the area of the sports goods business. This was a specialized area with a niche clientele and did not always follow the sensitivities of the common economic factors in the market.[72] Initially the colonists and the Europeans formed their main customers. After they left, the void was filled by the expat community who accounted for the larger section of the clientele since the 1970s and remains so till the present. There were comparatively few players in the market. Among them, the Royal Sporting House was one of the most famous names along with the Chinese enterprise, the World of Sports. In fact, during the 1990s, the massive competition that ensued between the two affected the others in a similar business and gave them a hard time dealing with the competitive "price-wars".[73]

Most of the sports goods business progressed and flourished as part of the newly established companies in the post-independence era. The Royal Sporting House (RSH) founded by M.S. Gill and his son, J.S. Gill in 1969, was engaged mainly in outsourcing of sporting goods in the early years. When the son, J.S. Gill took over the reins of the business, he succeeded to incorporate it as the Sporting House Pte. Ltd. on 28 September 1977.[74] The opening of Royal House at Lucky Plaza, Singapore's most expensive shopping mall at that time in 1979, was a significant milestone achieved and there was no looking back. They tried to evolve constantly with the changing conditions suiting to the needs of active lifestyle of the clients and making some of the best brands available to the consumers. In the 1990s, they began to look beyond Singapore's new growth and market diversities and had successful operations in different countries like Malaysia (1989), Indonesia (1990), Brunei (1991), Dubai (1992), Hong Kong (1992), India (1993) and the Phillippines (1994).[75] In 2000, the company was listed on the main board of the Singapore Stock Exchange. At the turn of the century, business was further diversified into fashion, footwear, furniture, etc with "Novo" and "Mumbai Se".[76]

Another name, not as big as the RSH, was that of Weston Corporation. A family business started by his great grandfather who sold sports goods manufactured at Sialkot, modern Pakistan,

Anant Bir Singh, one of the present directors, along with his brother, inherited the spirit of business and competency to succeed in opening thirteen outlets in Singapore.[77] The business originally started with the name of Rose & Co. till 1950 when they were dealing in both the textiles and sports goods, but later decided to discontinue with the textiles. Dealing with both wholesale and retail business in sports goods, Anant Bir Singh is of the opinion that the present business has reached a stage when the needs and choices of the customers are extremely important. He also believes strongly in higher education for the younger generation, quite unlike many other Sikh businessmen, not only to bring about changes and innovations in the business and understanding the client better, but also as an option to fall back upon in the situation of a crisis.[78] They are currently focusing on the consolidation of their business and assets and streamlining it for the convenience of the future generations.

Other names in this business are that of Chopra Sports Pte. Ltd. (the business of Anant Bir's uncle who broke away from his father in 1983), Champion Sports, Crown Sports, etc. Since this was a kind of a monopoly business and served a specific upper strata clientele, not many opted for it. Incidentally, it was mostly the Sikhs who took up this trade which best served the interests of the Western expatriate communities as luxury products that were quite westernized in style and functions.

There were manifestations of other forms of diversified business interests too. A prominent name in the well-known circles of Singapore, Satpal Khattar, started his career as a professional lawyer. A student of the National University of Singapore (both for his LLB, Hons. and LLM degree), he was the founding partner and later consultant in Khattar Wong and Partners, one of the premier law firms of Singapore. Khattar Wong was established in 1974 and grew dynamically to provide comprehensive services in banking, finance and property, litigation, tax, shipping, construction and criminal law, corporate and securities law to a wide and diverse clientele.[79] Khattar remained a Senior Partner in the law firm until December 2000, and "commenced practice as a sole proprietor under the name and style of Messrs Sat Pal Khattar"[80] with effect from 1 September 2005.

Satpal's father came to Singapore in 1932 and had a sports goods shop here, which was closed down during the Japanese aggression. They were in Pakistan at the time of the Partition and came to Ambala as refugees. Thereafter, they came back to Singapore to start afresh.[81] Satpal Khattar, now the Chairman and Director of Khattar Holdings Pte. Ltd., a group of company engaged in making investments, is again looking towards India of late and making frequent trips there to make broad based investments in various sectors there like banking, real estate and infrastructure and has also some interest in the auto and the manufacturing sectors.[82] He nourishes positive feelings about India's growth, feels comfortable on its soil both linguistically and culturally, and looks for opportunities there though he admits that there are bureaucratic hassles on the way. Interestingly, he had been allotted nine million shares of the HDFC Bank in India before it went public, some of which were sold off and some were retained.[83] He has also entered into a MOU with Sunsam Properties, a Kolkata-based real estate company for a Rs. 1,500 crore township project in Kolkata. The Hyderabad-based Surana Group has also roped in Khattar to make infrastructure investments of Rs. 150 crores.[84] In his own words, about 60–70 per cent of their investments are in India, 5–10 per cent in China, and the rest in Singapore, Malaysia, Vietnam and Europe.[85]

Satpal Khattar is a renowned name both in the world of business corporations as well as among different business associations. He is the chairman of Guoco Land Ltd., a public listed company in Singapore with headquarters in Hong Kong. He has been the Chairman of "Network India", a platform that encourages business linkages between the companies of Singapore and India, as well as the Director of "Savant Infocomm".[86] He is among the Board of Advisors to the SICCI, Director of the Institute of South Asian Studies (ISAS) and the Chairman of the Board of Trustees of the Singapore Business Federation and holds several other similar posts in different organizations.

Satpal's dynamic spirit and entrepreneurial vision has been successfully taken up by his son, Arvind Khattar, the Executive Director of the Khattar Holdings. At the launch of the Young Business Leaders Forum by the Singapore Business Federation, he, like a true successor, said: "With globalisation and changing market dynamics, I think it's very important that we start young, we start fast and we develop that dynamic nature (in) us."[87]

There were others too who were flourishing, like Shankar's Emporium Pte. Ltd., which was established in Singapore in 1957. It has been a leading trader in consumer electronic goods and household appliances since 1981 and is spread over many countries across the globe.[88] In 2004, it launched its own brand "Zaiko" in consumer electronics in various regular products like home and kitchen appliances, home theatre systems and many others.[89]

It is interesting to note that while several old trading firms had diminished and disappeared in this period, there were emergence of new trading enterprises in the 1970s and thereafter, who had prospered over the years and still remain as big names in the business community. However, there was a major difference between components of trade, operational methods and periphery of outreach in the two generations. While the former small traders mostly thrived on textiles and spices in the entrepot trade within the Southeast Asian waters, the next generation embarked assertively on diversification, technological advancements, incorporating professionals and looking aggressively beyond Asia. One such business venture, which started during the 1970s and emerged as one of the affluent enterprises by the turn of the century was the Sofeene Enterprises. This company had started as small textile agents in 1970 by Hanifa Shariff (present Chairman of the Company) and Ally Shariff (the present Managing Director).[90] From the 1980s, they expanded to other products like import of carpets, fabrics and fibres from Japan into the Indonesian market. In 1980, they also started operations in Hong Kong and Taiwan markets and established offices there as well as in Thailand and Vietnam in 2001. In 2004, their India office also expanded. They are now trading in products ranging from cotton, leather, paper, metals and alloys, agro products to chemicals.[91] They had been a pioneering company in importing Indian yarns into Singapore in 1974, and are at present one of the leading trading, sourcing and marketing agency with a turnover of more than US$100 million.[92] To quote Mr Hanifa: "Growth has no limit at Sofeene. I keep revising my vision. Only when you dream it you can do it."[93]

Besides the North Indian merchants and traders in general, some of the merchants in the Serangoon Road area have also made efforts to embark on a path of expansion and diversification in the context of retail trade and marketing. It would be interesting to look at a few examples from the area.

O.K. Mohamed Haniffa, who came from an agricultural background in Pudukottai in Tamil Nadu, started as a provision shop in the area and gradually ventured into retail textiles and other products and went on increasing the number of shops in Madras Street, Dunlop Street and Serangoon Road. With humble beginnings in 1962, Haniffa Textiles soon became a famous name in the Serangoon Road area. They not only did good business in saris, ready-made garments and Java batik sarongs, but also diversified to jewellery business opening the Jewel Palace in 1995 and also a Departmental Store in the area selling all kinds of consumer durables. They have also managed to open several branches in Malaysia (Kuala Lumpur, Selangor, Ipoh, Penang) and India (Chennai, Pudukottai).[94]

Hailing from Tanjore, Murugaia Ramachandra, the founder of Jothi Stores & Flower Shop (JSFS), came to Singapore in 1948 at the age of sixteen. He worked in Standard Times Press till 1958 and in 1960 he opened a very small shop (the same place where it stands today) selling betel leaves and other small items.[95] About a year later, he bought the neighbouring shop and started the flower business. He started his business with a rent of $55 and an initial investment of $1,000.[96] There was one shop assistant for the first two years which later increased to fifteen by 1990. In 1970, the business suffered heavy losses due to the Indonesian problem.[97] He, however, could successfully wade through the difficult years till 1975 and bought another new shop by 1981 and also managed to reduce his debts.[98]

The JSFS has a unique monopoly in the market. It has capitalized on the social rites and religious oriented products that sold with large profit margins to the very religious minded Indian population. Flower was an indispensible necessity in every event of an Indian's life, whether in birth, marriage or death. Added to it is the availability of all the necessary products for the rites and the rituals, decorative items, CDs, cassettes and statues under one roof which has added to the prosperity of their business. Ramachandra also mentioned about three other flower shops in his time, which did not survive. But he started with making $40–50 a day to $100 and more with the opening of the flower shop.[99] Of late, however, we find a number of flower shops in the vicinity, who seem to complement the business rather than give any competition of sorts.

Business took a new turn in 1985 when Ramachandra's son joined him. With a university degree in computer science, he efficiently steered the business to further prosperity. In February 1986, the Company became a partnership business between him, his father and his mother, R. Thanaletchimi.[100]

Rajakumar has had valued customer satisfaction immensely, interacting with them and receiving their feedback in maintaining and increasing his business. He is usually found behind the counter serving customers' needs and suggesting handy options to them. This helped him along with his foresight and toil to bring the business to a different level in his time. In his own words, "I found the niche market in Singapore where my business was already there. People don't have the time to do shopping for religious rites and puja ... priests used to give a long list of puja items, about 40/50 items, people have to spend about two/three days going up and down every shop to make sure that all the things are there for the prayers to be carried on well and people didn't have the time."[101] Rajakumar capitalized on the needs and the sentiments of the religious minded Indians to supply them with all the items under one roof. His shop also supplies the flowers to all the temples in Singapore. (There are twenty-five Hindu temples in Singapore at present.)

JSFS has gradually become a distributor for many Indian companies. It is also involved in wholesale and retail business of Basmati rice, beverages and Indian electrical household appliances and utensils. Jothi Holdings Pte. Ltd. was incorporated in 1992 with the same partners and purchasing offices were opened in Chennai and Mumbai. To further increase his business, Rajakumar wants to go into franchising in about a decade or so, brand his products and bring in the professionals.[102] He says:

Maybe in another ten to fifteen years down the road, I would
like to franchise the Jothi business out of Little India. And at that
point of time, I would like to create a lot of Indian entrepreneurs
who want to take the business and the Indian community
participate in that. That is the level what I'm looking at now.

Thus, with dynamism, modernization, innovations and foresight,
Rajakumar has efficiently managed to put his enterprise as one
of the leading business concerns in Little India.

At the opposite end of the big names, exist small and
medium-level business outlets in the area, which were founded
and managed to sustain themselves through the formative years
of Singapore and have also grown in their own limited way. One
such name is that of Anacaona Pvt. Ltd. set up by V. Damodaran
Pillai. Son of a labourer, he was deprived of higher education,
but trained in the methods of business by working as assistant
in shops. Eventually he started his first business by door-to-door
selling on his bike and later established the shop as it stands
today.[103] The items sold are very much similar to that of everyday
utilities in Jothi Stores, but done on a much smaller scale. This
initially started as a partnership business which was later taken
over by Mr Damodaran and he intends to pass it on to his son,
an engineer by education, in about five years' time.[104] Similar
outlets and even smaller ones are quite a few in the area.

Interestingly, the Serangoon Road merchants maintained
relations with India on a much more regular basis than the
merchants on the High Street, as India continued to be a sourcing
base for their saleable products in the retail market for local
consumption as well as retirement options and philanthropic
activities. In a way, they remained attached to the Indian soil
in more ways than one. In the Chettiar society, for instance, a
marriage can only take place only if it is approved by one of the

temples in the Chettinad village in Tamil Nadu in India to which the family is affiliated. In their system of conservative customs, marriages can only take place in the designated temple grounds, or, has been made flexible to the extent that the original temple permits the temple overseas to give the garlands for exchange during marriage. Any intermarriages, though increasing, are still not accepted or entertained within the gambit of their caste norms.[105] This is almost incredible keeping in view that the Chettiars had been one of the oldest of the Indian commercial communities to be spread across the waters of the Indian Ocean in Southeast Asia. The children of the present and earlier generation have also received high education in the West and opted out of the moneylending business to a great extent, but have not been able to recast the strictures of the caste system entirely. It has, thus, been inevitable for the community to maintain close relations with their ancient village in India, irrespective of political or other factors.

IV. CONCLUSION

The post-independence period and the later years witnessed a lot of changes as to the players in the ethnic Indian business ventures as well as their modes of operation and diversifications. While many of the past opportunities were lost, it also opened new vistas for undertaking and furthering commercial interests in the post-colonial world. The preference of Indians over the others, at times by the colonialists for their familiarity with the English language, was then utilized and diverted towards the greater global outreach. In fact, it has been adequately acknowledged that the transnational outreach of ethnic Indian business had been wider and more extensive than that of the other races during this period.

However, when the PAP government took over with some trails of the British legacy in administrative and legal matters, the larger systems had changed and priorities became different. Under the new political structure, changed policies and increased industrial modernization, Indians found it increasingly difficult to keep up with the changed make-over and, consequently, with few exceptions, gave way to the new players in the fore.

Indian businessmen did not flourish as much as their Chinese counterparts. It is believed that "the average Indian businessman is more easy-going and less shrewd than his Chinese counterpart; he can't think big and he can't gamble".[106] Experts believe that this was also a reflection of the Indian character. We have the examples of the Tamil moneylenders who possessed a lot of wealth, but for different reasons, failed to make good use of it. As the politician and businessman, Inderjit Singh puts it, "For the Indian community, we have not seen the partnership and collaborative spirit of the Chinese where the professional with the knowhow get the support of successful businessmen where both benefit from new business opportunities."[107]

Trading remained the main area of business activities for the ethnic Indians, however, with a new rhetoric. The intra-ethnic viability of the commercial community and their homeland linkages and support from the subcontinent were severed with the establishment of new political relationships. The older generation of the Indian community was more involved in the process of sociological interactions, re-adjusting and re-bonding in the new political set-up, where they had to choose between the citizenship of either country. The new generation of offsprings, who were born and brought up on this soil, chose to be a Singaporean in mind and soul only to be virtually linked with the subcontinent through its culture (somewhat modified to the Singaporean milieu), cuisine, religion and music. Besides, the environment of the Cold War and the political tensions in the region prevailed upon and reshaped the interstate relationships. This was also the era when ethnic Indian companies ventured into setting up of manufacturing units outside Singapore. Those who progressed did so with changed dynamics than before leading to an increased gap between the generations as also communication with the subcontinent. It may be mentioned here that almost all of the successful second-generation Indian businessmen in Singapore that we have discussed in the chapter, started with their first generation being involved in the textiles trade mainly, from where they eventually diversified into new business opportunities.

In the "considerable loosening" of the "foregoing colonial social order", as K.S. Sandhu puts it,[108] there has been a substantial human movement of one racial enclave into the other, especially in the post-1965 phase in Singapore. In modern Singapore, the economic progress, education and language policies, urban development and the formation of the Housing Development Board (HDB) estates helped to diffuse the "enclave" mentality of the people to a large extent. The newer generations were more educated, partly as an effort of their own consciousness as well as the persistence and stewardship of their parents aiming at a better living. The old patterns of division on caste-based lines or wealth-oriented distinctions began to get blurred paving way to a more secular approach based on meritocracy under the independent nation. The ethnic walls began to crumble and were "increasingly subsumed under the overarching presence of the state, nation building, and the creation of a common Singapore ... identity".[109]

The political and economic circumstances of the 1960s and the early 1970s in Singapore were very testing indeed. On one hand, the challenges of nation-building brought forth a revolution of sorts with the dynamic economic policies, infrastructural facilities, foreign policy incentives, and educational innovations. The challenges transcended both on the domestic front as well as in the whole of Southeast Asia, the repercussions of which were seriously felt in Singapore. For Singaporean Indians in the trade of textiles and spices, the days of monopoly trade were over. In the march towards self-sufficiency and nation-building, as we have already seen, both Malaysia and Indonesia began to encourage indigenous industries reducing the dependence on Singaporean traders drastically and putting up the barriers of custom duties. In addition, Sukarno's Indonesia carried out a policy of "confrontation" against what it called the "neo-colonialism" in the vicinity[110] both in political and economic fields, thus posing great difficulties to the traditional trading activities. The profit margins began to dwindle, so many in the next generation concentrated more on the previously neglected spheres of education and professional services, and eventually relocated themselves abroad.

In the phase of structural adjustments for the Indian business communities, the new business and enterprise that emerged depended much on contemporary market demands like those in the case of electronics. The encouragement of the growth of the tourism industry also led to ethnic Indian participation in related business and hospitality industry, which still continues as a lucrative sector of enterprise. However, competing with the multinational companies in a free market economy not only requires the money but equally, dynamism of thought and actions, and few Indian businesses were equipped with the required professionalism at this stage. The Government-Linked Companies that emerged in the post-colonial phase had a significant presence in Singapore's corporate sector and gave substantial competition to the private enterprises. The Singapore-based Indian companies chose rather to navigate beyond the borders to less competitive and lesser developed terrains with a price advantage, and many were successful in doing so.

Most ethnic Indian entrepreneurship was based on family business groups with the hereditary succession. Over the decades, education began to receive due importance, something which the earlier traders and merchants did not focus on, thus emphasizing more on hands-on experiences and business acumen. The primary importance of education has brought in a vast array of changes within the traditional trading community. If on the one hand, it brought in the possibilities of incorporating a more professional approach and technical advancement within the family business pattern, on the other hand, it has often led to dissociation of the educated younger generation from the stereotype of their forefathers. They would want to experiment with innovative ideas either on the business front, or excel as professionals. This has resulted in many enterprises, especially the smaller, closely guarded family business entities to dwindle and ultimately perish. Thus, closures of many enterprises was not because of the lack of competency or bankruptcy, but in many cases, because of the inability to handle domestic transitions and assimilate the thinking process of the new generations within the hereditary format of the family business patterns. This was common both for the North and the South Indian business communities where corporatization has remained the biggest challenge.

In the sociological construct of Singapore, there ensued a new kind of negotiation among the dominant entities. The homeward bound tendencies of the Indians had to be replaced with the settlement patterns in the Singaporean milieu. They had to accommodate cosmopolitanism and modernization along with their traditional social and religious sentiments. There was also the economic tension of survival and success. As has been discussed, some middle and small level enterprises and the ones more orthodox with lack of foresight, succumbed to the transition, but that was not the case with all. Many succeeded in the competition with modernization, diversification, collaborations and globalization as we shall continue to see in the forthcoming chapters, and actively participated in accelerating the economic climate of Singapore.

Notes

1. C.M. Turnbull, *A History of Singapore, 1819–1975* (Oxford, Kuala Lumpur: Oxford University Press, reprinted in 1979), p. 308.
2. Ibid.
3. Lee Soo Ann, *Industrialization in Singapore* (Victoria: Longman Australia Pty Limited, 1973), p. 12.
4. Chong Li Choy, *Multinational Business and National Development: Transfer of Managerial Knowhow to Singapore* (Singapore: Issued under the auspices of ISEAS, Maruzen Asia, 1983), p. 63.
5. Ibid.
6. Ibid., p. 67.
7. Ibid., p. 60.
8. Foreign direct investments were allowed both in trading and services, but for the retail sector, government preferred 51 per cent stake of a Singaporean partner.
9. Chan Kwok Bun and Ng Beoy Kui, "Singapore", in *Chinese Business in Southeast Asia: Contesting Cultural Explanations, Researching Entrepreneurship*, edited by Edmund Terence Gomez and Hsin-Huang Michael Hsiao (London: Routledge, 2003), pp. 41–43. The authors wrote from the Chinese business perspectives which were applicable to the Indians too.
10. One such example was the business and wealth of Pakirisamy Pillai who was the owner of prime properties in the Orchard Road area and was also into financing business. However, things changed in the face of new rules, regulations and modern methods, and the next generation, unable to reorganize their fortunes, lost it. This

information is based on an interview in February 2008 with Brian Shegar who is one of the close descendants of Pillai.

11. "They are especially sensitive to signs of any excessive ascendency of Chinese identity, language and culture, resulting inevitably, as they view it in a relegated status for their own languages and cultures. Behind this all is the ultimate fear that Singapore will be turned into an essentially Chinese Singapore, a Third China." Raj Vasil, *Asianising Singapore: The PAP's Management of Ethnicity* (Singapore: Heinemann Asia, 1995), p. 5.

12. George Abraham, "Indians in South-East Asia and the Singapore Experience", a paper presented at the International Conference on "Contribution by People of Indian Origin (PIO) in the Development of the Countries of their Adoption", Indian Council for International Cooperation, New Delhi, India, 12–13 February 2000.

13. Susumu Awanohara, "A Home for Genuine Effort", *Far Eastern Economic Review*, 23 November 1979, p. 40.

14. "The Switch to New Industry for Indians", *Malay Mail*, 15 April 1970.

15. "New $10 m Holding Company is Launched", *Sunday Times*, 5 April 1970.

16. Apart from the Census reports of the years concerned refer to Nirmaljeet Kaur, "Indians in Multiracial Singapore, 1945–1980: A History of their Occupational Pattern" (B.A. honours thesis, History Department, National University of Singapore, 1982/83).

17. Girishchandra Kothari, Oral History Recordings, Accession no. A000549, Reel no. 14, National Archives of Singapore.

18. Ibid.

19. Ibid., Reel no. 12. Chhatru Vaswani, the Honorary Secretary of the Sindhi Association, and a businessman himself, in his conversation with the author on 14 May 2009, reiterates that *tobralco* was especially popular with the Chinese ladies. Similarly *tricolene*, another example of one of the finest quality of cotton cloths from England, and quite expensive too, was popular with the Chettiars,

who bought them in large quantities when going to India on their annual vacation.

20. Kothari, op. cit., Reel no. 14.

21. B.H. Melwani, Oral History Recordings, Accession no. 000146, Reel no. 4, National Archives of Singapore.

22. The intricacies of inter-ethnic network even prior to the coming of the colonists in Southeast Asia has been discussed by Rajeswary Ampalavar Brown in her chapter on "The Growth of Trade, Trading Networks and Mercantilism in Pre-Colonial South-East Asia" in her book, *Capital and Entrepreneurship in South-East Asia* (Houndmills, Basingstoke, Hampshire: The Macmillan Press Ltd. and New York, St. Martin's Press Inc., 1994), pp. 1–20.

23. Kothari, op. cit., Reel no. 14. Kothari gives a vivid account of his business initiatives, his earning of substantial profits as well as his downfall.

24. Interview with Chhatru Vaswani dated 14 May 2009. Vaswani has been intimately involved with the Sindhi Merchants Association and is a trader in specialized electronic items like the camera. When asked why he would not employ an assistant as he had been running a one-man show all along, he replied that he was apprehensive of the fact that he would have then lost his contacts to the employee who would, once mastered the nuances of business, more often than not, start his own business. That was what seemed to have been the most common practice.

25. Arumuga Muthuvellu, Oral History Recordings (in Tamil), Accession no. A001175, Reel no. 4, National Archives of Singapore.

26. Vandayar is an endogamous group within the *Kallar* caste from Madurai district in Tamil Nadu, India.

27. Suzanne Ooi, "Changing Face of Indian Business", *Sunday Times*, 24 November 1985.

28. Ibid.

29. Exhibition panels, *Cash, Credit and Collateral, Money-lending in Singapore, 1820s–1930s: Some Perspectives from the Koh Seow Chuan Collection*, Level 10, Lee Kong Chian Reference Library (Donor's

Collection), National Library, Singapore, 7 May to 7 August 2007.

30. A. Mani, *The Changing Caste Structure Amongst the Singapore Indians* (M.A. thesis, Department of Sociology, University of Singapore, 1977).

31. M. Ramachandra, Oral History Recordings (in Tamil), Accession no. 001122/03, Reel no. 1, National Archives of Singapore.

32. Rethnavelu Suppiah, Oral History Recordings (in Tamil), Accession no. 001161/03, Reel no. 1, National Archives of Singapore.

33. Ibid. Their shop was initially situated at 45, Serangoon Road till 1977 and then shifted to the present location at 73, Serangoon Road. The initial rent was about $35–$40 which gradually increased. They later bought over the place.

34. In India, the goldsmiths are a specialized category under the caste structure, where the specific techniques were handed down from the father to the son for generations.

35. Suppiah, op. cit. The interview was taken in 1990. Actually, there are very few who would come to Singapore at present under the Employment Pass category. I have discussed this further in one of my forthcoming articles on the jewellery business, "Beyond the Glitteratti: Indian and Chinese Jewellery Business in Little India".

36. The date was revealed by one of the employees during a conversation with the author at Batu Pahat in September 2008.

37. Interview with the owner of Gayatri Restaurant and the President of IRA(S), G. Shanmugam on 23 May 2009.

38. Penny Reutens, "The Grape Vine", in *Savour*, food magazine, published by the Indian Restaurants Association, Singapore, July–October 2003, p. 67.

39. Interview with the owner of Jothi Stores and Flower Shop (JSFS) and the President of Little India Shopkeepers and Heritage Association (LISHA), Rajakumar Chandra on 17 July 2008.

40. "Tekka Mall Gets New Name and Focus", article in the *Business Times*, posted on 6 August 2008 by agneschaw, <http://agneschaw.

wordpress.com/2008/08/06/business-times-tekka-mall-gets-new-name-and-focus/> (accessed 8 August 2008).

41. Michael Mukunthan, "Rajabali Jumabhoy", National Library Board, <http://infopedia.nl.sg/articles/SIP_859_2004-12-27.htm>.

42. "Historical Highlights", <http://www.royalbrothers.com/historicalhighlights.htm> (accessed 21 May 2008).

43. Ibid. The Royal Brothers Building was originally the DBS Securities Building. They purchased from them to house the group's headquarters.

44. "About Tolaram — History", <http://tolaram.com/about.htm> (accessed 22 May 2008).

45. Ibid.

46. "Businesses", <http://tolaram.com/Manufacturing_Petrochemicals.htm> (accessed 22 May 2008).

47. "Our Community Initiatives", <http://tolaram.com/community.htm> (accessed 22 May 2008).

48. "The Tolaram Group is co-owned by seven family related individuals", Mohan Vaswani, Vishamkar Adnani, Sajen Aswani, Haresh Aswani, N.K. (Sonny) Aswani, Yogesh Vaswani and Rajesh Vaswani; "Ownership Structure", <http://tolaram.com/about.htm> (accessed 22 May 2008).

49. "Kartar Singh Thakral", <http://www.sikh-history.com/sikhhist/personalities/kartar_singh_thakral.html> (accessed 28 August 2009).

50. Gurmukh Singh, "Singapore: Best in the East", in *The Rise of Sikhs Abroad* (New Delhi: Rupa & Co., 2003), p. 171.

51. Ibid.

52. "Thakral Story", *Straits Times*, 29 June 1996; Singh, "Singapore: Best in the East", op. cit., p. 171. The Thakral Holdings is one of the largest tourism-based groups of Australia owning a chain of hotels, resorts and shopping complexes there like the All Seasons Premier Menzies Hotel, the Wynyard and Retail Centre in Sydney, the Novotel on the Collins Hotel, Hilton on the Park and many others.

53. "Kartar Singh Thakral", <http://www.sikh-history.com/sikhhist/personalities/kartar_singh_thakral.html> (accessed 21 May 2008).

54. Ibid.

55. "Milestones", <http://www.thakralcorp.com/mile.asp> (accessed 14 March 2008).

56. "Thakral Corporation Ltd.: Milestones", <http://www.thakralcorp.com/about.asp> (accessed 14 March 2008).

57. "Kartar Singh Thakral", op. cit.

58. Ibid.

59. Ibid.

60. "Thakrals", <http://www.sikh.com.au/famous/men/thakral.html> (accessed 14 March 2008).

61. Singh, "Singapore: Best in the East", op. cit., p. 173.

62. "Chairman's Statement", Thakral Corporation Ltd., Annual Report 2006, p. 3.

63. Ibid.

64. Interview with Amrik Singh on 13 June 2008. The company has been known as A.S. Sachdev and Sons (Pte.) Ltd. since.

65. Ibid.

66. "Home", <http://www.parsram.com/home.htm> (accessed 29 August 2009).

67. Shobha Tsering Bhalla, "Spice Route to Success", *India Se*, December 2008, pp. 23–24.

68. Ibid.

69. Website of Pars Ram Brothers (Pte.) Ltd., <http://www.parsrambrothers.com/Home.htm> (accessed 16 June 2009).

70. "Home", <http://www.parsrambrothers.com/Home.htm> (accessed 16 June 2008).

71. Advertisement in a publication by the Singapore Indian Chamber of Commerce and Industry (SICCI), *Inauguration of the SICCI Building & Launch of EDC@SICCI*, Singapore, 8 March 2008.

72. This was suggested by a respondent who was engaged in business in this sector. He pointed to the fact that during the Asian Financial Crisis in 1997, the North Indians did not suffer as much as did

the others in the trading sectors as they could look for markets in Europe and America and at the same time source their products from Asian countries like Thailand and Vietnam. Inevitably, the profit margins went up.

73. Interview with Anant Bir Singh, Director of Weston Corporation conducted on 19 June 2008.

74. "Corporate History", <http://www.rshlimited.com/history.php> (accessed 21 May 2008).

75. Ibid.

76. Ibid.

77. Interview with Anant Bir Singh, op. cit. A large part of their manufacturing base is in China, Vietnam, Indonesia, Thailand and Malaysia and they do a lot of business in the South Asian countries.

78. Ibid.

79. "Overview", <http://www.khattarwong.com/> (accessed 15 June 2008).

80. "Professional Moves: New Law Firms", <www.lawgazette.com.sg/2005-10/Oct05-Notices_prosmov.htm> (accessed 16 June 2008).

81. Rasheeda Bhagat, "India is exciting, but not without hassels", *Hindu Business Line*, 4 July 2006, <http://www.thehindubusinessline.com/2006/07/04/stories/2006070400351100.htm> (accessed 16 June 2008).

82. Ibid. In the infrastructure sector, their investments are directed through Gateway Distriparks Ltd. (listed in India).

83. Ibid. The Khattars also have interest in the Centurion Bank in India and have invested in the Radisson Hotel in New Delhi.

84. V. Rishi Kumar, "Bhagyanagar Metals plans Rs 150-cr investment in infrastructure projects: Set to acquire HMT, NTC lands", *Hindu Business Line*, Internet Edition, 19 July 2005, <http://www.thehindubusinessline.com/2005/07/19/stories/2005071901960200.htm> (accessed 29 June 2008).

85. Ibid.

86. "Board of Directors", <http://www.savant-infocomm.com/aboutus.htm> (accessed 16 June 2008).

87. Article by Priyia Paramajothi, "Young Business Leaders Forum aims to nurture talent for Singapore", *Channel News Asia*, 8 September 2006, <http://www.channelnewsasia.com/stories/singaporebusinessnews/view/229332/1/.html> (accessed 17 June 2008).

88. "About Us", <http://www.shankars.com.sg/about.html> (accessed 27 March 2009).

89. Ibid.

90. "Sofeene — Achievements", <http://www.sofeene.com/aboutus_achievements.htm> (accessed 27 August 2008).

91. "Products", <http://www.sofeene.com/products_textiles_fi.htm> (accessed 27 August 2008).

92. "Sofeene — Company", <http://www.sofeene.com/aboutus_history.htm> (accessed 27 August 2008).

93. "Sofeene — Directors", <http://www.sofeene.com/aboutus_directors.htm> (accessed 27 August 2008).

94. In Malaysia, they operate under the Haniffa Textiles Sdn. Bhd. In Chennai there are three outlets under the same group: Singapore Hanifaa's and Greenland Exports Ltd. in Chennai and Green Palace in Pudukottai. This was told to the author during a fleeting conversation with Mr Haniffa in April 2008; their business card also gives the details of their outlets.

95. M. Ramachandra, Oral History Recordings (in Tamil), Accession no. 001122/03, Reel no. 1, National Archives of Singapore.

96. K. Ramaiyah, "The Place of Thirumakkotai in Singapore History", in *Our History in Singapore* (in Tamil), edited by A. Veeramani, Tenth Singapore Tamil Youth Conference Proceedings, The Singapore Tamil Youth's Club, 1999.

97. This problem has been discussed earlier. A lot of Indian merchants had to bear huge losses when the trade connections were cut off from Indonesia, mainly because a lot of their business was done on credit, which could not be recovered once the political situation stopped the trade.

98. Ramachandra, op. cit.

99. Ibid.

100. <http://www.jothi.com.sg/index.htm> (accessed 21 May 2008).

101. Interview with Rajakumar Chandra on 17 July 2008.

102. Twenty-five per cent of his products are already branded. Rajakumar Chandra, ibid.

103. This information is based on an interview with V. Damodaran Pillai conducted in Tamil on 24 June 2008.

104. Ibid.

105. This information is based on discussions with Dr Thinnappan, Fellow, South Asian Studies Programme (SASP), Faculty of Arts and Social Sciences, National University of Singapore, 16 May 2008.

106. Awanohara, op. cit.

107. Inderjit Singh, Member of Parliament and a businessman in Singapore in a questionnaire, 4 July 2008.

108. K.S. Sandhu, "Indian Immigration and Settlement in Singapore", in *Indian Communities in Southeast Asia*, 2nd ed. (Singapore: Institute of Southeast Asian Studies, 2006), p. 780.

109. Mani, op. cit., p. 789.

110. For detailed analysis of Sukarno's foreign policy, refer to Michael Leifer, *Indonesia's Foreign Policy* (London, Boston: Published for the Royal Institute of International Affairs by Allen & Unwin, 1983).

Chapter 3

TAKING STRIDES INTO THE FUTURE: TRANSITION AND TRANSFORMATION OF THE INDIAN BUSINESS COMMUNITIES

The challenges of modernization and industrialization that were successfully confronted by Singapore soon propelled her to one of the most prominent and economically stable nations of the East. However, at the end of the twentieth century in the post-Cold War scenario, she was further consumed by the resurgence of the two of the greatest ancient civilizations of the world — China and India. They were also two of the largest geographical entities of Asia with huge pools of thriving human resources. The new situation demanded re-establishing equations in dominance and power play amongst the nations and at the same time readjustments and rethinking of their respective foreign and domestic policies. Singapore was quick to respond to the changing circumstances and a globalizing India and its "Look East" policy followed by the new trends of migration offered propitious grounds to believe that the ethnic Indian communities would find new opportunities for competitive performances in professional and business ventures.

Indian economic liberalization preceded by the rapid modernization and opening up of China and the favourable global economic climate have been relevant to commercial groups and businessmen who would now spread their wings outside Singapore with greater confidence and bigger investments. Scepticism of the Indian bureaucratic system and a notion of Chinese impregnability had barred them from entering the respective markets (China opened up much earlier than India) which they could now venture into, given the changes in the approaches of the two giants. Opening up of investment opportunities in the face of improved political relations have also enabled many Indian and Chinese entrepreneurs to come into the region by opening representative offices, joint collaborations or independent corporate ventures. The influx has been quite remarkable in the case of the Indians, who have continued to be a minority population in Singapore. There have been new migrants who are Indian professionals in the field of telecommunications, computer engineering, education and banking, thus creating a new group of ethnic Indian settlers in the diaspora, and not only leading to their increasing importance as players in the economy but also creating sociological complexities. On the other hand, there was the existing traditional Indian business community who sought to make the best use of the favourable global economic conditions and continued to embark on further diversifications and expansions in the global milieu on the strength of the acquired stability in the past decades and wanted to assert themselves on a bigger footing. The new age brought in increasing number of migrants to the city-state, mostly professionals and businessmen with renewed interactions and negotiations in the sociocultural context as well. It would be interesting to examine the drivers and the historicity of the emerging scenario and also analyse the delicate balance of social construct and the prospects of economic viability that may lie ahead.

This chapter discusses the "new look" of the business communities and the Indian diaspora, the phenomena of transnational mobility, effects of the circulation of capital and labour, the emergence of "knowledge-based economy" followed by the new trends in entrepreneurship, and also mentions to some extent, the reconstruction of restructured urban spaces and identities.

I. EMERGENT TRENDS IN THE NEW CENTURY

Singapore's size and its geostrategic vulnerability had been reoriented with constant adjustments by its policy-makers to suit its needs to remain a major player in the Southeast Asian politics. In that context the Singapore Minister, S. Dhanabalan has pointed out, "Realism in international politics consists not only of acknowledging limits, but also recognising opportunities."[1] The *realpolitik* approach towards the foreign policy was aptly described by Lee Kuan Yew in October 1981 when he said that:

> In an imperfect world, we have to search for the best accommodation possible. And no accommodation is permanent. If it lasts long enough for progress to be made until the next set of arrangements can be put in place, let us be grateful for it.[2]

This is what Michael Leifer calls an "epigraphic statement" which "encapsulates the essence of Singapore's practice of foreign policy".[3] Singapore's foreign policy is also interpreted with perspectives of "liberal institutionalism" and "social constructivism" as has been done by scholars like Amitav Acharya[4] that calls for a different context of analysis. In its balance and distribution of power strategy in the new millenium, it was necessary for Singapore to share its economic dependency on China with another power of similar proportions. India, being the biggest economy of South Asia, in fact bigger than the rest of South Asia put together, provided the opportunity of such an engagement.

Right from the beginning, Singapore strived to put herself at the top ranks of global competition to mobilize the geopolitical vulnerability to an advantage. This vision was articulated by Foreign Minister Rajaratnam in his speech as early as February 1972 when he said, "If we view Singapore's future not as a regional city but as a Global City then the smallness of Singapore, the absence of a hinterland, or raw materials and a large domestic market are not fatal or insurmountable handicaps."[5] For the achievement of such a goal what was managed and facilitated were competitive standards of living, world-class infrastructural facilities and create opportunities for ushering in transnational and multinational enterprises. What started with the Trade Development Board (TDB) in the 1960s soon emerged as the dynamic Economic Development Board (EDB) later and was eventually joined by other facilitating organizations like International Enterprise (IE), Enterprise One, SPRING Singapore (especially catering to the needs of the SMEs) and the Singapore Business Federation (SBF). All these government institutions were singularly dedicated to promoting investment opportunities, collaboration facilities and other prospects of cooperation in the country, and reversibly for Singaporeans, about countries abroad, by informing and updating on government norms and regulations, providing e-links, resource libraries, networking opportunities, technical assistance or financing schemes and loan programmes to the interested investors. The main drivers of Singapore's trade policies have been the flourishing operations and functioning of existing market forces which would lead to a stable multilateral trading system. To develop itself as a prominent and successful international trading centre, Singapore has focused on identifying new markets, increased export of its services, diversified and safeguarded its imports and formulated successful Free Trade Agreements (FTAs) with strategic partners.[6] Singapore has FTAs with thirteen countries and ongoing negotiations with ten more. It also benefits from the trade agreements between ASEAN and ASEAN plus, thus giving preferential access to the markets of the partners of the FTA agreements. The CEPT Scheme (Effective Preferential Tariff) has helped remove the trade barriers to a large extent. Singapore forms a major player in the building up of economic integration initiated by ASEAN. A stable political set-up, efficient judiciary and maintenance of an important and successful operational base have given it a distinct advantage over any other countries interested in operating in Asia-Pacific region to use Singapore as a springboard to venture into the Southeast Asian waters.

Singapore has been successfully providing platforms and meeting avenues for global business networking. The Suntec Singapore Joint Marketing Alliance (JMA) and the Singapore Exhibition and Convention Bureau (SECB) have facilitated the efforts of the EDB and SPRING Singapore and others in this respect. Thus, it is not surprising that the "global events city" was chosen by the Union of International Associations (UIA) as the Top International Meeting City in 2007.[7] Singapore has also earned accolades for being the second most competitive country in the world[8] (*IMD World Competitive Yearbook 2008*), first rank for three consecutive years as the best in the world for "Ease of Doing Business" (World Bank, *Doing Business 2009 Report*) and also the "Best Business Destination City" (*DestinAsian Reader's Choice Award 2007*).[9] Singapore is home to around 7,000 multinational companies (MNCs), sixty international organizations and about 110,000 professional expatriates,[10] which makes it a favourable destination for skilled opportunity seekers. Apart from business, the country has successfully promoted itself as the choice tourist destination for many around the globe, thus increasing the prospects of mixing business with pleasure.

The rapid pace of economic progression of Singapore has been characterized by modern business practices and first world living environment on the one hand and falling fertility rates on the other, resulting in the increasing percentage of the aged population in the demography of the country. Thus, it was almost inevitable that to avoid the labour shortage, Singapore had to rely to a large extent on the services of foreign labour, both in the skilled as well as the unskilled and semi-skilled sectors. To ease the situation on labour demands, the retirement age was raised from fifty-five to sixty years in 1993.[11] Singapore also made continued efforts to decrease its dependence on unskilled labour by technological advancements in infrastructure and industrialization. However, Singapore's aim to develop as the regional and the global services hub and establish itself as the knowledge-based economy (KBE) has led to the facilitation of the immigration of skilled professionals in the country, especially in the sectors of education and research, computer services, finances and banking, information and communication technology (ICT) sectors and biomedical research. In its globalization strategy in the new century, it was relevant to emphasize on talent, education, innovative entrepreneurship, and upgradation to high-end manufacturing and services.[12] The change from labour-intensive economy to capital-intensive production and services brought about a change in the occupational structure and the "proportion of workforce in managerial, professional and technical jobs increased from 11 per cent in 1970 to about 40 per cent in 1999".[13] Singapore's foreign labour and migration policy has been framed in a manner to create opportunities both for the unskilled as well as highly skilled professionals with different set of rules. While the former is permitted only a short-stay status and are denied any permanent residency (PR), the latter had been encouraged to take up PR and are also offered citizenship on many occasions. This has led to a remarkable increase in the number of PRs over the years — about 76.1 per cent of the total population in 2000 were Chinese PRs whereas 14.9 per cent were Indian PRs,[14] which has been higher than the percentage of Indians in the total population. It also brings to light the undeniable fact that Singapore has been encouraging foreign talent for its growth and expansion, which has often been propagated and effectively propelled by the leaders of the country.[15]

The changing rhetoric in India coincided well with the Singaporean domestic and foreign policy initiatives and the emerging trends of Asian migration. It was further facilitated by the enhanced bilateral relations between India and Singapore. The nations' leaders took initiatives to revive the bonding of the yesteryears and emphasize on new growth trajectories. One of the initial concrete steps from the Indian side was taken by the then Indian Prime Minister, Atal Bihari Vajpayee, who, during his visit to Singapore, pointed out that "business leaders from India and Singapore have a historic opportunity to join together to reconsider their business strategies ..."[16] He also pointed out how Indian human resources could be beneficial to the Singaporean paradigm:

> It would help Singapore if it further strengthened its services sector, to cater to the needs of the global economy using Indian professionals. Since quality education is going to be a key driver of the economy in the new century, we could also think of

setting up extensions of India's world-recognized technology
and management institutions here. These could attract young
talent from around the world and train them to tap the high-
value opportunities in the Knowledge Economy.[17]

The intra-Asian wave of migration and "new" globalization trends
that coincided with the liberalization policies of the Indian
Government, came after about half a century of inward looking
economic policies arising out of scepticism and contempt for
British hegemonic assertion of two centuries that resulted in de-
industrialization and economic degradation. India's Southeast
Asian policy operated within the context of her foreign policy and
relations with the Big Powers. Nehru, India's first Prime Minister,
was against any regimentation, but at the same time refrained
from antagonizing Big Powers.[18] Also there persisted a sense of
preclusion against the nation states with communist lineages. It
was only after the end of the Cold War that India finally set out
to reconsider the import substitution policies and eventually took
the bold step of not only embarking on economic liberalization
from the 1991, but also realign with its Asian neighbours in the
Indian Ocean and the Pacific.

India had attempted to activate support towards the resurgence
of Pan-Asianism as early as the Bandung Conference in 1955, but
the nation states were not matured enough then to perpetrate
the idea, realize its significance and embark on such a trajectory.
The basic tenets around which the foreign policy of the Asian
states revolved was anti-imperialism, the communism factor and
the Cold War tensions. Most of them were primarily concerned
with their nation-building process which was mainly structured
on pro-Western lines. The ambivalence and complacency of the
Non-Aligned Movement (NAM) further separated India from
her Southeast Asian neighbours. The change of attitude came in

the 1990s with the initiation of the then Indian Prime Minister, Narasimha Rao and his Singaporean counterpart, Goh Chok Tong, and bilateral ties were formed both in econometrics as well as defence programmes.[19]

It might be noted here that Narasimha Rao and Vajpayee represented two different, rather opposing parties at the central government of India, but followed the same policy initiatives of economic liberalization, something which not only had rare precedents in the Indian democratic set-up, but also revealed the seriousness of India's commitments to befriend and explore beyond its waters. Vajpayee's approach was cautiously observed by the investors, businessmen and political leaders initially as they were concerned whether the "reform was deep-seated enough"[20] to herald a new dawn of bilateral relations. Vajpayee succeeded in conforming to the new faith and a major outcome of the visit was setting up of the "Singapore-India Joint Study Group" (JSG) which submitted its report in April 2003 during the visit of then Prime Minister Goh Chok Tong in India. Supporting and reiterating confidence in India's growth trajectory, PM Goh Chok Tong said that "Prime Minister Vajpayee not only kept to the course but also stepped on the accelerator.... India's leaders understood that there was no other credible option for the country to reclaim its rightful place in the world economic order."[21] Singapore and India have rightly walked the path of mutual collaborations and benefits to mobilize the ICT, research, finance and the education sectors in the island nation. Reversibly, India has also witnessed a lot of investments especially in the infrastructure developments from private enterprises as well as the GLCs (Government-Linked Companies).

The new century has been characterized by "global capitalism" and capital market liberalization, the impact of which has been truly incredible in the Asian countries. This rising market capitalism on the one hand plays a vital role in opening up of new vistas of business opportunities, and on the other, erodes the state paternity and socialistic elements that many of the state systems have been structured with. At the same time, the knowledge and information in the internet age is poised to narrow the gulf between the so-called rich and the poor nations. The increasing tendencies of market liberalization and competition have transcended boundaries and replaced the paradigm of conventional structural reforms by the individual nation states. The new rhetoric strives towards improved macroeconomic performances with institutional, infrastructural and regulatory support of different states. This has brought about a rethinking of governance and dynamism of state systems in their opening to global market forces, and contributed to porous state boundaries and transborder mobility.

The dissemination of the "new age" globalization and encouragement of capitalism and liberal market norms provides greater territorial spaces for interaction of market forces, especially in the fields of information technology, electronic media, financial sector and telecommunications, traditionally that have been a part of the service industry catering to corporations, but now developed into industries in their own right. They have joined with the conventional sectors consisting of commodities, manufacturing and mining to extend the market as well as to create the flexibility and competitiveness among the market players.

In the emerging scenario of capital market liberalization, pricing and profit margins have become extremely competitive and small geographical entities like Singapore have been striving to build an edge over the others not only to sustain but also to excel in their economy. Progressive entrepreneurs have to be constantly innovative in their approach and searching for fresh avenues and newer markets to make an effort to grab every opportunity that emerges. For this, they are dependent on the expertise of the professionals and consultants. Thus, the traditional family firms are fast evolving with corporate structures and professional advice. There has emerged direct relation between professionals and entrepreneurs in today's economy, who not only complement each other or act as combined force, but also influence to a great extent, the foreign domestic investment (FDI) interests and economic policies of their respective home governments. There has been an emerging trend in many of the companies in Asia as well over the last decade in which the managers and professionals, who are employees, are also given profit sharing incentives in the companies they work by the owners, thus making them directly responsible and accountable to the profits of the company. A positive development in this direction has led to a tremendous impact on the ethnic Indian community in Singapore. Figure 3.1 shows the interdependence of the different economic, social and political factors in the circulation of capital and professionals in a liberal market economy and the consequent effects on the transformations of its diaspora.

A few salient features of the new age economy may be pointed out in this context:

- Asian markets have been hotbeds of investments essentially due to cheap labour and abundance of resources.
- Technological innovations have shrunk geographical distances and created global opportunities.
- Pricing and profit margins of enterprises have become extremely competitive.
- Rise of global capitalism has led to the rethinking of foreign policy initiatives of different states and increased the momentum of regional cooperation.

Figure 3.1
Interdependence of Economic and Political Interests

Quite naturally, the increased parameters of business ventures have raised the scope and expectations of the Indian business diaspora in Singapore. This has been equally facilitated by the uncomplicated procedures for opening up new companies in Singapore with minimum bureaucratic hassles, fewer regulations and transparent and efficient administrative system, lower taxes, both personal and corporate. While traditional business continue to exist and flourish on the one hand, a new generation of innovative ventures with mergers, acquisitions, collaborations, or just small time, independent first generation enterprises have emerged, making the community more spacious, flexible and accommodative to recent changes. Though trading remains an important business for the community with some venturing into manufacturing in different parts of the globe, many ethnic Indians are also engaged in outsourcing, shipping, consultancy, hospitality, legal assistance, ICT sectors and others. This has resulted in the emergence of three distinct sections of ethnic Indian entrepreneurs in Singapore:

- Traditional family firms who have grown and flourished over the years.
- New generation of Singaporean Indian entrepreneurs.
- Indian companies who have acquired, invested and collaborated with the Singaporean companies.
- Professionals who have turned into the first generation of entrepreneurs.

The first category of businessmen has already been discussed at length in the previous chapters. Some companies had started off as early as the beginning of the twentieth century and still continue to do so with the required diversification and innovations. For most of the ethnic Indian companies trading still remains the main sector of operation, and many have been venturing into acquiring and setting up of manufacturing bases in different parts of Asia and the world. In fact, among the Singaporean businessmen and entrepreneurs, Indians figure prominently in extending their bases and trading interests to different parts of Asia, Middle East, CIS countries, African countries and to the rest of the world. With the enhancement of bilateral relations with India, many of these companies are also looking towards India to extend their business interests and investments there.

A number of new business entities created by the local Indians have also emerged during this phase. They are the first generation of businessmen venturing out with the new trends that have emerged and at the same time, dabbling with trading as well. Efficiently shuttling between being an active member of parliament and an entrepreneur, Inderjit Singh, Singapore Member of Parliament, has been successfully blending his political career with the entrepreneurial zeal. He started his career in business with a trading and distribution company in August 1997 which has been continuing for more than a decade now. It has spread over thirty-nine countries in Africa and Southeast Asia, headquartered in Singapore with seven overseas offices elsewhere.[22] Keeping the trend of the new business sectors, he soon started the high technology and semi-conductor business in February 1998. Two other companies were started in 1999, but later sold and shut down. He continued with his expansionist spree by opening companies providing software solution products (2000), "development and manufacturing services of semiconductor products and electronic manufacturing service" (2001), which is headquartered in Singapore and employs about 1,300 people including different cities of the Philippines, the United States and India, and yet another company dealing with electrical consumer products (2006).[23] His business ventures have been an intelligent assortment of the traditional businesses and modern trends.

Another example of the first generation business during this phase could be that of Delta Exports Pte. Ltd., a company that was started in 1993 dealing for more than a decade with synthetic rubber, metals, minerals, agricultural products and chemicals. They are one of the few Singapore companies to focus on CIS countries with branch offices in Moscow and Kiev. Keeping well with the footsteps of diversification and expansion, they have joined hands with the Wilmar Group, the largest palm oil producer in Asia to set up a palm oil refinery at Yuzhny, Ukraine[24] as well as a joint venture (JV) with R1 International Pte. Ltd., the marketing arm of MARDEC, one of the largest global producers of natural rubber.[25] It has also ventured into pharmaceuticals in the CIS countries and invested in mines in Turkey. Delta Exports is an example of a typical, low profile local Indian company, yet progressive and modern with timely ventures into manufacturing and marketing.

It is also representative of the Indian companies who have risked, profited and managed resources from lesser known geographies, an aspect which has remained as an advantage with the ethnic Indians.

There also emerged a number of local Indian companies who diversified into manufacturing, but interestingly all their manufacturing units were being located abroad. As early as the 1970s, the Tolarams, as we have seen, had already set up their green field textile manufacturing plant in Indonesia and a petrochemical project in Africa, and have also entrenched themselves in Estonia. Olam, since its inception, was investing in agricultural products and commodities in Nigeria in a big way. The ventures of the Thakrals and Pars Ram Brothers have already been mentioned before. There are companies like Comcraft Asia Pacific Pte. Ltd., which is a manufacturer of various consumer and building products made of steel and aluminium. They have based their manufacturing units in Tanzania, Uganda, Kenya, Ethiopia and other countries. Other lesser known entities like Premchand & Sons have a plastic products manufacturing unit in Nigeria. These are some of the examples of local Indian companies abroad. Interestingly, they represent a large range of products as well as different geographies, with African countries being favourite destinations of many. We may now look at the other categories of business interests in the region and the consecutive effects on the Singaporean economy.

Indian companies from the subcontinent, quite in contrast to common beliefs, have made their presence felt in Singapore much before the current wave of euphoria in bilateral agreements and other government policy initiatives had plunged in action in the middle of the first decade of the twenty-first century. Their earlier presence has generally been overlooked as sporadic and individual initiatives. While it is true to certain extent, it has nevertheless helped in mobilizing the business diaspora as well as global expansion of the enterprises. There have been three categories of Indian companies which have made inroads into the island nation, the trend having geared up in the post-CECA phase. (CECA Agreement has been discussed in the following pages.)

- Merger and acquisitions (M&A)
- Collaborations and joint ventures
- Representative and branch offices, subsidiary companies and headquarters of the Asia-Pacific region

One of the oldest Indian companies to step into Singapore in a significant way was Tata Steel. Among the various foreign acquisitions by the Tata Group of Companies, Tata Steel acquired Singapore-based Natsteel for Rs.1,313 crores (approximately US$292 million[26]) in August 2004. It included 26 per cent stake of Natsteel in Malaysia's Southern Steel Berhard, which was a 1.3 million tonne steel manufacturer.[27] B. Muthuraman, the Managing Director of Tisco announcing the buyout from Singapore said that the acquisition would help secure better access to the Asian markets and extend the company's footprints to seven Asian countries including Vietnam, Singapore and Thailand.[28] With Tata Steel Limited's internal restructuring of its Asia-Pacific subsidiaries, the total business of Natsteel Asia Pte. Ltd. was transferred to Natsteel Holdings Pte. Ltd. from 1 August 2008.[29]

The Asian Paints (India) Ltd., even prior to Tata Steel, had acquired 50.1 per cent stake in 2002 in Berger International Limited (BIL), a holding company incorporated in Singapore. This gave it an opportunity to tap the emerging markets with the existing manufacturing units.[30] The then Asian Paints (India) Vice-Chairman and Managing Director, Ashwin Dani commenting on the acquisition said: "In line with our vision of becoming a leading player in the emerging markets, Berger International offers access to the high growth emerging markets."[31] This was the 22nd joint-venture/acquisition overseas for Asian Paints selling in more than forty countries. It also helped Asian Paints have a combined capacity of about 100,000 tonnes and twenty-seven manufacturing facilities globally.[32]

The India-Singapore JVs have been active in both countries ever since India has set on the path of economic liberalization. Initially, Singapore investments in India started in the ICT, infrastructure and the logistics sectors. What is however lesser known is the launching of a stock-broking firm by DBS as a joint venture in India in collaboration with India's Capital Trust Group way back in 1995.[33]

Insurance companies from India have also entered the Singaporean market. The India International Insurance Pte. Ltd. has been operating in Singapore since 1987, which is a company registered in Singapore and comprise of five Indian insurance companies — General Insurance Corporation of India, the New India Assurance Co. Ltd., the Oriental Insurance Co. Ltd., National Insurance Co. Ltd. and United India Insurance Co. Ltd.[34] Though their main focus is in the highly specialized class of Marine Hull Insurance as well as property insurance both within Singapore as well as the region, they also cover the various aspects of personal and corporate insurances.[35]

The Indian names that had made inroads into the shipping sector prior to the signing of CECA were the Tolani Shipping and the Orient Express Lines. Tolani Shipping (Singapore) Pte. Ltd. was incorporated into Singapore in September 2002.[36] This company, along with its sister concern in Mumbai, operates ten ships and is headed by Rohet Tolani, the Managing Director of the Company.[37] The Tolanis were one of those families who were displaced by the Partition in 1947 and settled in Mumbai with very little money to start with. This was the family's shipping venture that they started in the 1960s. Rohet Tolani worked for twelve years in his company in Mumbai before moving to Singapore, a place about which he is all praises. Prior to that he had studied and worked in the U.S.[38]

Mahesh Iyer of the Orient Express Lines came to Singapore even earlier. Transworld Shipping Services, founded in 1977 in India by R. Sivaswamy, Mahesh Iyer's father, expanded and flourished as separate agency companies dedicated to different shipping lines, ship repair and management business till 1983, when the group launched the common carrier feeder service under Orient Express Lines (OEL) in 1983.[39] Mahesh Iyer relocated to Singapore in 1999 to set up the Singapore regional office and hub for the group that expanded to cover areas in Bangladesh, east coast of India, Burma, Indonesia and Malaysia. The Sreyas World Navigation Pte. Ltd. was established in 2001 and the first ship was bought in 2002 — Orient Freedom. By 2004, OEL, with the regional office in Singapore and the management office in Dubai were operating a total of fourteen owned vessels and ten chartered vessels.[40] The group continues to expand and progress amidst increasing competition and challenges.

Trading, which has been the stronghold for the Indian businessmen for generations in the Southeast Asian region, has also been taken up by many recent Indian companies based in Singapore. Part of the US$24 billion Aditya Birla Group, Swiss Singapore Overseas Enterprise Pte. Ltd. was incorporated in Singapore way back in 1978 as a timber trader in Singapore and Malaysia. It had gradually expanded to deal with transnational bulk commodity trading along with diversified portfolio of products such as "petroleum products, sulphur, fertilizers, timber logs, steel and steel scrap, coal/coke, iron ore, chemicals".[41] With almost three decades of experience, it has become a "trading powerhouse" of more than a billion dollar (US$) turnover moving about 7MT of cargo across the globe from Southeast Asia to the Middle East and Africa and also to Canada.[42]

MMTC Transnational Pte. Ltd. (MTPL), incorporated in Singapore in 1994, is a wholly owned subsidiary company of MMTC Limited, a Government of India undertaking under the Ministry of Commerce and India's largest international trading corporation.[43] Its diverse field of business activities include "minerals, metals, steel and pig-iron, fertiliser and fertiliser raw materials, coal and coke, building materials like cement and clinker, ferro alloys, industrial raw materials, chemicals, agri-products, edible oil, engineering products, bullion, etc".[44] Right at the turn of the century, MTPL had received the prestigious Approved International Trader (AIT) status (later known as the Global Trader Status) by the government of Singapore in April 2000.[45]

The CECA Agreement facilitated the influx of Indian companies in Singapore to a much larger extent than what was taking place earlier. A general review of the Agreement might be helpful in further assessing the developing economic scenario.

The Comprehensive Economic Cooperation Agreement (CECA)

The recommendations of the JSG attempted to strengthen the economic links between Singapore and India covering a wide range of sectors from telecommunications, healthcare, real estate, port and trade logistics, transportation and others to promote trade, investments and tourism.[46] The JSG also proposed that "CECA be an FTA-plus arrangement" which implied that negotiations would go "beyond tariff reduction on merchandise trade into other areas of trade negotiations, *viz.*, services, investments, standards and movement of natural persons".[47] Discussions on trade facilitation relating to customs flexibility, open skies agreements as well as MRAs in certain sectors like electronics, agricultural products and telecommunication equipments were also recommended.

Negotiations of CECA took almost two years to be finalized, but it indeed created a milestone in the history of the bilateral relations between the two countries. This was a significant step that India took in stretching its arm out in involvement with Singapore and the Southeast Asian economic community. This was also the first bilateral agreement of its kind that India had entered with a high-income level Asian country.[48] Singapore had already emerged as the eighth largest foreign investor in India in 2002 (JSG Report), and the figures climbed up further in the following years. This agreement was the first of its kind for India which was an "all-encompassing economic pact"[49] and much more than a mere FTA.[50]

The present context of study does not provide us with the opportunity of discussing the pros and cons of CECA at length, but we may highlight a few points which boosted the growth trajectory in the bilateral econometrics. Kamal Nath, the Indian Commerce Minister in 2005 hailed it as an "economic cooperation pact; an economic engagement in various facets covering technology, industry and human resources".[51] CECA provided:

- Acceleration of trade exchanges, improvement of bilateral relations and a platform for entrepreneurs to make inroads on either side of the borders.
- A package of several agreements involving economic cooperation, science, technology and air services, trade

in goods and services, improved agreement on double taxation avoidance, intellectual property rights, media, tourism and flow of human resources.

- Encourage greater linkages and exchanges and set up a model for other members of ASEAN to build relations with India.

Under the provisions of CECA, both India and Singapore have relaxed the restrictions of entry of four categories of temporary entrants — business visitors, intra-corporate transferees, short-term service providers and professionals.[52] While business visitors could stay on for a period of two months (with an extension of one month) with a five-year multiple entry visa, short term service suppliers could reside for a period of ninety days and managers and executives under intra-corporate transferees have been permitted to reside in either country for the initial period of two years or the duration of contract, whichever is less. The professionals, in 127 specific categories, have been permitted residence for a period of one year or the term of the contract, whichever is of shorter duration. They are, however, subject to mutual recognition of qualifications agreements.[53] The human resources have thus been further mobilized with CECA and have paved way for a flexible business and professional diaspora in the country.

Post-CECA, both the countries are tapping the provisions of mutual benefits and optimizing their drive to pursue lucrative investment opportunities across the borders. The geostrategic location of Singapore at the crossroads of Asia and the trade junction has complemented the mutual goodwill that has been articulated by CECA and resulted in reciprocal economic advantages. Sustained encouragement and maintenance of the collaborative spirit between the states would further exploit the tremendous potential and opportunities paved by CECA.

The outcome of the political goodwill and mutual enhancement of bilateral relations has been tremendous and has been effectively visible in matters economic in both the countries. CECA called for immediate tariff elimination for 506 goods and phased tariff elimination for more than 4,500 items between 2005 and 2009.[54] Within a few months of signing the agreement, SBF and CII established a premier foundation to enhance relations and launched the Singapore-India Partnership Foundation on 14 January 2006. For Singapore, which is a small country where the ethnic Indians are a minority, such changes have brought about new dimensions of socio-economic perspectives which bear direct relation to the resident ethnic Indian population. It has opened floodgates of opportunities to the business sectors and the professionals alike. Referring to the overwhelming response in the recently held PBD (Pravasi Bharatiya Divas) in Singapore in October 2008, which was mainly a business-oriented conference and networking opportunity provided for the Non-Resident Indians (NRIs) and People of Indian Origins (PIOs), Dr S. Jaishankar, then India's High Commissioner to Singapore had said, "At this stage there is no saturation point — we have to keep growing. It is growth without a ceiling and a lot of it is relationship driven."[55]

II. CHANGES BEYOND CECA

The change in the trends of the Indian business diaspora situated in Singapore was accelerated by the change in government policies and the most important of which might be the signing of CECA agreement between the two countries, thereby leading to quantum jump of trade & commerce between the countries, which in turn prompted business entities from both sides to look for new opportunities at the other country, thereby leading to a transition of Indian diaspora in the past decade or so in Singapore.

Figure 3.2

Singapore-India Trade Figures

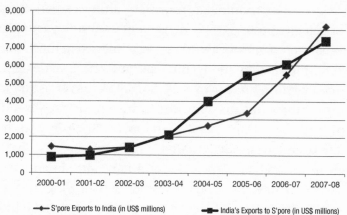

Source: Export Import Data Bank, Department of Commerce, Ministry of Commerce and Industry, Government of India, <http://commerce.nic.in/eidb/ecntcom.asp> (accessed 29 December 2008).

Indian enterprises venturing abroad and making their presence felt has been a recent phenomenon in Asia and around the world. The advantages that the Western MNCs have traditionally enjoyed with their cutting-edge technologies, global marketing skills and the successful know-how of branding have been challenged by the lesser known Indians in the twenty-first century. However, it is in the non-traditional sector of services that the Indians are mostly making their mark, though with few exceptions. The new Indian entrepreneurs in the Silicon Valley provide ample proof of the rising trend. In Singapore, there have been many factors which have contributed to the change. With the changes in the bilateral relations between the two countries, Singapore's encouragement of Indian entrants and liberalization policies of India, Indian companies have sought to seek out new markets in the Asia-Pacific region not only to increase their business periphery and accelerate growth but also to consolidate their position better in terms of multinational enterprises. They have been involved in different sectors like offshore drilling, freight forwarding and logistics, software technology, real estate, airline carriers, tourism and hospitality business. The merger and acquisition activities of the Indian companies are mostly being witnessed in the financial, telecom, information and technology, and to a lesser extent, in the manufacturing sector in Asia. Singapore serves as the ideal gateway to these Indian companies to anchor themselves further in the East. Tata Consultancy Services (TCS), Tech Mahindra, Satyam Computers, NIIT, Godrej, Gati and several other big names in the Indian corporate world have already entrenched themselves in Singapore and are spreading their wings further in the Asia-Pacific region. There are at present around 3,600 Indian companies (this is a 2008 figure and has been rapidly increasing) located in Singapore. An increasing trend of rising outflow of FDI into the region bears testimony to this. There has also been a constant rise in the bilateral trade figures which has almost doubled in three years from S$13 million to S$24 million in 2007. Singapore has continuously encouraged and facilitated the growing trade linkages. Mr Lim Hng Kiang, Singapore's Minister for Trade and Industry had said in 2004, "We believe that India should move from the No. 11 spot to become one of our top five trading partners",[56] and India has been able to make significant achievements in the same direction.

In June 2006, one of the leading transnational engineering and construction group of companies with headquarters in India, Punj Llyod Limited (PLL) had acquired 88 per cent stakes in Sembawang Engineers and Constructors Limited (Semb E&C), a wholly owned subsidiary of Semb Corp Industries, a company with headquarters in Singapore since 1982 and having far reaching operations in Southeast Asia. The acquisition was carried out by Punj Llyod Pte. Ltd., a wholly owned subsidiary of PLL, who acquired the remaining 12 per cent of the stakes by the end of 2006, leading to the total cost of the acquisition at around S$40 million.[57] This has enabled PLL to further widen its outreach in the Asia-Pacific region besides the Middle East, Europe and other areas across the globe.

Strides Arcolab, an Indian pharmaceutical company founded in 1990 with headquarters in Bangalore, is one of the largest soft gel capsule manufacturers in the world. In 2006, it signed an approximately Rs.60 crore deal (US$13.55 million[58]) to acquire the Drug Houses of Australia (Asia) Pvt. Ltd. (DHA), a Singapore-based generics company.[59] DHA, the wholly owned subsidiary of Haw Par Healthcare Ltd., was established in 1969 and has been one of the branded generics players in Singapore, Malaysia and Hong Kong. It has a manufacturing facility at Jurong and Strides would obtain its fourteenth manufacturing facility spread across the globe.[60] The existing small presence of Strides in the Southeast Asian markets would inevitably be enlarged with the acquisition.

Since the turn of the new century, India's outsourcing firms had been acquiring companies with dominance and established local presence in the markets that they catered to. There has been a significant trend to move the Indian IT firms to rise up in the value chain to compete with the likes of IBM, Accenture and others. Keeping in tune with the foreign companies' acquisitions spree, India's fourth largest software exporter, Satyam Computer Services, apart from its U.S. acquisitions, has acquired the Singapore-based Knowledge Dynamics, a company providing consulting solutions in the business intelligence space in 2005.[61] This involved a cash deal of approximately $3.3 million.

Singapore is already India's largest trading and investment partner in the ASEAN region. The constant increase in bilateral trade figures further emphasize on the willingness and the goodwill to exploit the potentialities of the resources available to both the countries. This would naturally pave way for joint collaborations and joint ventures in entrepreneurial endeavours on either side of the borders.

Prominent among the JVs that came more recently are Singtel's JV with Bharti Telecom and Singapore Technologies Telemedia's JV with Modicorp, apart from the major investment by Ascendas in the Information Technology Park in Bangalore. Singapore businesses have also been looking out for the biotechnology, pharmaceuticals, information and technology, healthcare, media and entertainment sectors and delegation from Singapore has often visited major cities in India to look out for the viabilities of investments.[62] We may mention here some of the JVs signed between the entrepreneurs in diverse sectors.

The Kalyani Group, a leading enterprise in auto component in India had signed a JV agreement in November 2006 with ST Kinetics (Singapore Technologies Kinetics) Ltd., Singapore, one of Asia's largest defence companies catering to products and services for defence, homeland security and commercial markets.[63] The JV, in which the Kalyani Group will have majority stakes, will offer the Kalyani Group an access to ST Kinetics' growing portfolio of products. "The JV will be engaged in the design, engineering and manufacture of high technology and critical systems for the Indian Defence market."[64] The Kalyani Group, which has 74 per cent stake in the JV will invest $4.44 million, whereas, ST Kinetics with 26 per cent equity, will invest $1.56 million for the running of the JV and development projects.[65]

In the healthcare sector, the Pacific Healthcare Holdings Ltd., a listed company of Singapore and a leading healthcare provider in Singapore entered into a Joint Venture agreement with the Wadia Group in India in September 2006 to expand its operations in India to Mumbai and later on to other cities. With both the enterprises having equal business stakes in the JV, the business plan has been laid out in two phases, first, a Cosmetic Medical Specialist Centre in phase one to be followed by a full-scale Medical Spa in phase two.[66] The specialist centre would be set up at Worli, Mumbai at a cost of S$1 million and will spread over a 7,000 square feet of land. The Wadia Group's investment would be carried out through their private arm, Nowrosjee Wadia & Sons Private Limited. The Director of the Wadia Group, Jeh Wadia said:

> Healthcare is a sunrise industry with increasing demand for excellence. Our partner, Pacific Healthcare is an established premier healthcare group which has created a unique model of combining both medical and wellness services under one roof. We are confident that this collaboration will positively impact the cosmetic medical landscape in Mumbai and then other cities by offering a combination of medical services with total wellness programmes for men and women using world class specialists and facilities.[67]

Another sector which offers huge potential of joint business is the education sector. In May 2008, Educomp Solutions Ltd., one of India's largest education company and Raffles Education Corp., the largest private education group in the Asia-Pacific region, declared two JVs, one in China for K 12 business and the other in India for professional education. The Raffles Group already has its operations spread out in around nine countries in the Asia-Pacific region including the ownership of the Oriental University in Langfang, Hebei province in China.[68] The aim and the prospects of the JVs have been amply elucidated by the CEO of the Raffles Education Corporation, Chew Hua Seng, who referring to the China JV said, "The JV will help us to expand our portfolio of products for the China market, providing seamless end-to-end learning solutions from K 12 to higher education."[69]

Similarly, of the JV in India, he said, "With over 657 million youths, India has the largest population of young people in the world. Through this partnership, we hope to nurture the required talent for India's growth."[70]

Turning to the more conventional sectors in business and enterprises, two of the largest of the commodities' giants in their respective countries, Adani Exports Ltd. of India and Wilmar Trading Pte. Ltd. of Singapore have formed a JV to set up the largest integrated edible oil refinery at Mundra port with a capacity of 600 tonnes per day as well as *vanaspati* (hydrogenerated vegetable oil) manufacturing capacity of 100 tonnes per day.[71] They are now aiming to set up another plant with a capacity of 1,200 tonnes and a 4MW captive power plant.[72] Their business spans across many categories of edible oils, of which the soyabean oil had been most lucrative. The logistics expenditure of the company imports including crude palm oil, sunflower oil and soyabean oil had been considerably cut down due to its proximity to the port facilities. Adani Global has two wholly owned subsidiaries out of which one is Adani Global Pte. Ltd. at Singapore. It might be mentioned in this context that the Singapore Investment Corporation Pvt. Ltd. has also invested a sum of 120 million dollars in the development of the Mundra port and the SEZ being developed by the Adanis.[73]

There has also been a JV agreement between Globe Detective Agency and Mainguard International of Singapore in 2008. The Globe Detective Agency, the largest and the oldest of the Indian Private Security Agency focuses on the business verticals of private investigations, industrial security and security systems. The Director of Globe, Sachit Kumar, talking about the JV reiterated, "This JV will help us to extend our services in Australia, Bangladesh, Hong Kong, China, Indonesia, Japan, Korea, Malaysia, Singapore, Phillipines, Sri Lanka, Thailand, Taiwan and Vietnam."[74]

The above examples of joint ventures and business collaborations reveal a mutual growing interest of both the nations to tap the innumerable potentialities in diverse sectors. It might be pointed out that apart from the JVs, there has also been substantial investments by Singaporean companies in India where a lot of ethnic Singaporean Indian entrepreneurs are involved. The Thakrals' involvement in developing the Gurgaon Technology Park in Gurgaon near New Delhi, or Satpal Khattar's investments in HDFC Bank and other real estate and infrastructure projects have already been mentioned earlier. There are also companies like Savant Infocom[75] and Network Inter Business Services who have interests and investments in India. The aim of this growth trajectory remains the same — expansion of market throughout Asia and beyond, increasing global competitiveness by sharing investments and technology and eventually contributing to the larger picture of a rapidly developing Asia.

In another category of Indian companies, we have names of numerous business establishments in wide ranging sectors that operate in the capacity of branch offices, representative offices, wholly owned subsidiaries of the parent Indian companies or even headquarters of the Asia-Pacific regions. Examples abound in plenty with some prominent names who have had a presence of more than three decades, but most of them are more recent entrants since the 1990s. Here, we might also reflect on the diverse business interests that have come from India to the global city-state.

Globally acknowledged and eminently visible, the Indian IT professionals and companies have made their presence felt in a remarkable way in different nook and corner of the world, and Singapore is no exception. The market for Indian outsourcing is growing with the advantages of the command over English language, good quality web designs and minimum development cost and the offshore software outsourcing is already more than billion dollar business. India's production of skilled technology has blended well with Singapore's increasing demand in the information and communication sector resulting in the increasing presence of the Indian companies on this island. Singapore and India have already made headway in collaboration and cooperation in the ICT sector and both the countries have also signed an MOU on Third Country Training Programme to conduct joint training courses in Cambodia, Laos, Vietnam and Myanmar.[76] A large number of software companies have come to Singapore like the Tata Consultancy Services, HCL Technologies Singapore Pvt. Ltd., NIIT Technologies Pte. Ltd., Satyam Computer Service Ltd., Polaris Software Lab Pte. Ltd., Infosys Technologies Limited, I-Flex Solutions Pte. Ltd., Hexaware Technologies Asia Pacific Pte. Ltd., Nucleus Software Solutions Pte. Ltd., Birlasoft Limited, Zensar Technologies (Singapore) Pte. Ltd. and many others.

Finance and banking is another sector which has seen the growing involvement of the Indians in recent times. Some of the Indian banks have continued to operate in Singapore since its pre-independence days. The Bank of India, United Commercial Bank, Indian Overseas Bank and the Indian Bank have been operating in Singapore under full banking licence. The provisions of the CECA has further liberalized the financial services and strengthened the bilateral cooperation between India and Singapore. The State Bank of India has been given QFB (Qualifying Banking Status), while Bank of Baroda and Axis Bank run their offshore operations in Singapore.[77] (This information is restricted to the years 2008–09 and has been through other changes since then.)

The entrenchment of the Indian companies in Singapore has been witnessed as we have seen earlier in the shipping sector too. Mercator Lines (Singapore) Limited, Indian owned international dry bulk shipping company with a modern fleet of eleven vessels,[78] forms another of the prominent examples. Engaged in servicing large thermal-based power plants and steel companies directly, the company offers full logistic solutions to their customers from load port to the point of usage in India. With a focus primarily on India and China, they are involved with transportation of dry bulk commodities like coal and iron ore.[79] Mercator was one of the first Indian shipping companies to be listed in the SGX in December 2007. It may be mentioned here that only a few of the Indian companies can be listed in the SGX as they are restricted by the Indian regulations which stipulate that only those firms listed in the domestic exchanges could be listed offshore. Meghami is another Indian company that is listed on SGX.[80] Indian companies have increasingly been interested in listing at the Singapore Stock Exchange for fund raising. The SGX had become a shareholder in the Bombay Stock Exchange in the early part of 2007. The Singapore time zone falls between that of Japan and India and thus provides opportunity for raising funds for companies with good track records, thus facilitating Indian offshore companies seeking funds.[81]

Other players in the field of freight forwarding, courier and logistics operations have also had a rising presence in Singapore. One such prominent example is that of Gati, which started a cargo management company in 1989,[82] stepped into the Singapore soil in 2006. With eighteen years of experience in express distribution and supply chain solution business in India, Gati International, the global operations wing of the company, has located its regional headquarters in Singapore (Gati Asia Pacific Pte. Ltd.) with offices in countries like China, Japan, Hong Kong, Thailand, Nepal and Sri Lanka, thus pursuing a policy of seeking partners in other countries and expanding its market share.[83] Mahendra Agarwal, the MD and CEO of the company reiterate its policy when he says that "Singapore is the best place in Asia-Pacific for an Indian company looking to expand outwards."[84] It is involved in point-to-point distribution solutions, complex end-to-end integrated logistics solutions and supply chain management to and from India and a base in Singapore complements its "India-centric" business model with connectivity in the region. It has also received the Regional Headquarters Award by EDB on 6 May 2008.[85]

One of India's largest domestic courier company, First Flight Couriers Ltd., established in November 1986 forms another example of the extension of its Indian arm into Singapore and the region. It has been engaged in providing with business services of warehousing, inventory management, supply chain and distribution channels along with travel assistance services in its tours and travel division.[86] Singapore has a branch of its eight international offices.

There are several other examples of Indian trading companies incorporating and subsequently establishing themselves in Singapore which, unfortunately, cannot be discussed due to space constraints. However, it might be mentioned that several Indian companies have shown equal competence in other fields of business too, like travel, tourism and hospitality, consultancy services, media and education. There are branch offices of the Government of India Tourist Office and offices of Jet Airways, Air India and Indian Airlines on the one hand and local representatives of The Taj and the Oberoi Group of Hotels in Singapore on the other. Similarly, Zee Network, Sony Entertainment, Star Gold and Star Plus provide with the uplinking facilities in Singapore serving a large Indian clientele, both expatriate and local. Big Indian names in the real estate sector have also entered the Singapore arena. DLF, one of the pioneering real estate companies in developing townships and group housing in India and Asia's third largest real estate developer, opened its first overseas office in Singapore in 2008 to serve as a platform for the Group's expansion in other parts of Asia.[87] In the education sector, Indian schools have already been mentioned at the beginning of the chapter. Besides there are management institutes offering their degrees in Singapore like the S.P. Jain Centre of Management and the Xavier Labour Relations Institute (XLRI), Jamshedpur, India.

The movement of the large number of Indian companies has also induced the Indian Chamber of Commerce to come into Singapore. The CII had signed an MOU with the IDA as early as 1 November 2000 "to promote closer link between the new economy sectors of Singapore and India"[88] and continues to play an important role in facilitating networking platforms and

Figure 3.3

Comparative FDI in Singapore from Select Asian Countries

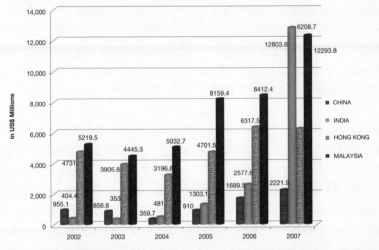

Note: Data incorporates Foreign Direct Equity Investment and net lending from Foreign Direct Investors to their investment enterprise in Singapore.

Source: Singapore Department of Statistics, 27 July 2009, <http://www.singstat.gov.sg/stats/themes/economy/biz/foreigninvestment.pdf> (accessed 4 September 2009).

other activities. FICCI, the other prominent Indian Chamber is represented by George Abraham (Regional Representative) and has also been instrumental in mobilizing networking platforms for business communities on either side of the borders.

III. THE FLEETING AND THE FLEXIBLE DIASPORA

Highly skilled Indian professionals have had a tendency of outward bound migration, especially to the West, owing to the dearth of adequate jobs and opportunities in the home country. They have been on the move looking for opportunities with locational advantages and favourable policy initiatives to address their upwardly mobile financial cravings and gaining a higher status of living. The "flexible", "globe-trotting diaspora", as we might call them, have tried to adapt to different urban spaces and settings in different periods of time. A part of the "fleeting diaspora" also managed to get entrenched to the soil of their migration. The success of Singapore Government's domestic and foreign policies, the free market economy and the structural facilities that it provided along with a modified migration policy made it a lucrative destination for professionals as well as entrepreneurs alike.[89] The Singaporean policy encouraged the outward-looking Indians to now look for opportunities nearer home, where familial grounds of language, cuisine, religion and customs already existed with an affordable and good quality of life, low taxation, safe and clean environment, easy learning facilities and large options of leisure and recreational activities. An Indian resident could enjoy all the technological advancements of the West with almost all amenities of homeland available. The proximity to home and familiar culture had been an added advantage of the Indians over the other expatriates who would consider the suitability of Singapore as a choice of residence and profession. Mercer (Mercer Human Resource Consulting, Worldwide Quality of Living Index, 2007) has ranked Singapore on top of the list for the best quality of life in Asia,[90] which has naturally attracted expatriates as a desired destination.

Singapore has also attracted a large number of Indian students over the years. It has been considered an ideal place for higher education in Asia with the situation of some of the renowned global institutions, which have opened branches in the global city, at affordable costs in comparison to U.S or Europe. At the same time the students have been provided with all the state-of-the-art facilities, a global faculty, safe and clean environment with efficient enforcement of rules and regulations, and above all, an Asian value system and cultural pattern. This is especially comforting to those Indian parents who are sometimes intimidated by the lifestyle of the Western youth. Whether it is the NUS Business school, INSEAD or the S.P. Jain Centre of Management, a large number of Indian students in the undergraduate and the postgraduate and above level have lately made their presence felt in this city-state. Besides, the large number of companies operating from the place also gives them exposure to different employment opportunities. According to the Area Director, Singapore Tourism Board, Chennai: "In a way, an education in Singapore plugs students right into the forefront of the global economy."[91]

The "India fever" has caught on in Singapore in a way that has also encouraged one of Singapore's most sought after high schools, Victoria Junior College (VJC), to introduce the India studies programme in its curriculum to give a better insight to India's politics, history and culture to "give students a distinct advantage and the confidence to do business in and with India" as opined by Chan Poh Meng, principal of VJC.[92] Raffles Junior College (RJC) and some other schools already have bicultural courses on India, but in the new course in VJC, students have the option of taking up India studies for four years instead of the usual two-year A-level programme, which would give them a better insight to Indian system of politics and governance and how it has evolved along with the economy. The government is also working on the establishment of the India Heritage Board on familiar lines of such a centre as the other races. Such steps go to prove the encouragement and efforts of the Singapore Government not only to create spaces for the Indians to mobilize and steer the country's economy, but also gear up the coming generations to engage in the business and employment opportunities generated by "Asia's awakening giant".

The Asian renaissance, catalysed by the rise of India and China and the open-door policy of India enhanced the intra-Asian mobility of the human capital resources and helped in the emergence of a new generation of professionals that is young, ambitious, mobile and adjustable. The traffic of these skilled professionals were not only headed from the subcontinent, but many home-bound Indian migrants from the West decided to situate themselves in Singapore, a place which could provide them with the ultra-modern facilities of living and yet secure them from typical Western lifestyles and culture. The days of pretentious fashion of being employed in the West are over. The competitive salaries and standards of living in many of the Asian states, which emerged with the Asian resurgence, could be another reason for them to retreat to their original Asian background. Deliberating on the rise of new professionals may apparently seem like a digression from the current perspectives of the business diaspora, but this group of migrants have considerably influenced the shaping of the present demography of the diaspora in the country as well as intimately participated in the modern mechanisms of business operations. Many of these flexible professionals have successfully turned into first generation entrepreneurs and settled down in

ception for Pandit Jawaharlal Nehru in the Indian Chamber of Commerce, 27 May 1937. Sitting on
nditji's left (black coat) is Mr M. Jumabhoy, the President of the Chamber.
urce: Reproduced with kind permission of the Singapore Indian Chamber of Commerce & Industry.

e First General Meeting of the Indian Chamber of Commerce, Singapore, held on 15 September 1935.
rce: Reproduced with kind permission of the Singapore Indian Chamber of Commerce & Industry.

Guests at Tea-party for Seth Govindram Fatehchand at Sindhi Merchants Association, 5 July 1941
Source: Collection of J.B. Rupa. Courtesy of National Archives of Singapore.

A Chettiar Chamber of Commerce Dinner most probably at the Raffles or Adelphi Hotel
Source: Nachiappa Chettiar. Courtesy of National Archives of Singapore.

The present Singapore Indian Chamber of Commerce & Industry building at Stanley Street.
Source: Reproduced with kind permission of the Singapore Indian Chamber of Commerce & Industry.

Perspective view of High Street buildings, 12 January 1965
Source: Ministry of Information, Communications and the Arts. Courtesy of National Archives of Singapore.

Stalls along Serangoon Road, 8 July 1975
Source: Singapore Press Holdings Ltd. Reproduced with permission.

Serangoon Road, Little India, 1980s
Source: National Archives of Singapore.

Provision store and flower shop at Campbell Lane, Little India, 1980
Source: National Archives of Singapore.

V.K. Kalyanasundaram & Sons Pte. Ltd., 1980
Source: National Archives of Singapore.

Picture of High Street shops, 2 December 1964
Source: Ministry of Information, Communications and the Arts. Courtesy of National Archives of Singapore.

The High Street in 2008.
Source: Photo taken by the author, 18 October 2008.

High Street/North Bridge Road, 1 May 1979
Source: Collection of Urban Redevelopment Authority. Courtesy of National Archives of Singapore.

Little India just before Deepavali
Source: Photo taken by the author, 18 October 2008.

Singapore River and High Street Centre, 1 November 1976
Source: Ministry of Information, Communications and the Arts. Courtesy of National Archives of Singapore.

Changing landscapes: Singapore River at present
Source: Photo taken by the author, 18 October 2008.

Market Street — mainly pre-war shophouses, 1970
Source: Collection of Chu Sui Mang. Courtesy of National Archives of Singapore.

Buildings at Market Street, 1980
Source: Collection of Ronni Pinsler. Courtesy of National Archives of Singapore.

Market Street — Chettiar moneylenders, 6 November 1975
Source: Singapore Press Holdings Ltd. Reproduced with permission.

Reflections of the past — inside the kittingi at 5 Tank Road
Source: Photo taken by the author, 25 October 2008.

Old order and the new: the Nagarathar Building at 5 Tank Road retains the *kittingi* shophouse structure.
Source: Photo taken by the author, 25 October 2008.

The Bharat Building houses two of the Indian banks in the Central Business District area of Singapore.
Source: Photo taken by the author, 17 January 2011.

Symbols of the past: figures of an ethnic Indian moneylender transacting business with an ethnic Chinese client in the present backdrop of IndoChine Restaurant at Boat Quay.
Source: Photo taken by the author, 18 October 2008.

Some Forms of Paper Credit in Colonial Singapore

The two most popular means of paper credit were the I.O.U. chits and the promissory notes, the latter largely used by the Chettiar moneylenders in their regular financial operations. The three promissory notes illustrated on the pages that follow are from the late nineteenth century showing transactions with the Chettiars irrespective of race or religion. Apart from revealing the date of issue, amount of credit, names of signatories and the rate of interest as 24 per cent per annum on an average, the third note is slightly more detailed on the clauses relating to the loan instalments.

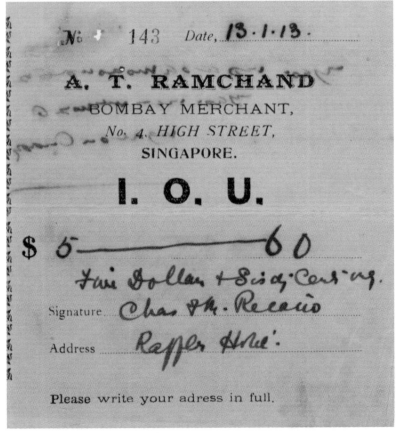

IOU chit by A.T. Ramchand.
Source: Koh Seow Chuan Collection, National Library, Singapore.

Promissory note — transaction between a Chettiar and a Chinese, 11 September 1893.
Source: Koh Seow Chuan Collection, National Library, Singapore.

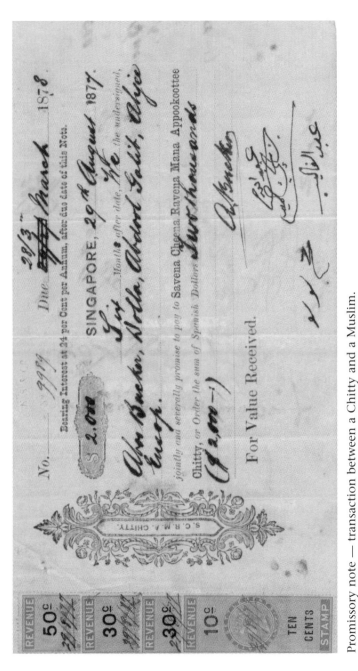

Promissory note — transaction between a Chitty and a Muslim.
Source: Koh Seow Chuan Collection, National Library, Singapore.

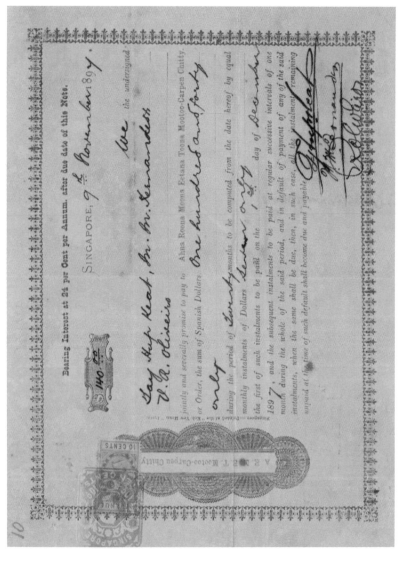

Promissory note — transaction between a Chitty and a European, 9 November 1894.
Source: Koh Seow Chuan Collection, National Library, Singapore.

Singapore facilitated by the alignment of various factors that are in the process of discussion.

A demographic profile of the new diaspora is very difficult to come by as they are an extremely agile group, and their inflow and outflow from the country is taking place from and to various directions around the globe. Also the intra-professional mobility and venturing into business and first generation entrepreneurship makes it impossible to get the right figures in different sectors of their occupational engagements. However, there has been a qualitative change in approach towards the Indian diaspora in the new century. The media has come to play an important role in arresting the new developments. Apart from extensive media coverage on business and political developments of India and the Indians around the globe (for example, *Business Times* has a regular page allotted to India-related news), there has been a monthly magazine for the global Indian diaspora, *India Se*, launched from and based in Singapore, and *Tabla*, a weekly newspaper published by Mediacorp in Singapore. As the first ever Hindi radio channel in the region, "Big Bollywood 96.3 FM" was launched in July 2008 in Singapore by Adlabs Films, India's biggest FM radio licence holder who had tied up with Singapore's leading broadcaster, MediaCorp, to lease its airtime and facilities.[93] The *Rupee Room*, the Bollywood styled discotheque, attracts all cross-section of ethnic Indians residing in the country as well as others. Besides, the frequency with which the Indian schools are expanding their branches, also points out to the demand of Indian style education and the subsequent business generated by it.[94] The visible changes set off with the rise of the ethnic Indian population have managed to bring about significant changes in the diaspora.

The complementarities shared between Singapore and India on human resources have been rightly acknowledged by both

Table 3.1
Resident Indians in the Singapore Demography

Year	Total (no. in '000)	Indians (no. in '000)	Percentage of Indians to Total Population
1990	2,735.9	194.0	7.1
2000	3,273.4	257.9	7.9
2008	3,624.7	323.4	8.9

Source: *Population Trends 2008*, ISSN 1793-2424, Singapore Department of Statistics, Ministry of Trade and Industry, Republic of Singapore, <http://www.singstat.gov.sg/pubn/popn/population2008.pdf> (accessed 4 September 2009).

Table 3.2
Average Household Income of Indians in Singapore

Year	1990 (S$)	2000 (S$)	Change (%)
National Average	3,076	4,943	60.69
Resident Indian	2,859	4,556	59.35

Source: <http://en.wikipedia.org/wiki/Demographics_of_Singapore#Household_income_distribution> (accessed 3 May 2009).

countries and concretized with the manifestation of signing of the CECA in 2005. The treaty has provided a smooth access to different professional occupations[95] on either side of the border with Mutual Recognition Agreements. This has helped Singapore to feed in the inadequate indigenous skill of managerial and technical expertise to fulfil its objectives of becoming a competitive global outsourcing market.

IV. PROFESSIONALS TURNED ENTREPRENEURS

It had long been a tradition with many first generation Indian entrepreneurs in Singapore to begin their careers as employees in different firms and eventually starting on their own with meagre capital but well-known contacts, and opportunizing being well-versed in the nuances of that particular business. The story of the transition of professionals to entrepreneurs in contemporary times is somewhat similar, although there are several factors to be considered before drawing upon comparisons. The earlier employees could not be termed exactly as "professionals" whereas the present generation in discussion are professionals with high level of education and acquisition of skills. They have been playing important roles in the decision-making and forward-looking approaches in their respective organizations, at the same time financially more stable and capable in making inroads into the entrepreneurial world.

Besides the osmotic pull of Singapore with its advantages, the new generation of Indian entrepreneurs also complement the characteristics and emergence of the new class of rising Indian entrepreneurs in the home country and across the globe. The age old dominance of the inexorable traditional trading community or the *bania* and *vaishya* caste of India has given away to a modern, techno-savvy and a professional business class. Harish Damodaran, in his book, *India's New Capitalists*[96] brings forth this change in the paradigms of business and entrepreneurship in India though he tries to interpret the changes on a caste-based analysis, which might not be an ideal way of looking at it. What cannot be negated, however, is the emerging trajectory of casteless endeavours of ambitious and skilled individuals making the most of situational advantages. Keeping in line with the process of "Sanskritization"[97] and breaking conventional social hierarchies, the entrepreneurial sector have also witnessed new players in the traditional dominance of business and enterprise. The emergence and flourishing of the service industry, the rich talent pool of the English-educated middle class and access to capital through venture capitalists have had a major role to catalyze the transformation.

Just as there was a situational advantage back under the colonial aegis for traditional Indian merchant communities to make the best of the geopolitical location, overarching and connecting umbrella of British administration and the demand for textiles and spices across the Indian Ocean and beyond, there has emerged a similar situational advantage, in different paradigms, especially at the turn of the century, where the recent trends of diversified interests, especially in ICT, finance and education sectors require the skills of professionals along with entrepreneurial capabilities to survive. Starting a business at present is about honing new skills and innovations and also working on value-addition to one's product as well as efficient marketing to survive and excel amidst cut-throat competition. The talent pool of the globe-trotting skilled Indian professionals has been successful in picking up the trend. The Silicon Valley Indian entrepreneurs played a vital role in setting up of the trend. Vinod Khosla of the Sun Microsystems or Sabeer Bhatia, the pioneer of hotmail.com are names which are familiar to one and all.

In the present scenario of professionals-turned-entrepreneurs in Singapore belong both the categories of the local Singaporean Indians as well as the new Indian immigrants who have chosen Singapore as their new base. Though the trend was initiated by the migratory global Indians and is a comparatively new phenomenon, many of the local Indians also decided to tread on similar paths and achieved remarkable success. All the entrepreneurs in this category have had some common advantages:

- Accumulated experience in their own field of expertise
- Capabilities of investments
- Useful global contacts, whether in government or private sector

However, the new entrepreneurs find a challenging task to survive the global competitive market. Not only are there a large number of similar players trying their hand at business with innovative value-addition, the employees (professionals) are also throwing up increasing tests of sustenance. The support of the globally mobile group of knowledge workers could act as an advantage, but at the same time become vulnerable and unpredictable to hold back the slippery employees who are forever in the search for greener pastures. The most obvious restraining factor would be the lucrative compensation package with the increasing number of incentives and additional benefits that they can offer. This has resulted in the steep vertical rise of the living standards of the professionally-educated middle class in the region.

The KSP Group of Companies formed in the 1990s is one the best examples of participation of professional ethnic Indians, embedded in the Singaporean soil for more than two generations, in the field of entrepreneurship. It was initially headed by Gopinath Pillai, Haidar Sithwalla and Satpal Khattar, a trio of Singaporean Indians who are civil servant, diplomat and lawyer by profession, and some of whom also have had experiences in the private sector.[98] The KSP Investments is a privately held company with four main subsidiaries — AEC Education (PLC), a listed company in U.K., Savant Infocomm Pte. Ltd., Windmill International Pte. Ltd. and Eastcom Systems Pte. Ltd.[99] AEC is engaged in providing educational programmes and solutions to various countries including Singapore, Savant focuses on IT and education, Eastcom provides with the cost management solutions for the industry, while Windmill is an international trading company.[100] While the function of different subsidiary companies are varied and complex, they are in tune with the modern trends of the demands in the service sector as well as involve with trading and supply chain logistics.

Another prominent name in this category would be that of George Abraham. Having served as the CEO of the Singapore Indian Chamber of Commerce and Industry (SICCI) for more than two decades, he has recently embarked on the entrepreneurial path. He set up an international business consultancy company, George Abraham & Associates Pte. Ltd., which assists Singaporean companies in linking business in the region and also works with the UN agencies "in small and medium enterprise development and capacity building for institutions in emerging countries".[101] The GA Group Pte. Ltd. comprises of George Abraham & Associates Pte. Ltd., East & Asia Pacific Trade & Industry Publications Pte. Ltd., which is involved in business and trade related publications and Global Indian Business Network Pte. Ltd., which works towards promoting trade and investment between India and Southeast Asia. As part of its networking programme, the company organized the Distinguished Technopreneurs Forum at Singapore in 2005,[102] Global Indian Business Summit @ Global Entrepolis Singapore in 2006 and 2007, and such other events in the consecutive years.

A successful example in the field of pre-school education is that of the Modern Montessori International (MMI) Group in 1989 in Singapore at the initiative of the Chairman and CEO of the organization, Dr T. Chandroo. Dr Chandroo started his career in the private sector working for a Singaporean company, but he was destined to play a far more important role in the entrepreneurial world and initiated the Europe-based system of teaching to pre-schoolers in the region. With the principal office in London, Modern Montessori International (MMI) has twenty-five pre-school centres in Singapore with many more in the region as joint ventures with other groups as in Thailand and India. It has also diversified into other Early Childhood Education courses and Diploma in Montessori Method of Education.[103] It is an ISO-certified and Singapore Quality Class (SQC)-accredited SME in Singapore. "Through franchising and joint ventures with powerhouse business partners, the MMI Group is able to position itself as a strategic and significant player set to make a difference in an industry that sees its importance exponentiation over time."[104]

Natarajan & Swaminathan, a firm of certified public accountants, is an example of how a professional accounting firm (established in 1950) expanded swiftly in recent years with increasing number of associate companies to cater to the growing demands of the Indians who sought to establish their business in Singapore. R. Narayanamohan, who had joined the firm in 1976 after completing his professional education in India, eventually took over to head the firm in 1990s, and has been successfully running it as its owner and managing director since then.[105] Providing "one-stop service to Indians", as Narayanmohan describes his firm, Natarajan & Swaminathan originally provided with statutory audit, tax work and company incorporation to its clients. With the increase in the influx of Indians, Mohan Management Consultants Pte. Ltd. was started in 1990 to help the new entrants with immigration necessities, maintain books of accounts, provide secretarial services, and also provide with tally services and training. They went on adding services according to the needs and demands of the clients. Mohan BPO Services Pte. Ltd. was started to cater to the back-office processing. This was, however, very different from what was done by business process outsourcing (BPOs) in India. They did back-office processing for those Indian companies which were small and did not need or want to take up office spaces or hire employees. Documentation work and such other activities were taken care of by the company. Besides, they also started the Mohan HR Pte. Ltd. to find jobs for the expatriates and their families when they moved to Singapore. Mohan Properties Pte. Ltd., established in 2008, was set up to manage properties for the NRIs and the Indian diaspora in Singapore.[106]

Narayanmohan, belonging to the previous generation of settlers in Singapore, is amongst the few, who has been intimately connected with the operations and necessities of the "older" migrants and the "newer" diaspora alike. His recent appointment as the Chairman of SICCI brings hopes of further attempts at interactions and exchanges within the Indian business community.

The participation of the new generation of professional immigrants in Singapore, who has been trying their hands at business and entrepreneurship, can be envisaged in varied and diverse fields of interests. The more trendy entrepreneurial choices for the professionals at present are those in the new-age sectors of e-commerce, IT operations, supply chain logistics, cost management solutions, multimedia marketing, consultancy services and education. A large number of firms has emerged and continues to climb the ladder of success in this area. Especially in the IT sector, firms like Emerio Corporation or Optimum Solutions, emerging in the 1990s, have been extremely successful. The CEO of Emerio, Harish Nim, an Indian Institute of Management (IIM) and Indian Institute of Technology (IIT) graduate, had started from a one-man show in 1997 to expand its company to employ more than 1,300 employees at present.[107] It is involved in consulting and IT services, which includes business intelligence services, infrastructure solutions, software services and others, and is spread over fourteen countries including delivery centres like Singapore, Malaysia, the Philippines, Indonesia, Thailand and India in the region.[108]

A similar, but a smaller entity, Techcom Solutions Pte. Ltd. had been started in 2003 by a chartered accountant duo, T.R.V. Rajan and his wife in the field of IT business. It has been rapidly expanding as IT solutions provider and other professional services and has managed to spread into a number of countries like Thailand, Malaysia, the United States and India.[109] In Singapore, some of their clients include Tiger Airways, UBS and Canon.

Interestingly, the new generation has been equally interested to plunge into the traditional areas of trading in commodities, chemicals or that in logistics, real estate or restaurant business. A very prominent name in the commodities trade is that of Vijay Iyenger, the former President of the SICCI. With the degrees from IIT-Mumbai and MBA from Cornell, he worked with Countercorp when he came to Singapore in 1986. He set up his business, Agrocorp International Pte. Ltd. in 1990 with a meagre capital of S$25,000.[110]

Iyenger describes his company as "a niche player focussing on certain markets where we have strong expertise ... that we leverage on".[111] His business primarily focuses on the countries and traders rather than a thin spread of commodities. A few economies that they concentrate on are Myanmar, Bangladesh, India, Indonesia, Pakistan, Turkey and Malaysia.[112] Agrocorp has earned various accolades for its progress and success. It has been approved of the AIT status by the TDB in 1995, ranked among the most successful of the Singapore-1000 companies for 2000–01 and has been awarded with Enterprise-50 since 1999.[113]

The story of Rajul Patel, at one-time a finance professional, who moved to Singapore in 1999, and eventually started the Chutney Café[114] at Church Street is remarkably different. They have adapted to the basic style cooking of the North Indian popular dishes using the clay oven, and also offer some fusion cuisines from the Chinese, African and European palate.[115] It caters to people from all walks of life and suitable to all pockets.[116] A large number of Indians are plunging into the restaurant business, especially focusing on the North Indian and fusion cuisines with innovative ambience in the offering and targeting both the middle-level and high-end customers.

V. CONCLUSION

The past two decades has been a period of transition for the Indian entrepreneurship, both in the subcontinent as well as in the world stage. The forces of changes have been many — from government policy changes, globalized capitalism, Asian resurgence and emerging market geographies, to mention a few. Singapore has been prompt to engage India in steering the direction of these global changes to that of mutual benefit and cooperation. In fact, the government initiatives were very much related to the combination of emerging factors in the business environment, which had a direct and an indirect impact on the ethnic Indian business community. Singaporean Indian companies are no more shying away from establishing business contacts with India. Following the decades after the independence, local Indian companies had avoided looking towards India for furthering their business interests due to the inward looking policies of India and comparatively weaker bilateral links with India leading to difficulties in transborder activities, except for the retail dealers in the Serangoon Road, whose demand-supply chain had always depended on the Indian links. With the recent trend set by Singaporean companies to strategize and build on a part of their business operations with South Asia and the Indian subcontinent, we might draw a familiarity with the situation of the Indian companies during colonial times utilizing the commercial linkages and advantages of the native country, however, keeping in view the changes in paradigms and in the *modus operandi*.

This chapter also gives us glimpses of the rising excellence of the Indian professional class, many of whom have sought to have a home in Singapore and also diversified into the field of business activities. The meteoric rise of the professional class, mainly due to the technological advancement of the service sector and its intrinsic involvement with entrepreneurship, has redefined much of the conventional entrepreneurial paradigms and necessitated the corporatization of the traditional family-business patterns. Those family businesses that have survived, have done so by maintaining a delicate balance of highly-skilled professionals as employees at the management level, maintaining amity and cohesive spirit in the family and efficiently holding onto the reins of the business. The close collaboration of the business houses and the professional class to create an edge in the world of cut-throat competition has been felt like never before. This inevitable nexus has, perhaps, lured a large number of professionals to try their hand at business, a task that many have undertaken with great confidence, panache and success.

What has also been witnessed in the current phase is the participation and situation of a large number of Indian companies in Singapore. This has brought in a large number of first generation Indians who have extended their arms to Singapore and the region. Triggered off by the business interests, it has also rejuvenated and mobilized the cultural linkages of India with the Southeast Asian region and presented prospects of reshaping the process of cultural exchanges in the future.

It is interesting to note that the number of JVs and collaborations between Indian and Singaporean companies have increased remarkably over the past decade. It may, however, be pointed out that the inter-ethnic relations within the business environment of Singapore prevailed at different stages of history irrespective of the structures of the business models of operational mechanisms. Representations on the board of companies have usually cut across ethnic lines, some examples of which have already been discussed.[117] However, generally speaking, the inter-ethnic relations for the past decades have been more at the market level, but such relationships are increasingly being witnessed at the corporate and structural level with the present generations with improved professionalism and the mindset of a global outreach. Also, inter-ethnic relations and participation exist in the day-to-day running of the business. However, the extent of the interplay of econometrics and socio-political imperatives as well as the psychological factor or the involvement of human element then needs to be analysed, which is, perhaps, beyond the scope of the present research.

Notes

1. S. Dhanabalan, then Minister for Foreign Affairs at the talk at the NUS Forum, Lecture Theatre 11, Singapore, 27 November 1981.
2. Quoted from Michael Leifer, *Singapore's Foreign Policy: Coping with Vulnerability* (London: Routledge, 2000), p. 162.
3. Ibid.
4. Amitav Acharya, *Singapore's Foreign Policy: The Search for Regional Order* (Singapore: World Scientific Publishing Co. Pte. Ltd. and Institute of Policy Studies, 2008).
5. Chan Heng Chee and Obaid ul Haq, eds., *S. Rajaratnam: The Prophetic and the Political* (Singapore, Graham Brash and New York: St. Martin's Press, 1987), p. 227.
6. Rajesh Mehta, "Economic Cooperation between India and Singapore: A Feasibility Study", RIS Discussion Paper no. 41, New Delhi, 2003.

7. <http://www.visitsingapore.com/publish/stbportal/en/home/btmice/ip_archive/Dec08/ip_online/indust...> (accessed 12 December 2008).

8. The first in merit is the United States.

9. <http://www.visitsingapore.com/publish/stbportal/en/home/btmice/ip_archive/Dec08/ip_online/indust...> (accessed 12 December 2008).

10. Interview with Kiran Bhandari, Area Director — Southern India, Sri Lanka and Maldives, Singapore Tourism Board (STB), Chennai, *The Hindu*, 27 March 2008, <http://www.hindu.com/thehindu/holnus/006200803272172.htm> (accessed 31 March 2008).

11. Amarjit Kaur, "Order (and Disorder) at the Border: Mobility, International Labour, Migration and Border Control in Southeast Asia", in *Mobility, Labour Migration and Border Controls in Asia*, edited by Amarjit Kaur and Ian Metcalfe (London: Palgrave Macmillan, 2006), p. 37.

12. Seema Gaur, "Indian Professional Workers in Singapore", in *Mobility, Labour Migration and Border Controls in Asia*, ibid., p. 194.

13. Ibid., p. 195. Different categories of visas and work permits granted to the students, workers and professionals are discussed by Arunajeet Kaur, "Singapore's New Indians: Attracting Indian Foreign Talent to Singapore", in *Rising India and Indian Communities in East Asia*, edited by K. Kesavapany, A. Mani, and P. Ramasamy (Singapore: Institute of Southeast Asian Studies, 2008), pp. 625–26.

14. Brenda S.A. Yeoh, "Singapore: Hungry for Foreign Workers at all Skill Levels", Table 2, <http://www.migrationinformation.org/Profiles/display.cfm?ID=570> (accessed 2 December 2008).

15. Minister Mentor Lee Kuan Yew had pointed out on one occasion: "There are four million people in Singapore; one million of which are foreigners. You get rid of this one million and many will not find jobs." *Business Times*, 13 November 2003.

16. Speech of Prime Minister Shri Atal Bihari Vajpayee, Singapore-India Business Forum, Singapore, 8 April 2002, <http://mea.gov.in/speech/2002/04/08spc01.htm> (accessed 3 December 2008).

17. Ibid.

18. For further details of India's foreign policy with Southeast Asia in the Cold War period, see Asis Kumar Mazumdar, *Southeast Asia in Indian Foreign Policy: A Study of India's Relations with Southeast Asian Countries from 1962–82* (Calcutta: Naya Prokash, 1982).

19. The first joint naval exercise between the two countries was held in December 1992. Niranjan Khilnani, *New Dimensions of India's Foreign Policy: Prime Minister Narasimha Rao's Era X-rayed* (New Delhi: Westvill Publishing House, 1995), p. 57. Joint naval exercises have become a regular feature now and involves the participation of multiple countries in the region.

20. Acceptance address by Singapore Prime Minister Goh Chok Tong for the Jawaharlal Nehru Award for International Understanding on 9 July 2004 at Rashtrapati Bhavan, New Delhi, India, <http://app.mfa.gov.sg/pr/read_content.asp?View,3970> (accessed 20 September 2008).

21. Ibid.

22. Inderjit Singh, Member of Parliament, Singapore, in answers to a questionnaire prepared by the author on 4 July 2008.

23. Ibid.

24. "Corporate Profile: DELTA's Group of Companies", <http://www.deltaonnet.com/delta%27sgroup.htm> (accessed 7 September 2009).

25. Ibid.

26. At the approximate exchange rate of 2004–05, Ministry of Commerce, India.

27. Sanjeev Nair, "The Tata Group leads India Inc's great acquisitions sweepstakes", 16 February 2005, <http://www.domain-b.com/industry/general/20050216_acquisitions.html> (accessed 6 January 2009).

28. Ibid.

29. "A Proud Nation Builder", <http://www.natsteel.com.sg/about_history.htm> (accessed 18 January 2009).

30. "Asian Paints Acquires 50% in Berger Intl.", *Financial Express*,

6 September 2002, <http://www.financialexpress.com/news/asian-paints-acquires-50-in-berger-intl/56581/> (accessed 18 January 2009).

31. Ibid.

32. "Asian Paints to Buy 50.1 pc Stake in Berger International", *Hindu Business Line*, 6 September 2002, <http://www.thehindubusinessline.com/2002/09/06/stories/2002090602480100.htm> (accessed 6 January 2009).

33. "DBS Launches Brokerage Venture in India", *Business Times*, 11 September 1995.

34. <http://www.iii.com.sg/index.cfm?GPID=9> (accessed 24 March 2009).

35. Ibid.

36. "Credit Report", <http://www.lloydslist.com/lmiu/companies/tolani-shipping-singapore-pte-ltd/20001839311-report-summary.htm;jsessionid=487E344004BC2A4BE5BB8F3FCB1857F6.5fa4e8cc80be35e2653c9f87d8b8be45bf6ba69a> (accessed 3 September 2009).

37. "Rohet Tolani", *Tabla*, 29 May 2009.

38. Ibid.

39. Madhu Madan et al., "Smooth Sailing: Mr Mahesh Iyer", in *Singapore Indian Entrepreneurs: Dreams to Reality* (Singapore: Singapore Indian Chamber of Commerce and Industry, 2004), p. 97.

40. Ibid., pp. 97–98.

41. "About SSOE", <http://www.swiss-singapore.com/about.htm> (accessed 2 April 2009).

42. Ibid.

43. "MMTC Transnational: Profile of an Indian trading company", <http://www.mmtclimited.com/grp_mtpl.html> (accessed 2 April 2009).

44. Ibid.

45. Ibid. MTPL's growth then shot up by 28 per cent from S$248 million in 2002–03 to S$318 million in 2003–04. G. Srinivasan, "MMTC Singapore arm posts record turnover — Makes foray

into sophisticated, competitive markets", *Hindu Business Line*, 2 April 2004, <http://www.blonnet.com/2004/04/02/stories/2004040201050400.htm> (accessed 2 April 2009).

46. M.G. Asher and S. Srivastava, "India and the Asian Economic Community", RIS Discussion Paper no. 51, New Delhi, 2003.

47. Rahul Sen, "The India-Singapore Comprehensive Economic Cooperation Agreement: A Good Beginning towards an Enduring Relationship", *ASEAN Economic Bulletin*, vol. 20, no. 2 (August 2003): 180.

48. Ibid., p. 180.

49. Alka Chadha, "CECA Implementation: A First Look", ISAS Working Paper no. 9, Singapore, 7 February 2006.

50. Rakhee Suryaprakash, "Singapore-India Relations: CECA and Beyond", SAAG (South Asia Analysis Group) Paper no. 1493, 10 August 2005.

51. Indrajit Basu, "India, Singapore ink pact", *Asia Times*, 2 July 2005, <http://www.atimes.com/atimes/South_Asia/GG02Dfo3.html> (accessed 6 August 2008).

52. Sanchita Basu Das and Rahul Sen, "Singapore-India CECA: Rationale, Overview and Implications", in *Investors Guide to India-Singapore Comprehensive Economic Agreement*, edited by Mohan Pillay (Singapore: Reed Elsevier (Singapore) Private Limited, 2005).

53. Ibid.

54. Vibanshu Shekhar, "India-Singapore Relations: An Overview", *IPCS Special Report* 41, June 2007.

55. The then High Commissioner of India to Singapore in conversation with Ms Shobha Tsering Bhalla, "Growth without ceiling", *India Se*, December 2008, p. 11.

56. Rasheeda Bhagat, "India-Singapore trade linkages must grow", *Hindu Business Line*, 28 April 2008, <http://www.thehindubusinessline.com/2008/04/28/stories/2008042851171600.htm> (accessed 6 August 2008).

57. "Punj Lloyd acquires the balance stake in Sembawang Engineers

& Contractors, Singapore", 19 October 2006, <http://www.sembawangenc.com/admin/spaw2/uploads/files/Media%20 Releases/19-Oct-2006.pdf> (accessed 19 January 2009).

58. At the approximate exchange rate of 2005–06, Ministry of Commerce, India.

59. "Strides to acquire Singapore generics co", September 2006, <http://www.bridgesingapore.com/strides.htm> (accessed 6 January 2009).

60. Ibid. Strides is involved in manufacturing and supply of soft gels in New Zealand and Australia and also has supply agreements with South African companies and market presence in the United States and Canada.

61. "Satyam eyeing $50m overseas buy", *Indiatimes-Infotech*, 14 April 2008, <http://timesofindia.indiatimes.com//tech/news/outsourcing/Satyam-eyeing-50m-overseas-buy-/articleshow/295060.cms> (accessed 6 January 2009).

62. One such twenty-two member delegation from Singapore visited New Delhi, Chennai and Bangalore in October 2004, which included many Singaporean-Indian companies. "Singapore Seeks JVs with India", *Financial Express*, 19 October 2004, <http://www.financialexpress.com/news/singapore-seeks-jvs-with-india/117308/> (accessed 20 January 2009).

63. "Kalyani Group enters into Joint Venture Agreement with Singapore Technologies Kinetics", <http://www.bharatforge.com/investers/JV_with_Kalyani_Final.pdf> (accessed 21 January 2009).

64. Ibid.

65. "Kalyani arm, Singapore firm sign JV agreement", <http://timesofindia.indiatimes.com/articleshow/299621.cms> (accessed 21 January 2009).

66. "Pacific Healthcare Enters into a Joint-Venture with Wadia Group, to set up Mumbai Cosmetic Medical Specialist Centre", <http://www.pachealthholdings.com/images/pdf/memorandum.pdf> (accessed 21 January 2009).

67. Ibid.

68. Both were a 50:50 JV for India and China, "Educomp forms two Joint-Ventures with Raffles Education Corp., Asia Pacific's largest private Education Group", <http://www.educomp.com/Downloads/Educomp-%20Raffles%20JV%20final%20India.pdf> (accessed 21 January 2009).
69. Ibid.
70. Ibid.
71. "Adani Exports to set up power plant at Mundra", <http://www.projectsmonitor.com/detailnews.asp?newsid=2880> (accessed 20 January 2009).
72. "Adani Wilmar to set up 1,200 tpd refinery — To expand edible oil biz; focus on export", <http://www.thehindubusinessline.com/2003/09/12/stories/2003091201341100.htm> (accessed 21 January 2009).
73. "Singapore delegation sees opportunity in port, pharma", <http://www.expressindia.com/latest-news/singapore-delegation-sees-opportunity-in-port-pharma/324727/> (accessed 21 January 2009).
74. "Globe Detective goes Overseas ... Sets up new joint venture in Singapore with Mainguard International", <http://www.indiaprwire.com/pressrelease/security/2008101614320.htm> (accessed 21 January 2009).
75. "About us", <http://www.savant-infocomm.com/aboutus.htm> (accessed 21 January 2009).
76. <http://www.bridgesingapore.com/sector_for_future_bilateral_trade.htm> (accessed 23 March 2009).
77. The CECA provisions also allow the opening of the Indian banking sector to three local banks giving them the opportunity to venture into big markets like India and develop new strategies of marketing and survival. The three banks — DBS Holdings, United Overseas Bank (UOB) and Overseas Chinese banking Corporation (OCBC) have been allocated fifteen branches (for three banks) for four years and also "permitted to acquire private Indian banks under the existing foreign investment policy framework". Sanchita Basu

Das and Rahul Sen, "Singapore-India CECA: Rationale, Overview and Implications", op. cit.

78. "Shipping solutions to India and Asia, website of Mercator Lines (Singapore) Limited", <http://www.mllsg.com/> (accessed 24 March 2009).

79. "About us, Business", <http://www.mllsg.com/about_business.html> (accessed 24 March 2009).

80. "Indian firms look at listing in Singapore SE", *India News Online*, 19 March 2007, <http://news.indiamart.com/news-analysis/indian-firms-look-at-15094.html> (accessed 24 March 2009).

81. Ibid.

82. Corporate company profile of GATI, <http://www.gati.com/corporate_company_profile.jsp> (accessed 31 March 2009).

83. "Gati increases market penetration in Asia-Pacific with Singapore as its base", 6 May 2008, <http://www.sedb.com/edb/sg/en_uk/index/news/articles/gati_increases_market.html> (accessed 31 March 2009).

84. Ibid.

85. Ibid.

86. "Profile of the Company", <http://www.firstflight.net/about.asp> (accessed 31 March 2009).

87. Brochure, DLF Group of Companies, 2008.

88. "IDA and CII to Promote Closer Ties Between Singapore and Indian Infocomm Industries", Singapore, 1 November 2000, <http://www.ida.gov.sg/News%20and%20Events/20061116152518.aspx?getPagetype=20> (accessed 2 September 2009).

89. In the phase of international mobilization of highly skilled professionals around the globe, Singapore, while opening its doors for such migrants, also had to contend with an outward bound populace mostly to the United States, Australia and also to Europe, thus creating different complexities to the already strains on the indigenous skilled labour in the country.

90. Interview with Kiran Bhandari, Area Director — Southern India, Sri Lanka and Maldives, Singapore Tourism Board (STB), Chennai.

D. Murali and R.S. Murali, "Positioning Singapore as a constantly reinventing destination", *The Hindu*, 27 March 2008, <http://www. hindu.com/thehindu/holnus/006200803272172.htm> (accessed 31 March 2008).

91. Ibid.

92. "Singapore school introduces India studies programme", <http://www. prokerala.com/news/articles/a18150.html> (accessed 23 December 2008).

93. "Bollywood now playing on a radio near you", *India Se*, August 2008, p. 23.

94. The Global Indian International School (GIIS) has three branches in Singapore and several in the Southeast Asian region. It offers Indian as well as international curriculum to the students. The other Indian schools providing secondary education in Singapore are the international branches of Delhi Public School (DPS) and the NPS International School.

95. Seema Gaur, op. cit., p. 207.

96. Harish Damodaran, *India's New Capitalists: Caste, Business, and Industry in a Modern Nation* (New Delhi: Permanent Black, 2006).

97. The term was coined by M.N. Srinivas while describing the upward mobility of the lower castes in the social ladder of India. For further reference, see *Social Change in Modern India* (Berkeley and Los Angeles: Orient Longman, 1966) and *Caste in Modern India and Other Essays* (Mumbai: Media Promoters and Publishers Pvt. Ltd., 2002) by the same author.

98. Initially started by Satpal Khattar, Haider Sithawalla and Gopinath Pillai, but later joined by David Ho, who, in the early years of his life worked in the Citibank, then Intraco before starting his company, Windmill International Pte. Ltd., an industrial bulk-commodities trading and logistics trading company. He later joined the KSP. Haider Sithawalla started his career as a civil servant and rose to the position of Deputy Secretary in the Ministry of Finance. He then joined the ACMA Industries Ltd. as GM and then MD before venturing into KSP. He is also the Non-Resident High

Commissioner to Mauritius and Zimbabwe. Similarly, Gopinath Pillai has interests in various companies in South and Southeast Asia as well as involvement with the education sector. He is at present the Chairman of the Institute of South Asian Studies (ISAS) and IT Services Cooperative Ltd. and had been the past President of the National University of Singapore Society. He is also the Non-Resident Ambassador of Singapore to Iran. Satpal Khattar is a lawyer by profession and has been associated with various companies and institutes, both government and private. He had also been associated with the law firm Khattar Wong and Partners. Interview with Haider Sithawalla (HS) by the author on 18 March 2009, <http://www.savant-infocomm.com/aboutus.htm> (accessed 6 April 2009).

99. Interview with Haider Sithawalla (HS), ibid.

100. Ibid. For more information on the different companies, see <www. aeceduplc.co.uk> (AEC), <www.savant-infocomm.com> (Savant) and <www.eastcom-systems.com> (Eastcom).

101. Interview with George Abraham by the author in March 2009; <http://www.nus.edu.sg/nec/_files/ed/The_GA_Group_Pte_Ltd.pdf> (accessed 6 April 2009).

102. Ibid.

103. "Corporate Network", webpage of Modern Montessori International (MMI), <http://www.mmi-malaysia.com/corp_network.htm> (accessed 14 March 2008).

104. "Leaving Giant Footprints in the World of Tiny Tots", a write-up, sent to the author, on MMI and written by the PR Executive for Chairman, Alan Tan, MMI, Singapore, 28 March 2008.

105. Interview with R. Narayanmohan, senior partner and head of Natarajan & Swaminathan, on 11 July 2008.

106. Ibid.

107. "Management Team", company website, <http://www.emeriocorp. com/harish.html> (accessed 6 April 2009).

108. "About us", webpage of Emerio, <http://www.emeriocorp.com/ harish.html> (accessed 6 April 2009).

109. Conversation with Mr and Mrs Rajan, 27 March 2008; homepage

of Techcom Solutions Pte. Ltd., <http://www.techcomsolutions. net/index.htm> (accessed 7 September 2009).

110. Madhu Madan et al., "From Strength to Strength: Vijay Iyenger", in *Singapore Indian Entrepreneurs: From Dreams to Reality* (Singapore: Singapore Indian Chamber of Commerce and Industry, 2004), p. 149.

111. Ibid.

112. Dipinder S. Randhawa, "Agrocorp International Pte Ltd", in *Best Practices, Experiences of Successful Local Enterprises* (Singapore: Productivity and Quality Research Centre, Faculty of Business Administration, National University of Singapore (NUS), 2000), p. 97; Vijay Iyengar's conversation with the author on 19 January 2009.

113. Madan et al., op. cit., p. 149.

114. Amrit Barman, *India Fever* (Singapore: Singapore Indian Association, 2009), p. 38.

115. "Chutney Café, North Indian Fusion Restaurant", <http://www. chutneycafe.com/> (accessed 7 April 2009).

116. "Singapore Small Business Directory", <http://www.sgsmallbiz. com/chutney-cafe-link-2188.html> (accessed 7 April 2009).

117. Khattar-Wong partnership is an example of such partnerships.

PART TWO

Chapter 4

BUSINESS ASSOCIATIONS AND ORGANIZATIONAL NETWORKS

Organizations and associations of merchants' bodies must have existed as long as the inception of the trading community, though the term "chamber of commerce" was only coined as late as the end of sixteenth century[1] and became popular thereafter. The "merchant-guilds" and "craft-guilds", the predecessors to the chambers of commerce, were quite common in medieval Europe as it was in early medieval India. Some names of the South Indian merchant guilds existed not only as prominent entities of trading interests,[2] but represented complex syncretic relationships between state, guilds and religious institutions.[3] Ancient India has also been replete with numerous examples of *srenis* or guilds with nexus between political authorities and the commercial interests[4] in the parameters of the complex hierarchical occupational structures of the caste system. There are several other names denoting merchant bodies like the *samuha*, *nigama*, *gana*, *pasanda*, *puga* in the ancient Indian texts, but the differences between them is not very clear.[5] Thus the essence and structure of merchant bodies was not a Western innovation, as is often believed, but readily existed in the parlance of the

socio-economic structure of ancient India[6] and continued into
subsequent ages. The hereditary nature of profession in Indian
guilds differed from the European guilds, where individual
preferences were given priority; nevertheless, choice of family
occupations was more common. The hereditary, linguistic and
regional base of the Indian merchant bodies perhaps helped them
to maintain the intra-ethnic bonding of the informal commercial
networks even during the colonial period parallel to the Western
chambers of commerce.

The basic mission of the merchant bodies has remained
the same through the times, which is to promote a conducive
climate of productive and profitable business operations in
the commercial interests of the community. The Chambers of
Commerce eventually evolved as a common protection group
to govern conduct of trade for specific mercantile interests as
well as influence legislation of respective governments or act as
pressure groups to benefit their trade and commerce. This chapter
focuses on the evolution of different business organizations
and associations in Singapore, especially those emerging out
of ethnic Indian bodies, through the colonial times into the
present generation of several networking groups and analyses
their contribution to the commercial community in different
phases of history.

I. EVOLUTION OF BUSINESS ORGANIZATIONS IN SINGAPORE

The rapid development of Singapore as a centre of entrepot trade
in Southeast Asia and the commercial connector between Canton
and Calcutta necessitated safeguarding the merchants' interests
on the island. As early as 1829, a merchant delegation met Lord
William Bentinck, the then Governor General of India, on his visit

to Singapore to emphasize the need for a local currency and voice their displeasure about what they felt was an encroachment on "free-port" doctrine.[7] Soon after in 1831, merchants jointly made a petition to the Parliament in London regarding the absence of adequate judicial measures for the Settlement resulting in the appointment of a Government Recorder in 1833.[8] There was also a continuous resistance of the merchant communities of the "free-port" of Singapore against any attempts of the East India Company in Calcutta to impose any kind of taxation. There were only minimal harbour and anchorage charges and the Company found no avenues to add to their revenues, the main beneficiaries of which were the British agency houses and manufacturers in addition to the Chinese merchants.[9] The British traders and merchants, often being well connected with their counterparts in India and Europe, were naturally influenced by the efforts of the merchants around the globe to establish themselves into Chambers of Commerce at major commercial centres around the world. The Singapore Chamber of Commerce was established in 1837, and in the first inaugural meeting convened on 8 February 1837, it was unanimously resolved that "all merchants, agents, ship-owners and others interested in the trade of the place" were eligible to be the members of the association.[10] Alexander Johnston (first Chairman), Edward Boustead and Alexander Guthrie were the founding fathers of the Chamber.[11] The Penang Chamber followed soon after on 23 February 1837 and the two Chambers were in close cooperation with each other. By this time, the British Chamber of Commerce had already been established in Calcutta in 1833, Madras and Bombay in 1836.

In the late eighteenth century, before the appearance of the Chambers of Commerce, commercial organizations known as managing agency houses emerged, especially in India and some Asian countries like China, Malaya and the East Indies,[12] where they catered to the interests of those foreign investors who did not prefer to reside in the colonies continuously and passed the governance and management of their enterprises to these agency houses in lieu of commission and other benefits. The "free port" of Singapore was attractive to many private European merchants who came to participate in the transhipment of goods between the East and the West and barter items like spices, pepper, nutmegs of the East with Lancashire cotton goods, Sheffield knives and other items of Victorian England.[13] "Agency houses functioned as trade intermediaries for European manufacturers in the marketing and distribution of manufactured goods, in turn securing raw materials and native produce for export to Europe."[14] They minimized the cost of business, allowing easy flow of goods without trade financing, at the same time benefiting merchants in Europe as well as agency houses in Singapore.[15] They were also providing shipping facilities, taking care of insurance and coordinating credit. Most of the early agency houses were involved in textile trading from Britain. There was a gradual increase of merchant firms from seventeen in 1834 to forty-three by 1846, out of which twenty were British.[16] Some of the prominent names of the early managing agency houses were that of Guthrie & Co., Boustead & Co., Paterson, Simons & Co., the Borneo Co., Behn, Meyer & Co. The firms were in the words of P.J. Drake:

> ... a funnel for trade credit originating in England, and it was this credit which principally enabled the merchants to do a business of value well above the total of their own resources. ... it was also necessary for the merchants to have contacts and financial dealings with Asian traders and producers and (after the advent of banks to the Straits ports) frequent recourse to the banks for discounting of bills of exchange and promissory notes or for overdraft accommodation.[17]

From the second half of the nineteenth century, British merchants were more involved in speculative trading in mining and plantation agriculture, and also promoting and floating company shares for public fund raising. This was a feature common to the managing agency houses in India who were intimately involved with the management of joint-stock companies and participating in the mining, shipping, jute and tea industries. But, unlike India, where it was virtually a British monopoly with little participation of the local merchants, at least in the initial years of its development, in Singapore, the speculative involvement was "in close conjunction with Chinese and other local merchants".[18] Drake gives the example of the firm, J.A. Russell & Co. which speculated in plantation development from funds advanced from Chinese friends.[19] The advantageous speculation of many of these merchant firms into the growing rubber industry made them intricately involved with the commercial expansion in Southeast Asia and eventually brought about structural changes in the forms of incorporations and amalgamations.[20] By the first decade of the twentieth century, British merchants were getting more involved with direct commodity production in Southeast Asia and textile trading receded to the background with increasing competition from the Japanese.

The agency houses thrived well in the first half of the twentieth century. During the First World War or the Great Depression, the fluctuating rubber prices did not actually change the nature or prosperity of these institutions. However, the political changes brought about by the Second World War and the consequences of the Japanese aggression brought about modification in their trends to cope with the new situation.

The advent of the Chamber of Commerce brought about a consolidation of the merchant communities on the island.

The Singapore Chamber, quite unlike the British Chambers of Commerce in India, which were exclusively dominated by the Europeans from the beginning, threw its doors open to merchants of different races. The first elected committee included Arab and Armenian merchants, Chinese traders and an American planter besides the Europeans.[21] The Chinese traders, with increasing population figures on the island, were quite involved with the Chamber at the beginning with some prominent merchants serving on their committee too. The Chinese merchants played an important role in the transhipment trade between the Bugis traders and the Arab and the Indian merchants, in the import trade of Western manufactured products and channelling them to other parts of Southeast Asia as well as in the export to the West of the primary commodities.[22] But by the end of the nineteenth century, most of them had opted to move out of the Chamber.

In the nineteenth century, the Chamber had become a mouthpiece to protest against the tin imports to Britain (1838), or carried out long drawn differences with the government in Calcutta on imposition of port duties and taxes. It was also initially opposed to the introduction of the Rupee currency on the island by the East India Company and remained a subject of dispute and concern till the British Straits Dollar was adopted at the beginning of the twentieth century.[23] The Chamber also dealt with the grievances against the Company's rule among other things until the transfer of power to London from India. The Chamber continued to play an important role in trade related matters till the beginning of the First World War, influencing or opposing government decisions where the benefits of trade were concerned. In the following years it was greatly involved with the rubber plantations and rubber auctions through the Singapore Chamber of Commerce Rubber Association as well as demanding protectionist measures to combat the recession in the 1930s.

After the period of the Japanese Occupation, the Chamber was revived with the restoration of the British after it had ceased to function for a brief period.

The Chamber of Commerce played an important role in the interaction of government policy and market forces in the economic development of Singapore. Of the island's mercantile community, which was mainly divided into the European and the Asian community, it was the former who actually participated and influenced the legislation process. Though the door was initially opened for all races in the Singapore Chamber, the Chinese, who formed the majority of the population, withdrew as has been mentioned earlier. They later formed their own chamber, the Singapore Chinese Chamber of Commerce and Industry in 1906, which was originally named the General Chinese Trade Affairs Association.

The Chinese compradors and financiers had played an important role in the supply and distribution network in Singapore and the rest of Southeast Asia. Similar participation of Indians in the distribution and supply chain also existed, even if on a much smaller scale, but has not been well documented in history. Indian trade contacts with Southeast Asia dates back much prior to the coming of the colonial rulers, and the increasing presence of the Indian trading groups on the island during the colonial phase had been boosted by volumes of trade between Singapore and India. According to Anthony Webster:

> About a fifth of Singapore's trade up to 1850 was with India, and consisted largely of Indian cotton piece-goods and opium, which generated a steady flow of silver and gold specie to Calcutta and Madras from south east Asia.[24]

Though Webster refers to the British participation in the trade, it is only natural for the indigenous Indian merchants to be involved

in the demand-supply chain from the subcontinent, given the kind
of well-developed intra-ethnic regional networks that existed.[25] In
fact, these merchant networks were quite extensively spread out
in the region with strong family ties and hardly any structural
or management changes over generations or little efforts in
diversification.[26] Relating to the strong Indian textile networks,
R.A. Brown writes that "their extensive connections enabled them
to switch between markets, responding to increasing frequency
of changes in demand for differentiated materials".[27] In fact, they
had strong nexus with the Japanese textile merchant networks
in Southeast Asia at a time when the Japanese posed serious
competition to Lancashire products in the Inter-War period.
Interestingly, Webster also points out that according to Fullerton,
"imports of Indian piece-goods were double the quantity of British
piece-goods, which were regarded by Malay consumers as inferior
in quality to the Indian product".[28] Furthermore, the opium trade
stimulated the flow of Indian capital into Singapore and Southeast
Asia through the ubiquitous Chettiars from South India, who
financed the Chinese traders and also invested in the tin and
rubber plantations at the beginning of the twentieth century.
Chettiars had been adequately visible with their well-established
financing networks throughout the region, but like all other
ethnic Indian trading groups, have been studied in segregation,
rather than in the integrated periphery of the interplay of market
forces and trading operations. In fact, it could also be argued as
to whether and to what extent the Indian business community
was integrated and accepted within the gambit of larger
economic complexities. The Singapore Chamber, for instance,
had conformed to the membership of mixed nationalities from
the very beginning, but in 1947, it had denied membership to
one "Sheo Prasad Sharma" using the ostensible reason that "it
was not the policy of the Chamber to admit members of those

nationalities who were able to join their own Chambers of Commerce."[29] Such ambiguities and discriminations marginalized the community further, not to mention the lessons learnt under colonial duress in the subcontinent.

The volume of trade and the number of participants in the trading sector of the ethnic Indian communities was far from negligible at the dawn of the twentieth century. In fact, the establishment of the Burhani mosque at the end of the nineteenth century in Singapore and the Subramaniam Temple of Chettiars at Tank Road even earlier (1859)[30] or Jamae Masjid built by the Tamil Muslims as early as 1826 bear testimony to the fact that there was a substantial presence of the Bohra and Tamil Muslim merchants and Chettiars, who were essentially hereditary business communities based in Singapore. The growing number of ethnic trade associations and their gradual enlargement not only ascertained their increasing participation and importance in trade and commerce, but subsequent involvement and influence in the process of legislation and governance in the island nation.

II. ETHNIC INDIAN BUSINESS ASSOCIATIONS SINCE THE TWENTIETH CENTURY

The European business community had the support of the global network of buyers and suppliers, logistical efficiency and financial backing, apart from the aggressive foreign policy of the government, which was undoubtedly much stronger than any network of individual clusters of Asian merchants. The Indian merchants had, undoubtedly, been beneficiaries of the advantages of easy extension of their trade linkages under the canopy of the same colonial governance, but they also had to bear the brunt of colonization, which meant being bereft of political and trading rights and privileges and being subject to incessant discrimination.

In the Straits Settlements, they were a minority community with the focus of the Asian merchant groups being mainly on the larger body of Chinese merchant networks. Indian traders existed as small, segregated, heterogeneous, regional groups, more often tied to the roots of the regional homeland and linguistic affinity than by any common trading interests.

The robust bonding of strong connectivity on the fundamentals of linguistics, religion, caste or class structure was typical of the subcontinent's social system. This intra-ethnic network catered to their business interests by providing the financial, logistical and human resource support. They were structured on the distribution and demand-supply network laid down by the colonialists, but functioned independently through their indigenous mode of operations, meeting the Western market system at some nodal points of contact. The adaptation of Western market functions came gradually and slowly. Even then, strongly religious commercial groups like the Chettiars remained a closed-knit, temple-centric group, neither confronting, nor collaborating with the mainstream of business trends and groups. For the Bohras too, the mosque was much more than a place of worship, serving as the place for social congregation or business networking. Thus, manifestations of business associations cutting across ethnic lines took a long time in coming. The earliest known associations of the ethnic Indians were mainly social and religious in nature like the setting up of the Hindu Paropkari Fund around 1908 mainly by the Gujarati community, as has been seen earlier in the first chapter.

The Sindhis were the first North Indian business community to form themselves into an association of merchants and traders, which was primarily the occupation of all Sindhis who came to Singapore. The **Sindhi Merchants Association** formed as early as 1921, laid the path for the formation of a more well-defined trade and business organization later, the Indian Chamber of Commerce. By 1939, there were twenty-one member firms and a property at Enggor Street acquired in 1938,[31] which served the purpose of "providing comfortable boarding facilities for the visiting Sindhis and for those, who were in transit — to their destination".[32] This was a unique measure adopted by the Sindhi community for facilitating the traders and merchants to carry out business activities in the region. When the premises of the Association shifted to 30, Oxley Road[33] and to 176, Neil Road in the 1950s, they continued to provide for the accommodation of the Sindhi transit passengers.[34]

The Association had been quite active and organized in its functions as a mouthpiece of not only the merchants but also for the well-being of the general public. It helped with free boarding and lodging to War time evacuees in transit from Japan to India.[35] The Government also involved and consulted the Sindhi Merchants Association along with the other Chambers on matters relating to imports, exports, incentives and quotas.[36] There has also been an interesting reference to one of the rules laid down by the Association. In the days of no labour rights or privileges, the Association had made closure of the shops one day of the week mandatory, any violation of which was met with a fine of $500.[37]

The Sindhi Merchants Association laid the foundation for other ethnic Indian merchant bodies and organizations that soon followed in Singapore. This association then relegated to the background and took up more social causes by restructuring itself, though business networking among the community continued within its premises, but more under the garb of social congregations. They had also started a magazine, *Sindhu* in the 1950s[38] under the auspices of the Association, which mainly dealt with the sociocultural issues. In 1953, as B.H. Melwani told the managing committee, there were about 186 subscribers all over Asia to the magazine apart from the complementary copies given to the members of the Association,[39] which threw light on both the extent of the Association's outreach as well as the increasing number of Sindhis in the Southeast Asian region.

The name of the Sindhi Merchants Association was changed to the Singapore Sindhi Association in 2004 when it was felt by the community that the organization did not any more remain solely a merchant body but had among its members many professionals, a newer trend with the younger generations, in the community.[40] The Singapore Sindhi Association accommodates about 500 members at present, most of whom are resourceful businessmen,[41] but has also started incorporating, among its members, many of the new age professionals within the community. The present Sindhu House, situated in Katong, was bought in 1955 to facilitate the Sindhi families living around the area and the business firms in the High Street to congregate conveniently for recreational, religious and spiritual gatherings. Social functions like marriages and engagement ceremonies continue to be held here, making it a centre for all Sindhi activities.

The **Indian Merchant Association (IMA)**, established on 21 November 1924,[42] was the first organization of the Indian businessmen which cut across regional and linguistic barriers of different communities from the Indian subcontinent and later came to be acknowledged as the predecessor for the Indian Chamber of Commerce to be followed in a decade's time. It was founded with thirty members and Bhujangilal Mehta was asked to convene its first meeting.[43] It comprised of mainly the North Indian merchants who came to form an identity of similar business interests. Apart from aiming to protect the trading interests of the community, as was the case with all the business organizations, the IMA also had the objective of playing a meaningful role in the social and economic development of Singapore. The Association was greatly involved in the Trade Commission appointed by the Governor of the Straits Settlements from 1933 to 1934 to enquire into the trade of the colony. Eventually, eleven years later, when IMA was under the leadership of R. Jumabhoy, the Association assumed the status of the Indian Chamber of Commerce on 26 August 1935.[44] The Presidents of the IMA were A.M.S. Angulia, Nomanbhoy Abdeali and Jivrajbhoy Parekh besides R. Jumabhoy.[45] Before going into further details on the Indian Chamber, brief attention may be diverted to the setting up of a very closed-knit and low profile, but adequately important, Chettiar Chamber of Commerce in Singapore.

The **Chettiar Chamber of Commerce** was established in 1928,[46] about seven years before the Indian Chamber of Commerce came into being. The reason for choosing that particular year and how it had helped in integrating the Chettiar commercial interests with the larger framework of the national economy is not very clear, since they were already established as a strong commercial group on the island since the nineteenth century.[47] However, it may have been possible that establishment of a formal business organization could have given them better negotiation capability with the government. Unfortunately, not much information can be found in the available reports of their Chamber. The Chettiars, especially the merchant-banking group among them, the Nattukottai Chettiars, as has been seen earlier, were inwardly attached to their *kittingis*, temple and their own caste of people as far as conducting their business was concerned. The clients, of course, varied from Chinese, Malays to Indians and even at times, British. Thus, it was only natural that the bigger concerns of the ethnic Indian community could not be identified or addressed by them, who mainly carried out the moneylending business and also invested in properties, thus operating within the economic spheres of Singapore and Malaysia, connected to the *Chettinadu* in India with social, philanthropic obligations and man power recruitment, and not really much affected with the trading rights and concerns of the larger Indian business community in Singapore. However, their huge investments in the plantation and mining industries in the Malaya Peninsula at the beginning of the twentieth century encouraged them to publish regular bulletins on the tin and rubber prices in Malaysia and Singapore, which had a lot of information and analysis on these commodities.[48] The Chettiars, perhaps, unintentionally, came to play an important role in the informal banking sector connecting themselves both with the industrial investments as well as petty individual debtors as suppliers of big as well as small sums of money through the incredible success of the "guarantor-promissory notes" chain, sparing the debtor of formalities and complicacies of western system of banking.

The Sikh moneylenders were said to have had an organization called the **Sikh Moneylenders and Businessmen Association** at Sophia Road, but unfortunately, very little is known about them. The most important among business organizations was, however, the development of the Indian Chamber of Commerce.

The establishment of the **Indian Chamber of Commerce (ICC)** on 26 August 1935 was a major landmark in the history of the Indian business community in Singapore. The body was exempted from registration under Ordinance 16 (Societies) of Malaya and the inaugural meeting under the Chairmanship of Rajabali Jumabhoy that was convened on 15 September 1935 as reported in the *Malaya Tribune* (17 September 1935).[49] The membership had also increased from 30 since the IMA in 1924 to about 50 in 1935 and rose to 62 by February next year and further up to 85 by the end of 1937.[50] M. Jumabhoy was elected the first President when the first general meeting of the Chamber was held on 6 February 1936, and at the next meeting the Chamber was registered under the Ordinance 155 (Companies) of the Straits Settlements. In the Memorandum that was signed in August 1937, there were nine signatories of whom two, P. Govindasamy Pillai and B.K.M. Ismail were South Indians.[51] The rest of them were from North India, but over the decades, the Chamber continued to incorporate a lot of members from the South Indian community.

The long history of the Chamber had witnessed several phases of triumphs, accomplishments and disappointments. The initial years were more focused on efforts to legitimize the institution as the credible representative of Indian business interests as well as the larger welfare of the nation, both to the community as well as the government. The task was an arduous and long drawn one, as even a decade later, R. Jumabhoy, the then President of the Chamber had been demanding equal rights and representations as such other organizations. In his words:

> This Chamber has time and again requested the local Government to accord the same privileges as given to the sister chambers, the Singapore Chamber of Commerce and the Chinese Chamber of Commerce in respect of their nominees in the Legislative Council, but so far without result. If a body that represents 90% of its trade cannot speak for its mercantile community, it is beyond my comprehension who could do so.[52]

The long battle eventually paid off when the Chamber got its representation in the Government in 1948, and R. Jumabhoy was appointed the first elected representative on the new Legislative Council.[53] Soon after, Jumabhoy suggested the alliance of all the Indian Chambers in the Federation of Malaya into a single body and a meeting to that effect was held on 27 March 1948 and decided in principle that a Federation of Indian Chambers of Malaya would be formed.[54] This effort, however, did not pay off successfully in the long run.

The first decade of ICC's formative years were involvement in its adjustment to local and international politics, especially with the outbreak of the Second World War and the Japanese aggression. It had started issuing the Certificates of Origin to the members since 1936 and to the non-members by 1937. The Chamber not only continued to function during the years of upheaval, unlike the International Chamber which stopped functioning for a brief period during the aggression, but in fact championed the setting up of Indian banks in the 1940s in Singapore.[55] The membership of the Chamber had, however, witnessed an all-time low in this period. The post-war membership of the Chamber included the Indian banks, insurance companies and others which were different from the earlier group of textile merchants and traders. This was reflective of the effective recognition of the Chamber among the larger Indian community. The Chamber was also greatly involved with the rehabilitation work after the War and other social aspects for the larger benefit of the community. In a Memorandum submitted by the Chamber to "The Carr-Saunders University Commission" in 1947, it emphasized on the importance and necessity of the establishment of the University for Malaya. It also made a request for the inclusion of Hindi or Tamil or both along with the Chinese and Malay languages in the Memorandum.[56]

Another important direction where the Chamber focused its attention in the initial years was finding a suitable property for the Chamber. It began with a rented room in the Malacca Street but moved to No. 4 Raffles Quay in 1937. Only in 1963, it acquired its premises in a three-storey building at 55 Robinson Road. In 1984, it moved on to a modern office space in the Tong Eng Building in Cecil Street, but it was only in 2007 that it acquired the present three-and-a-half storey of a heritage property at 31, Stanley Street with a much bigger space allowing it to set up the "Enterprise Development Centre" (EDC@SICCI) within its premises.[57]

With the onset of the next decade, the Chamber had become quite vocal about the trading interests of the merchant community. In 1952, it called on the Indian Government to abolish or reduce the prevailing duty of 25 per cent on medium and course goods as the Indian traders were already facing difficulties due to a fall in demand from the Indonesian markets. It voiced protests against the local government's ban on re-export of textiles to Hong Kong which further increased difficulties of the merchants already reeling under the effects of the lack of demand from the neighbouring states. After a lot of correspondences and negotiations, it was successful in uplifting the ban except on the export of cotton drills and cotton duck of any origin.[58] In 1953, the Indian Chamber, along with the Singapore Chamber of Commerce and the Singapore Chinese Chamber formed a Liaison Committee to cooperate on mutual trade and commerce issues. In the second half of the decade, the Chamber also submitted a Memorandum to the Singapore Port Commission highlighting difficulties faced by the consignees and deliberating on an efficient working of the Harbour Board.[59]

In the post-independence phase, the Chamber had been consulted on various issues by the government along with the other Chambers of Commerce. It made representations to various government bodies submitting memorandums on issues like the safeguarding of minorities in Singapore or commenting on Draft Companies Bill (1966) as also to the Salaries Commission.[60] Apart from liaisoning with the newly established government, the Chamber, in its efforts to look for newer markets for its members, met with several foreign delegations visiting the nation as well as hosted receptions for the different Heads of States or dignitaries, thus gaining international recognition as an effective business organization.

This was also the decade when most of the Indian traders faced huge difficulties when the days of the complete dependence on entrepot trade was over and many countries in the region had embarked on direct trade. The Indonesian policy of *Confrontasi*, where traders suffered huge losses in their trade with Indonesia, has already been discussed earlier. While Singapore still maintained its free port status, there had to be diversification to local industrialization and looking for new markets as the then President of the Indian Chamber, K.M. Abdul Razak reiterated:

> Singapore must ... build its new road to permanent and stable prosperity by opening up industries and accepting the challenge of an industrial competition with Asian and foreign countries.[61]

The Chamber supplemented the efforts taken by the government to take up new opportunities and different directions of business and trade.

Apart from the trading concerns of the community, the Chamber had also been generous in financial aid and active in welfare activities. The Chamber presented to the Government in August 1969 a cheque of $25,000 to start a scholarship fund for the students of technical courses, marking the 150th anniversary of the nation since the coming of Raffles. The scholarship would be named the 150th Anniversary Indian Chamber Scholarship Fund.[62] It went on to provide fourteen similar scholarships in 1971 for technical students of secondary three and four.[63] In 1978, the Chamber also gave bursaries of $200 each to fourteen trainees from the Industrial Training Board.[64] Earlier in 1969, the Indian Chamber had also donated 48,000 tons of condensed milk to the victims in West Malaysia.[65] It had also donated $3,600 to the Blood

Transfusion Service to buy twenty improved aluminium mobile beds.[66] Later in 1972, they also presented a cheque of $22,000 to the University of Singapore to purchase a foetal heart monitor for the Obstetrics and Gynaecology Department.[67] Glimpses of such contributions bring forth the integrated approach of the Chamber towards the larger community, much beyond mere mercantile interests.

The Chamber assumed the name of **Singapore Indian Chamber of Commerce (SICC)** in 1971. However, the decade of the 1970s did not witness much dynamic activities on the part of the Chamber. This was the period when the government had undertaken massive industrialization, which the trading Indian community was less likely to participate in. The Chamber tried to encourage more businessmen to break free from the trading circles and participate in the industry. Roop Vaswani, the President of the Chamber in 1970 said that the members were investing $10 million in a holding company to set up joint ventures,[68] which, however, did not make much of an impact. Nirmala Purushottam, in her unpublished monograph on SICCI, puts the situation in these words:

> The mark of the period's context can be said to be reflective of a steady, very confident government — who, no longer, needed to woo the private sector as much as it did in its early years. To add to this, as we have noted, the SICC's members were in no part a significant quarter of the industrialization programme that was dear to the heart of new economic directions.[69]

Representation existed, not as an automatic seat in the government committees, but sending SICC representative as and when asked to do so.[70] Trade, however, remained as a major contributor to Singapore's economy, and the Indian businessmen continued to flourish in this sector, albeit, with changes in components and composition. The ones who ventured into manufacturing did so as a part of their global expansion. Thus, the ethnic Indian business community did not, in real terms, become involved with the industrialization process of Singapore, partly because of scepticism in switching over to industrialization and partly because most of them had believed in short-term profit-making motives rather than investing in long-term projects. There were also no significant incentives from the government at this stage, the encouragement and promotion of the SMEs coming much later. This attitude of the Indian business community, however, changed gradually over the years.

The inclusion of SICC in the Singapore Federation of Chambers of Commerce and Industry in 1978 immensely helped in boosting the image of the Chamber. It formed a national body representing the commercial interests of the private sector and also became the member of the ASEAN-Chambers of Commerce and Industry (ASEAN-CCI). The Chamber held the "responsibility for the ASEAN-CCI Working Group on Trade (WGT) for Singapore".[71] J.M. Jumabhoy was appointed the Chairman and George Abraham, the Executive Director of WGT from 1979 to 1981. These were positions of great significance and prestige in terms of recognition in the larger Singaporean context. Jumabhoy, while chairing the 5th Plenary session of the Working Group on Trade on 14 December 1979 called on the ASEAN government to take measures to reduce red tapism, set specific goals for definite periods and aim at achieving them, to give directives to expedite matters on Trade and Tourism, and build direct contacts between government committees and ASEAN-CCI members.[72] J.M. Jumabhoy, who was the President of SICCI from 1978 to 1982, had earlier served as the Minister for Commerce and Industry in Singapore from 1956 to 1959. He was also the leader of the first overseas trade mission of the Singapore Federation of Chambers of Commerce and Industry to Bangladesh in October 1978.[73] The Chamber was later represented in the WGT by G. Ramachandran and George Abraham as Chairman and Executive Director respectively from 1987 to 1989.[74] The Chamber thus reinvigourated itself in the 1980s both in terms of the business activities as well as increasingly playing an important role in the national and the regional economy of Southeast Asia.

The Chamber was under the leadership of one of its most dynamic Presidents, G. Ramachandran, the son of Govindasamy Pillai. The appointment of a South Indian businessman was especially significant to the Chamber which had been usually regarded as the hub of the merchants originating from northern region of India. In fact, Ramachandran made efforts to bring in the Serangoon merchants and the Sindhi Merchant Association into the folds of the Chamber to "represent a true cross-section of Indian businessmen".[75] He expressed concerns of low representation of those younger members who had taken over family businesses and wanted to expand membership and wider representation of the community.[76] Ramachandran also "called for setting up a body to look into the needs of small businesses".[77] In March 1986, SICC submitted a paper to the National Productivity Board spelling out the problems of small traders and the need for their training.[78] The Small Enterprises Bureau (SEB) then decided to help fifteen members of the SICC to take part in training and consultancy programme to improve their marketing skills.[79] The Chamber was also represented on the Task Force on Small and Medium Enterprises (SME) set up by the EDB in 1987 for "examining, rationalising and evaluating the effectiveness of the various schemes" within or outside the purview of the Small Enterprises Bureau.[80] Thus, the issues of the SMEs which are effectively pursued under the aegis of the Chamber had its inception in the 1980s and successfully pursued by the future management body of the Chamber.

Another effort of the Chamber to bring about closer economic ties in the region was the formation of the Asia-Pacific Indian Chambers of Commerce and Industry (APICCI) as was discussed in a meeting on 8 October 1988 with thirty-seven participants from Thailand, Malaysia, the Philippines and Australia.[81] As the *Straits Times* reported, "It would mean increased opportunities to diversify into manufacturing through joint ventures with their overseas counterparts."[82] It also proposed to make Rupchand Bhojwani, the Chamber's President as the first Chairman "because of Singapore's extensive trading relations with the other countries".[83] The potential areas of mutual cooperation were manufacture of textiles and garments, food processing, household goods, consumer items and basic electronics. The major role assumed by SICC in this direction was backed by the EDB and its strategy, as pointed out by George Abraham, to drive the local companies to become "home-grown MNCs".[84]

In the same decade the Chamber had directed its activities in sending trade mission to various countries abroad, apart from India.[85] The East European mission that was sent had clinched $10 million worth deals in countertrade.[86] Besides, the Chamber served its members by maintaining a library, publishing Economic Bulletins, Annual Reports and the Directory of Members. The publications were given free to the members and also sent to other chambers and government departments and foreign embassies, both in and outside Singapore.[87]

The 1990s kept up with the momentum of the past decade along with opening up new vistas towards exploring its links with India in a major way. It witnessed a tremendous boost in the Singapore-India relations, and it was through mutual cooperation in trade and commerce that gave it a further thrust forward. Naturally, SICC came to play major role in the future bilateral engagements. Under the Chairmanship of M.K. Chanrai and the encouragement of Minister George Yeo, the Chamber spearheaded Singapore investments towards India. It also took the initiative of setting up an investment holding company during this phase, incorporating the Parameswara Holdings Ltd. on 26 May 1993 to undertake investments in India.

The prospects of increased trade and parallel enhancement of bilateral relations between Singapore and India with the "Look East" and liberalization policies of India added to the initiatives of SICCI to devote its attention towards India to a large extent in the forthcoming years. It helped organize a seminar at Madras in India in December 1990 on "Business Opportunities with Singapore",[88] setting up of the ASEAN-India Joint Sectoral Cooperation Committee meeting held on 7 January 1994 first at Bali, Indonesia and the next meeting at New Delhi in February 1995, that organized the first ever Global Indian Entrepreneurs Conference in Singapore from 19–21 June 1996 (aimed to "explore the political background" and "forge strategic partnerships" between India and the world). It also helped organize the fund raising fashion event, "India Today", presented by the National Institute of Fashion Technology (NIFT) from India on 10 September 1997,[89] among several other such initiatives taken by the Chamber. Various meetings and seminars were also organized to boost up the trade and entrepreneurial relationships between the two countries. The public seminar on "India: Rising Emerging Marketing" organized by the Institute of Southeast Asian Studies (ISEAS) and supported by the Chamber on 5 March 1999 may be mentioned in this context. It was sponsored by the Kewalram Chanrai Group and attended by more than 250 participants,[90] which revealed the spirit and intention of the business community in research to know more about the emerging and untapped potential of the Indian market.

The Chamber went through some modifications and changes during this decade. It came to be known as the **Singapore Indian Chamber of Commerce and Industry (SICCI)** from 1991 onwards. Also from 1992 onwards, the term "President" was substituted with "Chairman" according to the Companies Act and the SICCI's revision of its mergers and acquisitions (M&A).[91] It was also decided from the 1990s to bring about a change in the constitution to include the professionals as members of the Chamber along with the entrepreneurs, traders and merchants. The membership was thus changed to five categories — trading, retail, manufacturing, services and a general sector not covered in any other category.[92] In 2000, it had set up an IT section keeping in view the 150 Indian software companies that had set up operations in Singapore. SICCI had allowed individual membership, thus encouraging and paving way for the 10,000 Indian computer professionals then present in Singapore to join the Chamber.[93]

The Chamber was also involved in the non-business activities like financially supporting the Singapore Indian Development Association (SINDA) and its activities and helping to develop its re-training programmes for employment assistance and continues to help the association in various ways. The SICCI had also raised funds for the earthquake victims in Maharashtra, India in February 1994,[94] and supported the launching of the South Asian Studies Programme in July 1999 at the National University of Singapore.[95]

The SICCI continued with its efforts to make a difference to the business community both at home and abroad. There were "SME 21 Steering Committee" meetings to develop plans for the SMEs in the century ahead, ASEAN-CCI and the Australia Peru

Chamber of Commerce and Industry (APCCI) meetings to bring about different issues of concern as well as boosting up regional and cross-country trade among the members, and also the Trade Missions to countries like Myanmar (24 May 1999) and Sri Lanka (9–13 May 1999).[96]

At the turn of the new century, the SICCI vigorously directed its attention towards closer working of the Singapore-India trade and business prospects. It received and sent several trade missions to different regions of India, aiming to tap at different resources from the different provinces. There were other business missions to other countries too like in Sri Lanka, South Africa, Botswana and Namibia (along with the Singapore Business Federation (SBF) in April–May 2007), Maldives (along with IE in October 2007) or to China (joined by the Singapore Chinese Chamber of Commerce and Industry (SCCCI) in October–November 2007), but the prime focus of the present decade had been to look towards the opportunities in India, not only for the ethnic Indian community, but for the larger benefit of the Singaporean community as has been evident with the participation of the SBF, Chinese Chamber or IE, Singapore. In fact, it had joined hands with the Chinese Chamber on different occasions in taking business delegations to India (in January 2005 to Mumbai and Kolkata and April 2007 to Hyderabad, Bangalore and Mysore). It was also involved with the India-ASEAN Business Summits that were held in India in 2002 and 2003. SICCI organized a business forum for the then Indian Prime Minister, Atal Behari Vajpayee on 8 April 2002, which was attended by about 600 participants. From 2005, SICCI, along with the Institute of South Asian Studies (ISAS) launched a series of "Global Business Leader's Lecture", the first of which was delivered by India's Finance Minister, P. Chidambaram on 28 March 2005 (*The Decade Ahead for the Indian Economy*), the second being addressed by the Chief

Minister of West Bengal, Buddhadeb Bhattacharya in August 2005 (*Economic Opportunities for Singapore and India: The Way Ahead with West Bengal*). The speaker in the third Lecture was Kamal Nath, Minister for Commerce and Industry, India on 12 April 2006 (*India's Economic Emergence: Opportunities for Singapore*) and the fourth Lecture was addressed by Dayanidhi Maran, Union Minister for Communications and Information Technology, India on 23 June 2006. SICCI also hosted a two-day business summit as part of the "Celebrating India" week which was attended by the government dignitaries of both countries.[97] Above all, the SICCI had been instrumental in effectively liaisoning between Singapore and India in mobilizing the signing of the historical agreement between them — the India-Singapore Comprehensive Economic Cooperation Agreement (CECA),[98] in 2005. Of late, it has also opened a branch office in New Delhi to further promote mutual commercial interests, especially "function as a 'hand-holding' facility for Singapore firms, helping them to navigate the Indian market", according to Vijay Iyenger, the then Chairman of SICCI.[99]

The year 2002 was a significant year for the participation of women in the predominantly male bastion of commerce and business. The SICCI launched the Women's India Network (WIN) to encourage aspiring Indian entrepreneurs of the fairer sex as well as providing them with a platform for networking.[100] Besides, the SICCI had also launched publications on the profiles of some of the Indian entrepreneurs based in Singapore, *Singapore Indian Entrepreneurs: Dreams to Reality* in 2004.[101] Though it has not been an exhaustive compilation of all the ethnic Indian entrepreneurs, it does bring to light the extent of the achievements of some in the community and the diverse interests and sectors that they are involved it. Another publication by SICCI, *Business Directory of Indian Companies in Singapore* is a useful handbook for contacts and sectors of operations of the business community. Other efforts to encourage entrepreneurship by SICCI include the SICCI-DBS Singapore Indian Entrepreneur Awards (SIEA) and SICCI Youth Enterprise Award launched in 2006. However, perhaps one of the most significant achievements of SICCI in the present decade was the setting up of the Enterprise Development Centre (EDC@ SICCI) in March 2008, which was launched by Prime Minister, Lee Hsien Loong on the very same day as the inauguration of the new building at Stanley Street. It was set up within the premises of the SICCI and extended a range of services to the companies regarding solving financial issues, "market access activities", "business support resources", providing consultancy and advisory services, apart from developing contacts with similar business organizations in other countries and also collaborating with the government agencies at home.[102] SICCI continues to exist as the most dominant and important, if not the sole business organization representing the ethnic Indian business community in Singapore as well as linking itself with the government bodies as well as other chambers of commerce in Singapore and abroad.

Another arm of the SICCI, a wholly owned subsidiary, has been the "SICCI Trade Match Information Network Services", which organizes business missions to India and other places and facilitates networking among different business groups as well as gives related information through its in-house publications.[103]

The India-centric activities of SICCI, especially in the twenty-first century, had fitted well with the Singapore Government's initiatives to forge economic, political and strategic relations with India. The bilateral ties, further enhanced by the trade and commerce initiatives have generated a big exodus of Indian entrepreneurs and professionals (as has been seen in the earlier

Table 4.1
SICCI Membership Beyond 2000

Year*	No. of Members
2003	389
2004	499
2005	575
2006	615
2007	683
2008	747
2009	808

Note: *The figures denote the numbers in the month of April for the respective years.

Source: SICCI, "The Executive Director's Report", *Annual Report 2007–2008*, p. 25; SICCI, "Chairman's Message", *Annual Report 2008–2009*, p. 4.

chapter) to come into the island nation, thus necessitating the increasingly important role played by the Indian Chamber. The SICCI's efforts to launch the Pravasi Bharatiya Divas (PBD) Conference outside India in Singapore in October 2008 (this was the second time since its inception that PBD was being held outside India) and being successful in bringing more than 600 delegates from all over Asia-Pacific region and beyond, bears testimony to its growing global recognition as an important representative body of trade and commerce in the region. It has also been instrumental in supporting the inclusion of India in the East Asia Summit. However, the initiatives taken by SICCI earlier in the 1980s for the ASEAN-CCI and APCCI to accelerate trade and business in the region have, somewhat been relegated

Figure 4.1
Changes in the Composition of SICCI Members

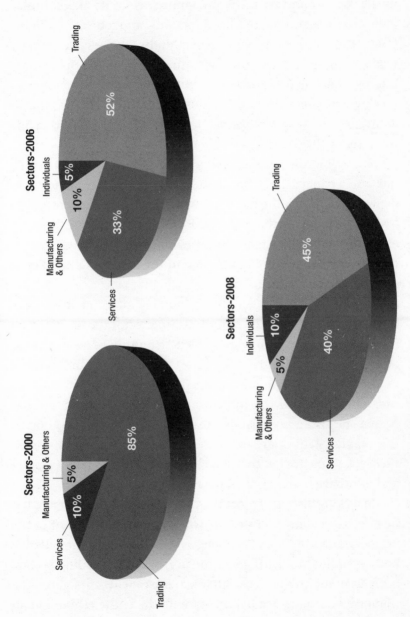

Source: Singapore Indian Chamber of Commerce and Industry (SICCI), *Annual Report 2006–2007*, p. 23; discussion with Predeep Menon, ED & CEO of SICCI on 4 February 2009.

to the background with the predominance of its "Look India" policy. The reshuffle of the directions and objectives of its policy calls for reorientation to maintain a balance, especially when keeping in view the increasing importance of regional interests and maintaining the significance of the Chamber in serving the larger interests of the community. This would, in addition, bear direct relevance to its efforts in promoting the interests of the SMEs.

The composition and character of members of the SICCI has also changed over the decades. If on the one hand, over dependence on trading has diminished and has been increasingly losing relevance in the globalized economy, there has been an emerging trend of a significant growth in the sector of services on the other, quite well manifested in the increasing number of members of SICCI in this sector.

It has also been seen that a number of companies have opted to venture into the manufacturing sector too, as has been mentioned before, though most of these units have been situated outside Singapore, both in Southeast Asian region, and as far as in the African continent. Although trading still remains an all time favourite with the Indian business community, there has been a shift from pure back-to-back trading to value-addition in the supply chain. Many of these companies have consolidated their position either at the sourcing point or at the target market and also have better control over the logistics.

In its long history of more than eight decades, membership has increased gradually and steadily with greater involvement of the business community and evolving as the successful representative body coordinating with governments and other trading bodies, both domestic and foreign. But for, at least the recent figures, the numbers do not, in reality, incorporate the entire ethnic Indian business community in Singapore. Whereas there are at present

Figure 4.2
SICCI Membership and the Indian Business Entities in Singapore: A Comparison

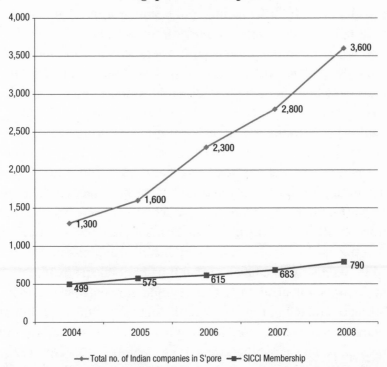

—◆—Total no. of Indian companies in S'pore   —■—SICCI Membership

Source: SICCI, "The Executive Director's Report", *Annual Report 2007–2008*, p. 25; discussion with Predeep Menon, then ED & CEO of SICCI on 4 February 2009.

around 3,600 Indian companies operating from Singapore, the total number of member companies remain much below that figure. The reasons might be diverse and multifarious. Many entrepreneurs and business houses, especially the ones that have been recently established either originating from India or other places abroad, have chosen to stay away from the

Chamber due to a difference in their attitude, principles, focus, areas of operation and several other reasons which are complex and should be discussed in a separate context of study. Besides, the members in SICCI include professionals at present, and the total figures might not be representative singularly of the total business community. Moreover, the Serangoon Road merchants have always had opted to stay away from the Chamber calling it to be a body representing different kind of interest groups. The Chamber had been more focused on international trading, venturing into new markets, promote manufacturing and deliberating on government policies and regulations affecting it, whereas the Serangoon Road merchants were concerned about day-to-day running of domestic retail business activities. Their business required sourcing for products which were channelized from similar directions like India or Malaysia. This is not to say that the varied interests of different business groups could not be addressed by the Chamber, or that it had not taken any initiative in this direction at all. In fact, P. Govindasamy Pillai, who had his business situated in the area of Little India, was one of the initial signatories to the Memorandum drawn up by the Chamber, and his son, G. Ramachandran served the Chamber (1966–68, 1973–74, 1982–84, 1985–86) as one of its most successful presidents. In fact, there were quite a few names among the members, even in the 1960s, in the import section of the Annual Report of the Chamber (1966) like G. Abdul Rahim Bros (82, Serangoon Road), S.S. Annamalai Bros (173, Serangoon Road), Kalaimangal Provision Store (1, Buffalo Road), K.S. Mohamed Haniffa & Co. (4, Campbell Lane), L. Natesan & Sons (11-D Campbell Lane), N.V. Navasivayam & Sons (122, Serangoon Road), Sri Thandapani Store (16, Campbell Lane) and others[104] who were doing business in the Serangoon Road area. Even now there are affiliations of Mohammad Mustafa & Samsuddin Co. Pte. Ltd. (the most prominent retail outlet of the area), GMT Jewellers Pte. Ltd., Nammavar Trading Pte. Ltd., S.I. Samy Trading Co. Pte. Ltd.[105] and some others, to mention a few shop owners in the area apart from the associate membership of the Indian Restaurant Association, Singapore [IRA(S)]. But there are differences, and the Serangoon Road merchants and traders have always had separate associations of their own like the Serangoon Merchants Association, the Indian Restaurants Association and other such bodies. Recently, these merchant bodies have joined together to form the Little India Shopkeepers and Heritage Association (LISHA).

The **Serangoon Merchant's Association**, as the name suggests comprised of the shopkeepers and the businessmen of the area of Little India, was started in the late 1980s. Among its founding fathers was Rajakumar Chandra's father, M. Ramachandra.[106] It was a much smaller and informal organization focused on intra-group business activities, addressing specific interests and concerns of a definite area of the ethnic India commercial activities. It comprised of the provisional stores, the flower shops, the vegetable vendors, retail cloth merchants, restaurants and the jewellery shops in the area. They took up issues like the increase of rentals of properties or the increasing dearth of workers and helpers needed to run their business. The older immigrant generation could not be adequately replaced by educated low skilled workers, who wanted to look for greener pastures with higher salary and status, at the same time they could not hire foreign workers either.[107] The Association was also involved in organizing various social and cultural activities like the Deepavali lightings along with the government bodies. R. Shanmugam had taken upon him efforts to run the association of about 100 odd members. Rajakumar joined as an ordinary committee member in 1987, from where he worked up to become the secretary in 1997 and president in 1999.[108]

The restaurant owners of the Race Course Road and the Little India area have had also formed an association of their own in 1998 to represent their own issues and concerns. This was different from the Restaurant Association of Singapore (RAS) established in 1980, and has been more a grouping of the ethnic Indian restaurant owners as the name **Little India Restaurant Association (LIRA)** reveals. It was initially started by Ramachandran of Ananda Bhavan Restaurant in the Little India area.[109] However, some restaurants have also associated themselves with the larger Singaporean union of the restaurants like Muthu's Curry Restaurant Pte. Ltd., which has recently joined the RAS as an ordinary member.[110]

LIRA had eventually changed its name to the **Indian Restaurants Association, Singapore IRA(S)** with a slight change in their constitution to incorporate members from other communities as members from all over the island. They have eighty-nine members on record at present, as had been revealed by their President, G. Shanmugam (since 2005), the owner of the Gayatri Restaurant in the area.[111] Though there have been talks about them joining the Restaurant Association of Singapore (RAS) as an institution body and do work closely at times, they participate in different kinds of activities. Whereas the IRA(S) is more involved with organizing the "Food Festival" in the Little India area, the RAS takes part in the "Great Singapore Sale".[112] The IRA(S) had also come out with its first publication *Savour* in 2007, which stopped soon after due to financial constraints. Apart from the funding problems, it has also been difficult to work in unity. Shanmugam is of the opinion that he had a more difficult role to bring the restaurateurs together than what is faced in LISHA. The latter would have participation from various trade and business, but for the members of IRA(S), they were all competitors in the same business. He believed that it could be overcome with maturity and time and pins hope on the younger generation who takes over their family business.[113]

At the turn of the twenty-first century, in September 2000, the different associations of Little India, at the behest of the Singapore Tourism Board (STB) made the effort to unite together under a single umbrella. This was part of the government's drive to start the redevelopment plans for Little India. Having taken on a similar project in refurbishing the old buildings in the Chinatown area, it was quite evident that the place had lost much of its old charm in the process. They did not want to let it happen with Little India, a major area of tourist attraction, thus involving the local associations in their redevelopment process. As a result, the Serangoon Merchant's Association and the Hindu Endowments Board, along with the cooperation of the Little India Restaurant Association,[114] formed the **Little India Shopkeepers and Heritage Association (LISHA)** in 2001 and Rajakumar became the first Secretary.[115] He is at present serving as the Chairman of the Association. Since the government was interested in promoting Little India as one of its major tourist destinations, the multi-ethnic and the multi-cultural character of the place received government support and also helped voice the concerns of the merchants and shopkeepers in the area. Situated at the Little India Arcade, in the heart of the activities in Little India and managed by the investment arm of the Hindu Endowments Board (HEB), LISHA would give the members of the association a priority in participating in the festival bazaars and carnivals, frequently organized in the area, and also access to different social and multi-cultural events organized by LISHA.[116] Members could also enjoy the benefit of free listing on the LISHA website as well as the eligibility of their staff and the family for LISHA study grants. In addition, the small businesses were provided with subsidies to participate in the festivals and the carnivals organized by LISHA.[117]

LISHA was very active in promoting and organizing cultural and heritage activities in the Little India area like the Vesak Day celebrations or the Deepavali lightings, thus bringing in not only tourists and Indians, but also a large number of other races in big crowds, indirectly booting up business in the area. This has been a more practical approach towards involving and helping the businessmen in the area who did not respond much to the activities relating to higher level of information and participation from the government initiatives, as they were small entities,[118] mostly looking for survival and adequate profit-making, not for big plans of expansion.

LISHA, as a representative organization of all the business in the area, had also tried to shed the garb of "India-centric" image of Little India. The *Little India: Events & Festivals* booklet that is jointly published with the STB is done so in English, Chinese and Japanese and is distributed globally by the STB.[119] Rajakumar reiterates this when he says, "When LISHA came about, we had members from Buddhist Temples and Mosques. ... We are a national organisation. ... We do not generally promote Tamil. ..."[120]

LISHA, as is quite evident, has been set up as an organization that is quite different from the SICCI in its motives and objectives. If there is no contradiction and opposition between them, there is also little room for assimilation and integration. It has been put quite simply and openly by Rajakumar, who is not a member of SICCI as yet, who says, "They are thinking on a different level — keen in bringing in overseas businesses and investing overseas. ... we understand the needs of the people of Little India. We need man power; we need finance and banks. ..."[121] The communication gap needs to be addressed more seriously.

Along with the merchant and business organizations, there have existed a number of socio-cultural organizations of ethnic Indians in Singapore, which, though not directly relevant to the present perspectives of discussion, might be mentioned in very brief, as they have continued providing veritable platforms for networking and interaction. However, since most of them are carved out on linguistic and regional lines, there is still a huge scope of intergroup interactions, which hardly takes place except in places of worship. One association, the Singapore Indian Association (established in 1923), forms an exception as one of the oldest of the social organizations of all ethnic Indians in general and still forms a meeting ground from people from all walks of life.[122] Few names of the regional organizations may be briefly mentioned below.

The Gujaratis had successfully organized themselves into their own association, however, quite late keeping in view that they belonged to one of the earliest business migrants in the region. In 1956, the Singapore Gujarati Yuvak Mandal was established which "comprised essentially the employees of the Gujarati business community".[123] In the 1970s, however, businessmen themselves became its members. At present, the Singapore Gujarati Society has a member base of 550 Gujaratis[124] out of the total population of around 2,800 in Singapore.[125]

Situated in the High Street Centre of Singapore is the Marwari Mitra Mandal, one of the most recent associations of ethnic India regional bodies, registered in 2005.[126] The Business Directory of the Association's website reveals participation and employment of its members in varied sectors like trading, metal and scrap business, IT services and consulting, banking and the like.[127]

Some of the other associations in Singapore are the Singapore Khalsa Association, which was mainly formed in the mid-1920s to promote cultural and sporting activities of the Sikhs here.[128] Singapore Telegu Association or Singapore Kerala Association,

Singapore Bengali Association, Hindi Society, Singapore, Kannada Sangha, Singapore, Singapore Malayalee Association, Singapore Telegu Cultural Society, and Singapore Tamil Youth's Club are some of the other similar socio-cultural and regional associations and had little to do with business activities except facilitating intra-group networking activities.

III. NEW PARADIGMS OF NETWORK

The onset of globalization and revolution in information technology has been able to bring the world much closer and facilitated the connectivity of the traditional institutional outfits with innovative approaches in unfolding untapped economic ties. Several informal networking organizations have thus emerged, working to bring different entrepreneurs closer along with the more formally structured conventional business associations. These organizations have emerged as mixed clusters with focus on region and trade, schools of professional training (especially applicable to the professionals and their alumni associations), sports, or simply social networks established, cutting across all ethnic lines.

Most of these groupings are much less rigid in structure and membership norms and offer flexibility of inter-group interactions. At the same time, they often exist virtually, with annual or biannual meetings, personal meetings, or just web-based interactions, thereby less imposing in matters of time and space on the members. These networking bodies, at times, have either facilitated or, have been mobilized by the conventional bodies of business associations. They are regularly connected by updated information on the web, with useful weblinks regarding government bodies, industry information, business directories and other business associations. One such website providing useful information to the ethnic Indians in Singapore has been launched by Confederation of Indian Industries (CII) called "Bridge Singapore",[129] the primary aim of which had been to encourage Indian companies to build new linkages and collaborations with Singapore, China and ASEAN. It also publishes monthly reports on the various perspectives of business in the Southeast Asian region. The CII has also launched the CII-India Business Forum (IBF) Singapore to be the "voice of Corporate India". "CII through IBF and its members would like to work towards further reducing the barriers and misconceptions that prevent exploitation of the immense potential that lies untapped in our economic ties."[130]

The efforts of the Indian Chamber (CII) to extend its facilitation in cooperation between companies and organizations in the Southeast Asian region through Singapore is an interesting example of Chambers of Commerce donning a new garb in consolidating the target business community. Similar steps have also been taken up by different government bodies. In Singapore, the IE has launched three different networking groups to focus on three different regions — Network India, Network China and Network Indonesia.[131] The objectives have been similar — to promote business linkages among the entrepreneurial world. Network India aims to "cultivate a fraternity of Singapore-based companies and entrepreneurs interested in business opportunities in India, to share timely information, ideas, opinions and experiences".[132] There has also been a joint initiative of IE and Contact Singapore in the formation of Singapore Indian Business Association (SIBA), which virtually connects entrepreneurs and businessmen in the region.[133] It was inaugurated in October 2002 at Chennai by Dr Vivian Balakrishnan, Minister of State, Ministry of National Development of Singapore.[134]

Apart from initiatives backed by formal institutions and government bodies, there are also semi-formal groups connecting businessmen and organizing occasional conferences and gatherings in association with chambers of commerce or government bodies, which has been effective in creating awareness among various trading interests. The Global Indian Business Network Pte. Ltd. is a part of the GA Group of Companies established by George Abraham, the previous Executive Director of SICCI.[135] The Global Indian Business Summit (GIBS) presented the Global Entrepolis, Singapore in October 2006 and subsequently in November 2007, and again in November 2009, which had been able to garner a considerable number of businessmen from the global Indian diaspora. It had also been successful in bringing them to interact with their counterparts from other communities as well. The main objective of the platform, supported by FICCI, one of the Indian Chambers of Commerce, had been best described in their website:

> The short term goal of GIBS is to engage successful **Diaspora Indian Entrepreneurs** to meet and generate profitable partnerships. The long term goal is to create a platform for diaspora Indian businesses to meet at least once a year, to generate intra-regional business prospects and to gain global recognition for successful role models.[136]

Almost on all occasions, these kinds of networking platforms have been attended by state dignitaries lending government support and encouragement on the necessity of such assemblies. The Global Entrepolis@Singapore was officially launched by the President of Singapore, S.R. Nathan.[137] Similarly, the PBD held in Singapore from 9–11 October 2008, organized by the SICCI, Ministry of Overseas Indian Affairs (MOIA) and the CII, was attended by Prime Minister, Lee Hsien Loong, Minister Mentor, Lee Kuan Yew, Senior Minister, Goh Chok Tong from Singapore and other ministers from India. The active participation of government dignitaries also brings them into conversations with the different business groups bringing forth the opportunities, difficulties or drawbacks of different rules and regulations and the need for further deliberations on the same.

Another interesting role in business networking is played by the much more informal organizational groups — the alumni organizations. Two of the most important ones in the present context of study are the Indian Institute of Management (IIM) Alumni Association and the Indian Institute of Technology (IIT) Alumni Association in Singapore, representing the two most globally reputed schools of higher professional learning in India. In fact, there are already existing exchange programmes between NUS Business School and IIM-Ahmedabad and IIM-Calcutta, besides the Memorandum of Understanding (MOU) between NUS Business School and IIM-Calcutta (April 2006).[138] The alumni associations mainly organize family-based social events, but the IIT Alumni also has an Entrepreneurship Club, which gives a helping hand in the exchange of ideas between the entrepreneurs or guide the potential and the ambitious entrants to the league. Every two years, the IIT Alumni Association also organizes an event supported by the government agencies and organizations of Singapore.[139] The IIM Alumni, on the other hand, runs an annual Business Plan competition among students, where the winners are announced in a grand finale organized by them. It is also interesting to note that many of the members are common to both the alumni associations, thus bringing about further integration among the entrepreneurial ventures of the Indian professionals.

There are various other informal social organizations like the "India Club" or "Golf Parivar" and increasingly many others which have emerged as successful networking outlets through social, cultural or religious gatherings. Another organization,

Professional Network of Young Indians (PNYI) was formed in 1994 to provide networking opportunities and platform for the exchange of ideas between the new entrants themselves and also with the established members of the community. However, it stopped being an active society in 2004 with the SICCI and other organizations taking up similar roles in a much bigger way.[140]

The networking organizations have facilitated the conventional business organizations to integrate and consolidate the ethnic Indian entrepreneurs on a regional and global level, rather than posing any challenge for them. In fact, many of the networking initiative have been supported and launched by different chambers, both from Singapore and India. On the other hand, the other groups of newly formed networking organizations like those of the alumni associations or other social groups are mostly representative of upper middle class in structure and composition and, at best represent, one section of the entrepreneurial community, albeit a significant one. Their functioning has been nurtured and nourished in sync with the changing rhetoric of the Indian diaspora and the improved bilateral relations, different aspects of which have already been discussed. However, the Chambers of Commerce need to play a more progressive role in consolidating numerous and varied interests of the Indian community at large.

IV. CONCLUSION

The task of integrating the Indian business community remains one of the greatest challenges of the Indian Chamber. The number of ethnic Indian associations, social or business, far exceeds the demographic minority status in Singapore. The regional nature of such large number of associations not only reveals the diversity of the subcontinent but also the kind of heterogeneity that exists. This diversity had been an inherent drawback for emergence of a cohesive community and has also brought about some hindrances in the participation in the larger economic system of the nation. It had been more visibly pronounced in the enclave structures of the colonial days, but diminished to a great extent by the Singapore Government in the post-1965 phase onwards when there was a more interactive and integrative approach. However, differences still exist between the SICCI and other smaller organizations in voicing any unified approach for the entire community. The SICCI's efforts in bringing about a positive difference to the whole Singaporean community has been witnessed in establishing and participating in bodies like ASEAN-CCI, APCCI or EDC@SICCI, but disparities have continued to exist, not only among the so-called "outward-bound trading groups" and the "Serangoon-Road merchants", but has been further complicated with the overlapping differences between the old time settlers or the "locals", as they are better known as, and the influx of the "new Indians".

It would also be interesting to look at the relationship of SICCI with the other major ethnic business associations in Singapore like the Malay Chamber of Commerce (MCC) and the SCCCI, though a detailed and a comparative analysis is not within the present purview of study. While there had been no major conflicts between them, each focusing on the interests of their respective ethnic bodies of business, there had not been any major collaborative efforts between them either, until in recent times. However, there was sporadic mention of unifying the businessmen of Singapore on certain occasions like the Vice-President of the Chinese Chamber, Yap Pheng Geck, in 1959, expressing hope of the formation of a unified chamber for all races of Singapore citizens.[141] The Chinese Chamber had also organized Malay classes for businessmen in 1959 though they were making efforts to spread the use of Mandarin among businessmen.[142] In the 1980s also there were efforts to promote interaction among the Chinese and the Malay Chambers in the field of "economics, education, culture and sports as areas of cooperation".[143] The strong links of the Chinese Chamber in China and the Malay Chamber in the Middle Eastern region was planned to be better utilized with this partnership. The two chambers were joining hands for the first time to become partners in a holding company (Sino-Malay Investment Holdings Company).[144] Under the leadership of the SCCCI President, Linn In Hua, initiatives were also taken to discuss with the Indian Chamber ways of "strengthening cooperation" between themselves and also with the Malay Chamber.[145] In the meanwhile, the Singapore Federation of Chambers of Commerce and Industry (SFCCI) had been formed in 1978 as the umbrella organization comprising of the three chambers as well as the Singapore International Chamber of Commerce (SICC) and the Singapore Manufacturers' Association (SMA), so the joint initiatives of the chambers were carried out under the auspices of the Federation. In the early 1990s, dispute arose regarding its leadership when the SCCCI and MCC protested against G. Ramachandran, nominated by the Indian Chamber, to be selected for the second term. Govindasamy Ramachandran had earlier served as its president for a two-year term from 1986.[146] Ramachandran later won the election by a majority of three votes to two in a secret ballot,[147] but the objections persisted. The SICC, on the other hand, continued to reaffirm its support to his election[148] and differences carried on for some time before it could be solved. Later in 1991, when the Indian Chamber amended its constitution to include the professionals among its members, the other chambers lauded its efforts, but did not feel it necessary to replicate with a similar move in their respective chambers.[149] However, at the turn of the new century, there have been efforts to create a better understanding between the chambers and more networking opportunities. Joint business missions have been organized by SICCI, SCCCI, SBF and others for India and China, and the Indian Chamber's subsidiary, SICCI Trade Match, works towards co-organizing such joint missions.[150] Also many Indian businessmen have in their managerial team and Board of Directors, Chinese entrepreneurs and professionals, paving way for closer interaction between different ethnic business interests.

The new Indian entrepreneurs have been facilitated by the advantageous changes in the political, economic and social scenario in Asia at large. They are more technologically advanced, professionally competent and tend to grow as transnational entities in a globalized market. The objectives and focus of action between the present age business migrants and the older ones residing in Singapore for two generations or more (except a few cases) have developed differently. Thus there have emerged Indians doing business in Singapore and looking forward to Southeast Asia and beyond; and Singapore Indians and others shedding their scepticism to interact with Indians in the sub-continent. As a major trading community, they were already used to looking for fresh avenues in different nook and corners of the world. For SICCI, there are a number of Indian companies and banks who have been their members for many years now and many new companies have also joined the Chamber. The Chamber's efforts to promote the SMEs has been a realistic approach in integrating different interest groups. At the same time it has also joined hands with the Indian Chambers to promote business networking. Joint efforts of SICCI and CII, the Indian Chamber, have also been seen in organizing big events like the PBD in Singapore in 2008.

Such endeavours of interactions and addressing issues relevant to different sections of the community would go a long way to further consolidate and incorporate diverse interest groups within the community, and help to identify their strengths and weaknesses and accelerate business activities to a higher level.

Notes

1. The *Chamber de Commerce* of Marseilles (1599) was the first organization to use this name from where it spread to the other parts of France and Germany and then to the rest of Europe.
2. Some important names were *Ainnurruvur, Manigramam, Nagarattar* and *Anjuvannam*. Local guilds were commonly known as *nagarams*. For further details on the functions of medieval Indian guilds, refer to Meera Abraham, *Two Medieval Merchant Guilds of South India*, South Asian Studies No. XVIII, Manohar, New Delhi, 1988.
3. Tansen Sen, *Buddhism, Diplomacy and Trade: The Realignment of Sino-Indian Relations, 600–1400* (Honolulu: University of Hawaii Press, 2003), p. 158.
4. Romila Thapar, *A History of India: From the Discovery of India to 1526*, vol. I (London: Penguin Books, 1966), pp. 112–13.
5. B.R. Sabade and M.V. Namjoshi, *Chambers of Commerce and Trade Associations in India*, Gokhale Institute Study (Poona, India: Asia Publishing House, 1977), p. 26.
6. Kiran Kumar Thaplyal, "Guilds in Ancient India (Antiquity and Various Stages in the Development of Guilds up to AD 300)", in *Life Thoughts and Culture in India*, edited by G.C. Pande (Delhi: Munshiram Manoharlal Publishers Pvt. Ltd., 2001), pp. 995–1006. Thaplyal in his article has tried to show with substantial literary evidence the presence of these institutions in ancient India.
7. Roderick MacLean, *A Pattern of Change: The Singapore International Chamber of Commerce from 1837* (Singapore: Singapore International Chamber of Commerce, 2000), p. 18. Trade was generally carried out in Spanish dollars and Dutch guilders.

8. Ibid.

9. Ibid., pp. 19–23.

10. Charles Burton Buckley, *An Anecdotal History of Old Times in Singapore, 1819–1867* (Kuala Lumpur: University of Malaya Press, first published in 1902, reprinted in 1965), p. 313.

11. MacLean, op. cit., p. 22.

12. Vera Anstey, *The Economic Development of India* (London: Longmans Green & Co., reprinted in 1957), p. 113.

13. Loh Wen Fong, *The Singapore Houses of Agency, 1819–1900*, B.A. (Hons) Academic Exercise, Department of History, University of Malaya in Singapore, 1958, p. 8.

14. Chan Heng Kong, *Singapore's Political Economy: A Case Study of Social Costs in a Market Economy* (Melbourne: Universal Books, 2005), p. 98.

15. Ibid. Many of them started as small merchants themselves. Guthrie, for example, came to Singapore in 1820 and set up a shop selling woollen cloth and Sheffield axes. He later started another business with a partner in 1823 with the sole proprietorship of Guthrie & Co., a name which eventually became renowned among the business communities in the region and beyond. MacLean, *A Pattern of Change*, op. cit., p. 27.

16. C.M. Turnbull, *The Straits Settlements, 1826–67: Indian Presidency to Crown Colony* (London: The Athlone Press, 1972), p. 180.

17. P.J. Drake, *Currency, Credit and Commerce: Early Growth in Southeast Asia* (Aldershot: Ashgate, 2004), p. 51.

18. Drake, op. cit., p. 55.

19. Ibid.

20. Ibid., p. 57.

21. MacLean, *A Pattern of Change*, op. cit., p. 29. Syed Abubaker was the Arab merchant; Isaiah Zecharia, the Armenian merchant; Kim Guan and Gwan Chuan were the Chinese traders; while Joseph Balestiaet was the American pioneer planter.

22. Chan Kwok Bun and Ng Beoy Kui, "Singapore", in *Chinese Business in Southeast Asia: Contesting Cultural Explanations, Researching*

Entrepreneurship, edited by Edmund Terence Gomez, Xinhuang Xiao, and Hsin-Huang Michael Hsiao (New York: Routledge, 2003), p. 40.

23. MacLean, *A Pattern of Change*, op. cit., pp. 43–45.

24. Anthony Webster, *Gentlemen Capitalists: British Imperialism in South East Asia, 1770–1890* (London: I.B. Tauris, 1998), p. 112.

25. We have already discussed the Sindhi and Gujarati merchant groups among others in a previous chapter and the strong intra-ethnic networks that existed.

26. Rajeswary Ampalavanar Brown, *Capital and Entrepreneurship in South-East Asia* (Houndmills, Basingstoke, Hampshire: The Macmillan Press Ltd. and New York, St. Martin's Press, 1994), p. 203.

27. Ibid.

28. Webster, *Gentlemen Capitalists*, op. cit., p. 115.

29. MacLean, *A Pattern of Change*, op. cit., p. 123.

30. Sri Thendayuthapani Temple, as the Chettiars call it, is believed to have been established after thirty-five years of the coming of the Chettiars to Singapore. C.M. Turnbull mentions this in her book, *A History of Singapore, 1819–1975*, webpage of the "History of Sri Thendayuthapani Temple", <http://www.sttemple.com/STT/english/history.asp> (accessed 13 May 2009).

31. Singapore Sindhi Association, <http://www.singaporesindhi.com.sg/aboutus.php> (accessed 8 May 2009).

32. Ibid.

33. Minutes of the Extraordinary Meeting of the Managing Committee held on 13 July 1951, unpublished records of the Sindhi Merchants Association, vol. 1, no. 4.

34. Minutes of the Managing Committee Meeting held on 12 November 1951 where the resolution was unanimously passed to purchase the Neil Road property by the Association, unpublished records of the Sindhi Merchants Association, vol. 1, no. 14.

35. Minutes of the meeting of the Sindhi Merchants Association held on 30 May 1946, unpublished records of the Sindhi Merchants

Association (Sindhi language). Mr Chhatru Vaswani has kindly translated the relevant texts in Sindhi for the author.

36. Minutes of the meeting of the Sindhi Merchants Association held on 17 October 1946, unpublished records of the Sindhi Merchants Association (Sindhi language).

37. Resolution passed in the minutes of the meeting of the Sindhi Merchants Association held on 28 October 1946, unpublished records of the Sindhi Merchants Association (Sindhi language).

38. Information based on conversation with Chhatru Vaswani, Honorary Treasurer, Singapore Sindhi Association on 15 May 2009.

39. Minutes of the Adjourned Meeting of the Managing Committee held on 15 September 1953, presided over by D.T. Assomul, unpublished records of the Sindhi Merchants Association, vol. 3, no. 6.

40. In conversation with Chhatru Vaswani, then Honorary Treasurer, Singapore Sindhi Association on 15 May 2009.

41. Singapore Sindhi Association, <http://www.singaporesindhi.com. sg/aboutus.php> (accessed 8 May 2009).

42. The Indian Chamber of Commerce (ICC), Singapore, *Report for the Year 1947.*

43. Singapore Indian Chamber of Commerce and Industry (SICCI), *SICCI's 80th Anniversary volume, 1924–2004* (Singapore: SICCI, 2004), p. 17.

44. "Introduction", in *Inauguration of the SICCI Building & Launch of EDC@SICCI* (Singapore: SICCI, 8 March 2008), p. 53.

45. Singapore Indian Chamber of Commerce and Industry (SICCI), *Trading with Singapore: Special 60th Anniversary Issue of the SICCI* (Singapore: SICCI, 1986), p. 12.

46. "History of Nattukottai Chettiars", <http://www.sttemple.com/STT/ english/chettiars.asp> (accessed 11 May 2009).

47. As has already been mentioned, the Chettiars' Temple or the Sri Thendayuthapani Temple at Tank Road was established in 1859 in Singapore by the Nattukottai Chettiars. Homepage of Sri

Thendayuthapani Temple, <http://www.sttemple.com/STT/english/stt_menu.asp> (accessed 11 May 2009).

48. "History of Nattukottai Chettiars", <http://www.sttemple.com/STT/english/chettiars.asp> (accessed 11 May 2009).

49. SICCI, *SICCI's 80th Anniversary volume*, op. cit., p. 17.

50. Ibid., p. 20.

51. The other signatories were M. Jumabhoy, Dayaram W. Vaswani, Gulamhusen Najmee, F.H.M. Nakhoda, Dhanpatrai, N. Manchharam and V.M. Shah. Ibid., p. 18.

52. Speech delivered by R. Jumabhoy, President of the Chamber at a Joint Tea Party in Honour of H.E. the Governor-General and H.E. the Governor of Singapore at the Victoria Memorial Hall on 26 February 1947 at 5.15 p.m. The Indian Chamber of Commerce, Singapore, *Report for the Year 1946*, Appendix VIII.

53. *Inauguration of the SICCI Building & Launch of EDC@SICCI* (Singapore: Singapore Indian Chamber of Commerce and Industry, 8 March 2008), p. 56.

54. The Indian Chamber of Commerce, Singapore, *Report for the Year 1947*, Memorandum submitted by the Indian Chamber to the Carr-Saunders University Commission, Appendix VIII, pp. 38–42.

55. Ibid., The Indian Overseas Bank Ltd. opened its branch in Singapore in 1940, p. 56.

56. The Indian Chamber of Commerce, Singapore, *Report for the Year 1947*, Appendix VIII.

57. *Inauguration of the SICCI Building & Launch of EDC@SICCI*, op. cit., p. 54.

58. SICCI, *SICCI's 80th Anniversary volume*, op. cit., p. 26.

59. Memorandum submitted by the Indian Chamber of Commerce, Singapore to Singapore Port Commission by P.S. Rajaratnam, Secretary Indian Chamber of Commerce on 14 September 1957, *Report for the Year 1957* (Singapore: Indian Chamber of Commerce, 1958), Appendix XXII.

60. *Inauguration of the SICCI Building & Launch of EDC@SICCI*, op. cit., p. 58.

61. "'Create Industrial Climate' Plea", *Sunday Times*, 31 May 1964.

62. "$25,000 to set up scholarship fund", *Straits Times*, 27 August 1969.

63. "Bursaries for 14 students", *New Nation*, 4 August 1971.

64. "Fourteen ITB students get Chamber's bursaries", *Straits Times*, 10 November 1978.

65. "Milk gift from Chamber to Malaysia", *Malay Mail*, 29 May 1969.

66. "Blood Bank to buy 20 aluminum mobile beds", *Malay Mail*, 29 November 1969.

67. "Varsity to get $22,000 from Chambers", *Straits Times*, 8 September 1972; "Dr. Toh is shown how the foetal heart monitor works", *Sunday Times*, 10 September 1972.

68. Roop Vaswani, in an interview with the Malay Mail, "The switch to new industry for Indians", *Malay Mail*, 15 April 1970.

69. Nirmala Puru Shotam, "A monograph commemorating the 60th anniversary of the Singapore Indian Chamber of Commerce", unpublished, SICCI, 1985, pp. 48–49.

70. Ibid., p. 49.

71. SICCI, *Trading with Singapore: Special 60th Anniversary Issue of the SICCI*, op. cit., p. 14.

72. SICCI, *SICCI's 80th Anniversary volume*, op. cit., p. 36.

73. Conversation with J.M. Jumabhoy on 20 March 2009.

74. SICCI, *SICCI's 80th Anniversary volume*, op. cit., p. 45.

75. "Changing face of Indian business", *Sunday Times*, 24 November 1985.

76. Boey Kit Yin, "Indian Chamber seeks to play bigger role", *Business Times (S)*, 13 March 1985.

77. Foo Choy Peng, "Manufacturers laud PM's call on productivity", *Business Times (S)*, 10 August 1985.

78. Anna Teo, "Woes of the trader", *Business Times (S)*, 6 March 1986.

79. Elaine Koh, "SEB aid for Indian chamber project", *Business Times (S)*, 2 July 1986.

80. SICCI, *SICCI's 80th Anniversary volume*, op. cit., p. 43.
81. Ibid., p. 45.
82. Shaun Seow, "Asia-Pacific body for Indian businessmen to be set up", *Straits Times*, 10 November 1988.
83. Ibid.
84. Chuang Peck Ming, "Aim to promote cooperation among Asia-Pacific countries: Regional Indian chamber formed", *Business Times (S)*, 19 August 1989.
85. In 1985, EDB had identified India as the area of growth for Singapore trade and businesses. "Team will tell all about trading in India", *Straits Times*, 30 July 1985.
86. G. Ramachandran in conversation with Suzanne Ooi, "Changing face of Indian business", *Sunday Times*, 24 November 1985.
87. Singapore Indian Chamber of Commerce, *Sixtieth Anniversary Memento* (Singapore: SICC, 1985), pp. 7–8.
88. Kevin Lim, "Businessmen in India form Indo-S'pore group", *Straits Times*, 14 January 1991.
89. SICCI, *SICCI's 80th Anniversary volume*, op. cit., pp. 51–56.
90. Ibid., p. 58.
91. *Inauguration of the SICCI Building & Launch of EDC@SICCI*, op. cit., p. 53.
92. Valli Subramony, "Indian chamber of commerce plans to extend membership to professionals", *Straits Times*, 19 June 1990; Narendra Aggarwal, "Indian chamber opening doors to self-employed professionals", *Straits Times*, 20 July 1991.
93. Narendra Aggarwal, "Indian chamber gives IT a boost", *Straits Times*, 1 May 2000.
94. SICCI, *SICCI's 80th Anniversary volume*, op. cit., pp. 51, 56, 57.
95. Ibid., p. 60.
96. Ibid., pp. 58–59.
97. All the information on the lectures has been taken from the section "About SICCI" in the SICCI publication, *Inauguration of the SICCI Building & Launch of EDC@SICCI*, op. cit., pp. 64–71.
98. Reference to CECA has already been made in the previous chapter.

99. Nirmala George, "SICCI opens India Office", in *Overseas Indian: Connecting India with its Diaspora*, official e-zine of MOIA, India, <http://overseasindian.in/2008/september/news/20081009-114022.shtml> (accessed 23 May 2009).

100. *Inauguration of the SICCI Building & Launch of EDC@SICCI*, op. cit., p. 65.

101. Ibid.

102. Ibid., pp. 78–79.

103. SICCI, "The Executive Director's Report", *Annual Report 2007–2008* (Singapore: SICCI, 2008), p. 27.

104. Singapore Indian Chamber of Commerce, Singapore, *Report for the Year 1966* (Singapore: SICC, 1966).

105. Singapore Indian Chamber of Commerce and Industry (SICCI), *SICCI's Membership Directory, 2007–2008* (Singapore: SICCI, 2008).

106. Interview with Rajakumar Chandra, owner of Jothi Stores and Flower Shop and the Chairman of LISHA on 17 July 2008.

107. "Feedback, Labour Crisis in Little India as the immigrant generation retires and no one wants to do the low paid jobs associated with traditional activities, aired in early 1988", <http://www.hsse.nie.edu.sg/staff/blackburn/heritageFeedbacklabourserangoon1988.html> (accessed 19 May 2009).

108. Interview with Rajakumar Chandra, op. cit.

109. Ibid.

110. Website of the RAS, <http://www.ras.org.sg/index.php> (accessed 20 May 2009).

111. Interview with G. Shanmugam, the President of IRA(S) and the owner of the Gayatri Restaurant on 23 May 2009.

112. Ibid.

113. Ibid.

114. G. Shanmugam, the present President of IRAS, revealed that IRAS works along with LISHA on different programmes in Little India but is not formally conjoined with LISHA; interview with G. Shanmugham, op. cit.

115. Interview with Rajakumar Chandra, op. cit.

116. "LISHA Faqs", *LISHA News*, a publication of Little India Shopkeepers & Heritage Association and Singapore Tourism Board, 2004.

117. Ibid.

118. Interview with Rajakumar Chandra, op. cit.

119. "LISHA Faqs", op. cit.

120. Interview with Rajakumar Chandra, op. cit.

121. Ibid.

122. Refer to Robert Godfrey and Samuel S. Dhoraisingham, eds., *Passage of Indians, 1923–2003* (Singapore: Singapore Indian Association, 2003).

123. Website of the Singapore Gujarati Society, <http://sgs.org.sg//history.htm> (accessed 8 May 2009).

124. Ibid.

125. <http://www.joshuaproject.net/peopctry.php?rog3=SN&rop3=103544> (accessed 8 May 2009).

126. The Association's website, <http://www.marwarimitramandal.com/aboutus.jsp> (accessed 20 May 2009).

127. "Business Directory", <http://www.marwarimitramandal.com/businessdirectory.jsp> (accessed 20 May 2009).

128. "About Singapore Khalsa Association", <http://www.singaporekhalsa.org.sg/cms/about-ska/evolution-of-ska> (accessed 20 May 2009). For further reference on SKA, see Tan Tai Yong, *Singapore Khalsa Association* (Singapore: Published for the Association by Marshall Cavendish International (Asia) Pte. Ltd., 2006).

129. <http://www.bridgesingapore.com/index.htm> (accessed 22 May 2009).

130. "CII-India Business Forum (IBF): Singapore", <http://www.bridgesingapore.com/india_business_forum.htm> (accessed 22 May 2009).

131. "What is Network India", <http://www.iesingapore.gov.sg/wps/portal/VenturingOverseas/IENetworks/NetworkIndia> (accessed 22 May 2009).

132. Ibid.

133. "SIBA — A Joint Initiative of IE and Contact Singapore", <http://www.e-siba.org/docs/vivian.html> (accessed 25 May 2009).

134. Ibid.

135. "The GA Group Pte Ltd", <http://www.gagrp.com/index.html> (accessed 23 May 2009).

136. <http://www.gagrp.com/gibs2007.html> (accessed 23 May 2009).

137. For other details of the conference refer to the article, "Greater Diversity at Global Entrepolis @ Singapore, 2006", *Entrepolis Daily*, 31 October 2006, <http://www.gagrp.com/gibsatges2006.html> (accessed 23 May 2009).

138. "NUS Business School Signs 'People Friendly' MoU with Top India B-School", <http://www2.bschool.nus.edu.sg/corpdev/bizleads/BIZ%20Leads%202006/May06/schoolnotes.htm> (accessed 23 May 2009).

139. Amrit Barman, *India Fever: The New Indian Professional in Singapore*, Book Series 2 (Singapore: Singapore Indian Association, 2009), pp. 57–58. In the conference organized in 2006, "IIT Industry Interaction", the author describes how the interactions became fruitful in future collaborations between Barclays Bank and IIT Kharagpur.

140. This information is based on correspondence with Shekaran Krishnan, Ernst & Young LLP. on 25 May 2009.

141. Mr Yap said, "I hope that in future there will be only one chamber of commerce to represent businessmen of all races who are citizens of Singapore"; "High Time for only one chamber: Yap", *Straits Times*, 31 August 1959.

142. "Classes in Malay for Towkays", *Straits Times*, 1 September 1959.

143. Tong Suit Chee, "Chinese, Malay Chambers Act to Promote Interaction", *Business Times (S)*, 6 November 1987.

144. "Chinese and Malay Businessmen Join Hands", *Straits Times*, 24 December 1987; "Business Across Races", *Straits Times*, 30 December 1988.

145. "Chambers of Commerce Deserve Support", *Straits Times*, 9 April 1987.

146. Diana Oon, "Who should be President?" *Business Times (S)*, 19 April 1991.

147. Ibid.

148. Tan Sung, "Do not tell us who should head SFCCI, says Indian Chamber", *Straits Times*, 18 April 1991.
149. Narendra Aggarwal, "Move for professionals: Others may not follow Indian chamber", *Straits Times*, 24 July 1991.
150. SICCI, *Annual Report 2008–2009*, p. 7.

Chapter 5

THE INDOMITABLE ENTREPRENEURS: THREE CASE STUDIES

The Indian diasporic business communities as we have seen, have traversed through the lengths of Singapore's history through different phases of triumphs and disappointments, achievements and failures. The emerging pattern that has been witnessed through the entry and exit of different business entities at different phases of history is one that is diverse enough to accommodate almost all sectors of enterprises that exist in Singapore. The success stories of different generations have had also imbibed the spree of globalization in different parameters that was partly inherent, partly catalysed by the constraints of the size of the domestic market of Singapore. This chapter deals with three different cases studies, rooted in different phases of Singapore's history (the different periods have been discussed earlier), and have continued to be prominent names in the contemporary business landscape of the nation with unique dynamics of their own. In fact, at present they all rank among the top enterprises of Singapore. They represent the diversity of ethnic Indian entrepreneurial talent and strong historic presence in this geographical terrain with a continuity that has been witnessed in the changes of business paradigms and environment affecting the whole community.

Ethnic Indian business firms have had existed in different shapes and sizes at different periods of time, and a generic representation of the magnitude of success and achievements of the entire community is indeed difficult. The three enterprises mentioned in this chapter — the Kewalram Chanrai Group, Mustafa and Chemoil are not only amongst the biggest names in Singapore at present, but also rank among the top forty companies in the Forbes list. Such examples would help to affirm the visibility and prominence of the community among the overlooming presence of the large Chinese business networks in Southeast Asia. It also asserts the incorporation of diversification, professionalism and corporatization of business entities and a successful and smooth transition of the conventional family business network patterns in the changing rhetoric.

Two of the three enterprises mentioned in this chapter were associated with trading at some point of their growth, a sector that the ethnic Indians have been most adept in different phases of history as well as contemporary times. The other business concern represents the retail business sector, which had existed in Singapore, targeting the Indian clientele mostly in a rather domesticated market scenario. However, rapid diversification and innovations among all the three business entities have had ramifications and manifestations in the development of a unique identity at a regional and global level in each of the three cases. Thus, the Chanrai Group of Companies had their inception in Singapore in the colonial days, growing parallel along with other names of its times like the Jumabhoys, Thakrals, Royal Brothers and others. Whereas most of them flourished rapidly during the initial decades, and some later demurred due to various different factors, Chanrais not only kept up their momentum, but increased it with diversification, manufacturing and restructuring. Mustafa gained into prominence in the retail sector at a period that was very challenging to many Indians engaged in business to survive, and managed to stave off competition with a unique business model that embarked on a course of diversification and consolidation and established themselves as a global household name in consumer business. They successfully challenged then established names like Sithi Vinayagar or Kalyanasundaram in the same Serangoon Road area and same kind of products, adding to the forces that drove these business concerns to extinction. Robert Chandran and his Chemoil, our third case study, represents the new generation of professionals venturing into enterprises. Though Robert Chandran is no more, Chemoil remains a progressive global leader in bunkering, oil trading and shipping. It also reveals how such emerging enterprises have made use of the advantages of the geostrategic location of Singapore and the conducive business environment that it provides to attract entrepreneurs from around the world. Chemoil has managed to outshine many others in the field in the perspective of foresight, vision and investment capabilities. All the three enterprises, though representing different generations of the Indian diasporic community, are connected to their homeland not only through the cultural roots, but also through business relations and philanthropy, and yet maintain their unique, indomitable status in the global entrepreneurial world. It may be remembered that due to considerations of timeline of research, the growth and development of the enterprises have been restricted to the end of 2008 and in some cases to the beginning of 2009 and have not taken into account the developments beyond that period.

I. KEWALRAM CHANRAI GROUP

The Kewalram Chanrai Group is a part of the globally extended Chanrai family business network, which had established its roots in Sindh about 150 years ago. Though set up in the Indian subcontinent, the Chanrais spanned across the globe in different parts of Africa, Europe or Southeast Asia. The Company deals with diverse sectors of distribution and manufacturing in textiles, commodities, agricultural inputs, real estate, IT-related products, transportation as well as manage environmentally friendly businesses. They have about 12,000 employees in over sixty-two countries across the globe.[1] The present patriarch of the Kewalram Group, Murli Kewalram Chanrai had steered the company successfully in its development and diversification across the continents. The formal helm of affairs of the Company now rests with his nephew, Narain Girdhar Chanrai, who took over as the present CEO of the Group in 2004;[2] he had been associated with the company for more than three decades.

Background

The story of the Chanrai family business began in 1860 with the opening of a small textile shop in Hyderabad, Sindh[3] by Jhamatmal and Thakurdas Chanrai, "two enterprising brothers" of a wealthy Sindhi *zamindar* (landowners) family[4] who were restless and adventurous in nature and became tired of leisurely life.[5] They founded the firm, J.T. Chanrai and started dealing with local handlooms, gradually expanding into wholesale and retail business along with a variety of other products. The Chanrais represented a typical *Sindhwork* firm[6] dealing with textiles and headquartered in Hyderabad from where they spread to Bombay (Mumbai at present) in India and dispersed across the globe with different family members in charge of different areas of operations. According to Markovits, "This dispersed structure is meant to maximize response to changing business opportunities worldwide...."[7] In characterizing the *Sindhworkies*, Markovits has further pointed out that the senior members were more like transnational families, the "lower echelons have ... tended to entrench themselves much more locally while maintaining international linkages which facilitate business."[8] This has been an important component in characterizing the diaspora.

The J.T. Chanrai brothers followed a similar pattern of progress. In 1865, they opened the Karachi branch and started dealing with pulses business, followed soon after by the Bombay branch in early 1870s.[9] Apart from trading in textiles and handicrafts, they began handling bullion and became commission agents.[10] The opening of the Bombay branch "merely impelled them to seek wider fields of activity, to reach out to new opportunities, fresh fields, greater achievements".[11] Soon they started with their global adventures when they "took over a running concern in Malta",[12] and later expanded to Spain, Gibraltar, Spanish Morocco, Ceuta (Atlantic port in North Africa), Tetuan, Melilla (Malija), Tangier (Mediterranean port in North Africa), and the Canary Islands.[13]

Business boomed during the last two decades of the nineteenth century, consequently the capital investments as well as the employees increased concurrently. During the Boer War, they opened an office in the British colony of Sierra Leone (West Africa)[14] and also in Lagos, Nigeria (in middle-west Africa) and at Accra, Ghana.[15] Not all of their ventures abroad were, however, successful. In 1904, they opened branches in Buenos Aires, Argentina and then in Rio de Janeiro, Brazil and Pentarenas, Chile, which did not survive for long, mainly for difficulty faced in shipping goods. Colon, opened in Panama in 1910, however, flourished, though closed down later in 1934 for difficulties in finding suitable managerial staff to be posted in the important trading post.[16]

It was time for the next generation to take over, which the sons of the two brothers successfully did. The Bombay office was reorganized and made the main exporting centre in India and they also established exporting centres in Yokohama and Kobe in Japan, which proved to be very useful for their expanding business, as has been mentioned in their *Centenary Souvenir* publication — "On the spot executives ... enabled to buy their requirements at more competitive prices and ship them to overseas markets, thus improving the quality of their exports, and saving considerable on insurance as well as on freightage".[17] After the end of the First World War, they continued with their expansions, but more carefully. In 1924, they took over the running business of silks and curios of Allomal Hassomal in Singapore and Indonesia and gradually set up offices in Saigon, Vietnam, Shanghai, Hong Kong and Canton.[18]

The enterprising spirit and the business acumen that spread across the continents helped the Chanrais to sail through the Depression years smoothly. "Chanrais rode serenely over the storm that wiped out the fortunes of others overnight."[19] Soon after, the two sons of Jamatmal died leaving their three children behind who separated from the family concern after taking their share in cash. The firm then became the sole property of the sons of Thakurdas — Ghanshyamdas and Hassomal.[20]

With the Partition of India in 1947, the firm closed down their Karachi office in Pakistan and relocated to India. The business assets were also divided into six shares and pragmatic rules were laid down.

> The firm's assets were split into six equal shares and each separating partner was told he could use the firm's name only

in the territory which fell to his share. In the territory where
he had not the right to use the firm's name, he was free to set
up a business under another name.[21]

Thus, the eldest son of Ghanshamdas, Kewalram, acquired the
right to use the name of J.T. Chanrai in Sierra-Leone, Ghana and
in London. In Lagos and Madras, Kewalram's company came to
be known as A. Kewalram & Sons, and in Osaka, it was called
Anglo-African Agencies.[22] This futuristic and professional approach
of the Chanrais, as far back as in the 1940s, was a unique and
innovative step to manage and maintain the family name and
went a long way to establish the business legacy worldwide and at
the same time avoid conflicts and differences amongst the different
shareholders. By 1948, Ghanshyamdas and his son, Kewalram
consolidated the diverse businesses under the Kewalram Chanrai
Group.[23] The Group was finally rooted in Singapore in 1976
when Murli Kewalram Chanrai, son of Kewalram came to settle
in Singapore and established Kewalram Singapore, the holding
company for the Group to serve their interests in the region.[24] This
was also the time Singapore embarked on his march to progress
and development, creating conducive business environment to
attract foreign investments and giving ample opportunities to
the entrepreneurs to expand and prosper as well.

Growth and Progress

Murli Kewalram Chanrai has been involved with the Group
for more than sixty years working in various places like India,
Indonesia, Africa, U.K. and Singapore, and served as an executive
chairman since 1976,[25] steering the company upwards in its
ladder of success. At a time when many of the Indian business
entities were battling for their survival, the Chanrais had been

successful in making the best of the situation. In fact, M.K. believed it had "good opportunities for business in the 1970s".[26] The company had already ventured into textile manufacturing in Nigeria earlier through "Afprint" in 1960, a textile printing plant. In 1972, it expanded with setting up of an integrated spinning mill. Subsequently, Afprint was listed on the Nigerian Stock Exchange.[27]

Taking advantage by positioning itself in Singapore, the Group expanded rapidly in Indonesia. They started with a modest spinning mill in Bandung, Indonesia in 1975 which eventually grew into a state-of-art facility textiles and embroidery production unit, fully integrating the manufacturing and finishing lines in the same location.[28] By the turn of the century, it had installed 60,000 spindles which produces about 24,000 tonnes of yarn annually and employ over 2,200 employees. The embroidery division had been set up in 1979 and produced fine laces; everything from designing and embroidery to stitching was done under the same unit with modern embroidery machines and computerized designing facilities, making it readily marketable at *haute couture* boutiques.[29]

By the beginning of the 1980s, the Kewalram Chanrai Group (KCG) spread over an extensive network in West Africa (Nigeria, Ghana, Sierra Leone), Far East (Hong Kong, Taiwan) and Southeast Asia (Singapore, Indonesia and Malaysia) and was involved with the diverse sectors of "manufacturing, wholesale trading, import and export, the management of departmental stores and supermarkets and even in financing ..."[30] In the same decade, the Group acquired Kewalram Oils in 1981 in Malaysia for recovering industrial grade oils from residues. In 1989, Kewalram Philippines was "established to manufacture synthetic blended yarns for weaving and knitting."[31]

The Group had extensive expansion and integration in Africa in the 1980s. They moved into the distribution business in this decade with Kewalram Nigeria taking up the distribution of Bridgestone tyres and opening showrooms and service centres for the distribution of Mitsubishi and Fuso vehicles catering to corporate and retail customers alike.[32] It also started dealing with other consumer products like electronics.[33]

In 1986, the Group opted for backward integration by going into cotton cultivation through "Afcott", which was launched in Nigeria to grow and gin cotton. "Afcott" later started dealing with both cotton and vegetable oil industries along with "Sunseed", which was established in central Nigeria in 1998 and even later in the "Springfield Agro", which dealt with total farming solutions in 2003.[34] However, the flagship project of the Kewalram Chanrai Group was the setting up of "Olam".[35]

Olam Nigeria Plc. was set up in 1989 by the Kewalram Chanrai Group as a non-oil export operation and to deal with agricultural commodities. It was initially set up to meet the foreign exchange requirements and earn hard currencies for other group enterprises based in Nigeria.[36] What began with the export of raw cashews to only one destination, India with just four customers and a seed capital of US$100,000[37] soon expanded to exports of cocoa, sheanuts and cotton from Nigeria. From a single product enterprise, it developed into "multiproduct, multinational, integrated supply chain manager" at present.[38]

Olam was incorporated in Singapore in July 1995 as Olam International Limited, a public limited company. It relocated its entire operations from London to Singapore in 1996. It was listed in the Main Board of the Singapore Stock Exchange in February 2005. While the management team has about 16.1 per cent share, Kewalram Chanrai Group holds a 23 per cent stake in the company at present.[39] The businesses for Olam stretches from confectionery and beverage ingredients to edible nuts, spices and beans, food staples and packaged foods as well as fibre and food products. The company incorporated a number of subsidiaries between 2005 and 2006 including EURL Agri Commodities, Outspan Peru SAC, Olam Shanghai and Olam Shandong.[40] By 2005, Olam had become the world's largest shipper of cashew nuts, controlling 25 per cent of the global trade.[41] Besides, it sources various other agricultural commodities like coffee, sesame seeds, rice and many others from around thirty-five different countries in the world and caters to customers like the Cadbury's, Nestle, Sara Lee, Mars and others.[42]

At the helm of affairs at Olam is Sunny Verghese, who is the Group Managing Director and CEO of the Company. He had started his career in KCG as a Project Manager in Nigeria[43] in 1986 to set up the company called "Afcott", dealing with mechanized cotton growing, which became the largest in Sub-Saharan Africa.[44] In 1989, he was entrusted with the task of building up the agri-business enterprise which was named as Olam. Olam was initially set up to generate "hard currency earnings for the group's manufacturing and trading interests in Nigeria".[45] Though he did not get big capital to start with, his experiences in the Nigerian market and the profile of the sprawling Chanrai business, already entrenched in the region for decades, helped in developing "emerging market sensibilities" and "distilled some lessons in terms of what works, what does not work" in those markets.[46] He worked on slim margins, but big volumes and established the company's presence in all the original markets to conduct regular crop surveys as a part of its risk management policy.[47] Olam has also grown by expanding into adjacent products and markets by 1993/94[48] and has provided value-added services and customized grades of quality according to the specifications of different customers. Sunny Verghese and

Table 5.1
Some Acquisitions and Joint Ventures of Olam International

Year	Location	Company Acquired/JV Formed
2007	U.S.	Acquired 100 per cent shares of peanut blancher and ingredient processor — Universal Blanchers (UB)
2007	U.S.	Acquired 100 per cent of Key Food Ingredients, a processor and supplier of dehydrates
2007	Australia	Acquired 100 per cent shares in Queensland Cotton Holdings
2007	Indonesia	Acquired 100 per cent stake in sugar refinery PT DUS
2007	Poland	Acquired 100 per cent in Naarden Agro, processor and supplier of industrial caseins
2007	West Africa	50:50 JV with Wlmar to form Nauvu Investments for investment in palm, rubber in West Africa
2008	New Zealand	Acquisition of 24.99 per cent of Open Country Dairy
2008	Cote D'ivoire	Announced acquisition of cotton ginning unit for US$5 million in Ouangolo region of Cote D'ivoire
2008	U.K.	50:50 JV with Wilmar to form Olam-Wilmar Investment Holding to acquire 20 per cent stake in Pure Circle Limited which is the leading zero calorie food maker.
2008	U.S.	Acquisition of dehydration facility from De Francesco & Sons
2008	India	Acquisition of sugar milling assets for US$9.9 million
2009	Argentina	Acquisition of peanut shelling and blanching company IMC for US$7 million
2009	U.S.	Acquisition of tomato-processing assets from SK Foods for US$39 million
2009	New Zealand	Acquired 14.35 per cent of New Zealand Farming Systems Uruguay

Source: <http://www.olamonline.com/investors/media_centre.html> (accessed 5 September 2009); information provided by the company dated 8 September 2009.

his team had been applying the principle of "farm-gate to factory gate" supply chain, managing risk at every stage, and continued to add new products and geographies to their business.[49] He believed in building on certain capabilities which would then become powerful competitors to expand across products and geographical boundaries, thus accelerating growth. As Sunny Verghese explains:

> ... we were growing across multiple vectors ... new product adjacency was one vector, new geographical adjacency was another vector, new value-chain adjacency was the third vector ... the different channels was the fourth vector ... and logic for growth was identified with ... adjacencies ... when the risk is low then you migrate into closely related adjacent business operations.[50]

This business model had worked very successfully for Olam to expand globally. Assif Shameen, in his article on Olam describes the company's position in the world market thus:

> Olam trades 17% of the world's cocoa, 16% of the world's cashew and 8% of the world's peanuts and dabbles in a host of other commodities, including sesame, beans, rice, sugar, dairy products, packaged food, cotton and timber. Olam is no small fry. It made $167.7 million profit on turnover of $8.1 billion in the fiscal year ended June 2008. It has been growing at a compound 25% to 30% a year for the past five years.[51]

The other associate company of the KCG is Redington, dealing with a completely different set of products, is the IT arm of the Group. Listed in India, it is a distributor of IT products and provides logistics and supply chain management in India, Africa and the Middle East.[52] The company was initially incorporated in

Singapore to deal with trade in PC components in the early 1980s, but later moved its base to Chennai, India in 1993,[53] when the Indian economy began to loosen up and the IT industry flourished. Redington (India) eventually acquired Redington Gulf FZE (Middle East and Africa) in April 2004, Redington Distribution Pte. Ltd. (Singapore, Bangladesh and Sri Lanka) and Cadensworth (India) Pvt. Ltd. in April 2005.[54] The company has emerged as the largest distributor of IT products in the Middle East and Africa and the second largest one in India.[55] Redington was listed in the Indian Stock Exchange in 2007 and has emerged as a leader in its key markets of IT and other technology products in Southeast Asia, Middle East and Africa.[56]

Another comparatively recent addition to the KCG is the EcoProcessors International Limited, established in 2004 as a holding company to set up and manage environmentally friendly business. This completely diverse group venture had been set up with a "commitment to develop sustainable business models".[57] It also signifies global trends and demands for the contemporary scenario of commerce and the flexibility and willingness of the KCG to do so. While the two companies in Malaysia (EcoOils processors Sdn Bhd. and EcoOils Sdn Bhd.) dealing with the recovery of vegetable oils from industrial residue to be further used as bio-fuels, bio-diesel, soap manufacturing and other purposes.[58] Another Company, Eco Water Management was founded in 2007 to provide water solutions in Africa.[59]

The KCG has also been involved in real estate and property development. The first industrial development project undertaken under the auspices of the Kewalram Realty Limited was the Kewalram House, a four-storey building covering an area of 17,666 square metres with the first two levels designed for storage and the next two levels designated for manufacturing facilities. It also housed a staff canteen.[60] Soon after, "Kewalram Hillview", a seven-storey industrial building and a terrace factory were also undertaken for construction by the Group.[61]

The Group also undertook property development projects outside Singapore, like Wisma Kewalram, the construction of a thirty-four storey office building by Kewalram Realty Sdn Bhd. in Kuala Lumpur, Malaysia in 1993.[62] Later, in 1997, the KCG launched an up-market apartment project, "Awanpuri" at Genting Highlands, near Kuala Lumpur.[63] Earlier in 1996, the Kewalram Chanrai Group went into a joint venture (JV) to build a residential tower at Alabang in Manila, Philippines.[64] The KCG had been earlier involved in a JV project to build a textile mill in Calamba, Laguna in the Philippines.[65]

The various undertakings of the KCG that have been mentioned above, are examples of the diversified entrepreneurial activities of the Group and, by no means form an exhaustive description of the company's ventures, which would require separate context and space. What is, however relevant, is to see the extent of the global spread of the company's enterprises through different generations, which seemed quite unaffected by the political or economic turbulences and turmoil at different times, ensuring success through aggressive and successful business model.

Corporate Philosophy

The KCG has not only been successful in building up an ever expanding loyal customer base with value additions at different stages, but has also been able to succeed at the efficient management of the family business pattern. The continuing generations of increasing family members and their effective incorporation in the in-house business is, perhaps, the biggest challenge faced by any family enterprises that have survived and prospered for almost

Figure 5.1
Kewalram Chanrai Group

KEWALRAM CHANRAI GROUP

GROUP COMPANIES

ASSOCIATED COMPANIES

AFRICA GROUP

KEWALRAM INDONESIA

ECOPROCESSORS INTL LTD., S'PORE

OLAM INTL LTD

REDINGTON (INDIA) LTD

KEWALRAM NIG LTD
CHANRAI NIG LTD
AFCOTT NIGERIA LTD
SUNSEED NIGERIA
SPRINGFIELD AGRO
AFPRINT NIG LTD
ECOWATER MGMT

PT KEWALRAM INDONESIA

ECOOILS PROCESSORS BHD, NILAI, MALAYSIA

ECOOILS SDN BHD, JOHOR, MALAYSIA

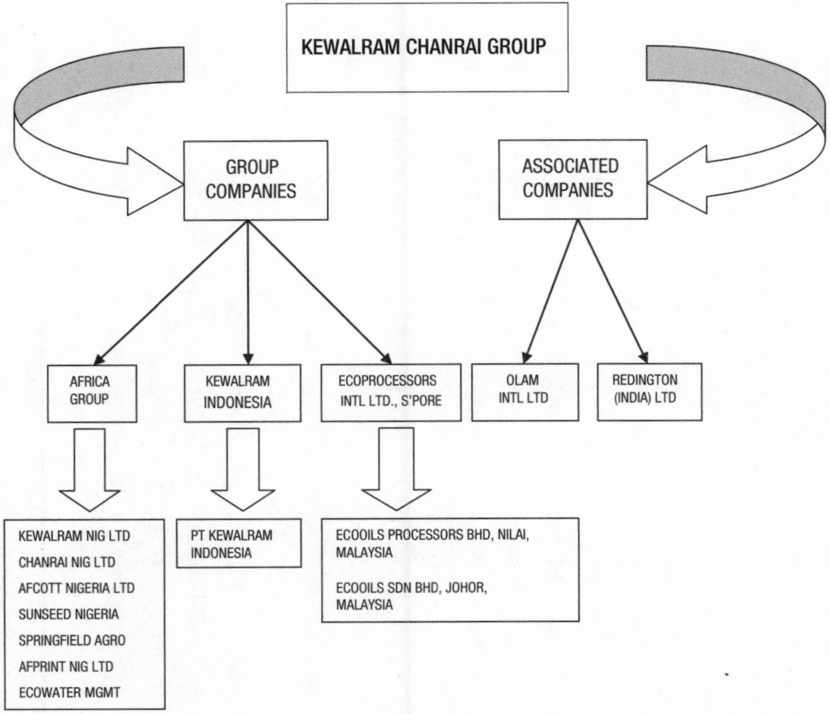

Source: <http://www.chanrai.com/> (accessed 9 September 2009).

one-and-a-half centuries. The KCG has managed it very well, especially under the leadership of M.K. Chanrai. In his opinion: "A family that does business together, grows together and in the process achieves a binding relationship that far supersedes all conflicts."[66] The veteran had also realized that the families do not plan their succession or their leadership[67] acceptable to all, which poses problems with the succeeding generations. The Chanrais, on the other hand, have been able to efficiently strategize at the right juncture and integrate members of the family with well laid-out norms and principles for ensuring the smooth transition from one generation to the next, which has paid off successfully in increasing the prosperity of the business. In the early 1990s, two nephews of M.K. had attended a seminar on family business and felt the necessity of a proper family constitution.[68] After much discussions and deliberations between the family members and with the help of a consultant, the family constitution was drawn up which proclaimed that the family business would never be broken up, competent daughters would be inducted and one had to qualify with the right aptitudes for business to be inducted into the Board. There would be a family council to look after the interests of all the members. A family member could also opt out of his business by selling shares to the Group or individual member at a price fixed by the Board.[69]

Professionals and professionalization have played a big part in ensuring the success of the KCG. The professionals have been entrusted with responsibility as well as confidence, besides the motivation that they received from the Board. What the Chanrais meant by professionalism "was not so much as hiring MBAs and Chartered Accountants and then putting them in their businesses, but really making a distinction between ownership and management".[70] From 1992 onwards, the KCG became a family-owned, but professionally managed concern.[71] They decided to allow the best managerial talent to steer their businesses. In reference to the steps of professionalization taken up by the KCG, Group's Director, N.G. Chanrai said, "We needed to send a clear message to our professional managers that there was going to be a fundamental change in the way we operated ... we would reward and recognize talents and there would be no glass ceilings."[72]

Such pragmatic and timely steps to bind the enterprise under the family tree is a rare example of a successful family business and provide lessons to many Asian entrepreneurs, both in the past and the present, to maintain consistency in matters of inheritance and leadership, at the same time, keeping in pace with the moving times.

Philanthropy had also been a part of the corporate philosophy. Talking about charitable contributions, M.K. had once said that a percentage of their profits goes to charity in all the countries where they do business.[73] The KCG is associated with a range of social work around the globe, like Jaslok Hospital and Research Centre in Mumbai, Kalyan Ashram Trust, London, and Kewalram Chanrai Foundation in Nigeria providing scholarships and bursaries to students there as well as involvement in different social services in Singapore.[74] Jaslok Community Ophthalmic Centre in Chennai and its twelve partner hospitals have served the community by performing more that 140,000 free eye surgeries. G.D. Chanrai Memorial Hospital and clinics in Yola, Nigeria have been providing pre-natal and post-natal care in its 24 healthcare facilities.[75] The Chanrai Group has also supported educational institutions. Besides providing merit scholarships in renowned educational institutions like the Lee Kuan Yew School of Public Policy, Singapore and Singapore Management University, they have also supported organizations like Child's Dream in Thailand to provide educational opportunities to under-privileged women of the Mekong Delta and also help the United World College to provide quality education to underprivileged children from Africa and Asia. They have also made donations to Singapore Indian Development Association (SINDA) in Singapore to support the needy.[76]

Business Model

The Kewalram Chanrai Group began by trading in textiles but soon ventured into dealing with processing of agri-products, textile manufacturing, real estate development, and many other diversified ventures over the years, though trading activities continued to fetch about 70 per cent of the revenues even in the early 1990s.[77] The expansion of the Group had been both vertical and linear in terms of products, process and global extent traversing through multiple continents. The success of any corporation, according to M.K. Chanrai, was to have a group of efficient managers who could be motivated and trusted.[78] Talking to Tan Sung (the *Straits Times*) about how he ran his vast business, he replied:

> I adopt the principle of management-by-objective, setting annual goals on turnover, profits and expansion plans for individual companies. I then sit back and monitor the progress through a comprehensive performance report submitted by the chief executive officers on the sixth day of every month.[79]

The KCG leadership had been quite a visionary in providing the space and the opportunity to the professionals to corporatize their successive ventures in the global market. The decentralization of authority from the family members involved had paid off well. The most outstanding example in this perspective was the case of "Olam", where Sunny Verghese, a marketing professional, was entrusted with the task of building up the company with a seed capital of just US$100,000. As has been previously mentioned, Olam soon grew into a business of $4.36 billion by 2007[80] under the able stewardship of its CEO, Verghese. In his own words: "We had a fairly simple understanding with the family that they won't force us to put any family-member in the business and they will never get involved with the recruitment at all. So the management will develop and identify the talent and recruit their men and all their staff."[81]

The focus of the KCG has been on the emerging economies, as had been rightly pointed out by R. Jayachandran,[82] Director of the Group and a part of the strong corporate team having had long association with the Chanrais. They have had extensive global expansions through different generations, but systematically avoided interacting with the competitive market forces in the developed economies; and rather tread on less familiar and difficult terrains, which was also far less competitive. In the words of Jayachandran, "We don't play in the developed world, we don't speculate and we have expanded in orderly fashion in the past."[83] He had also emphasized on the investment in technology and information[84] to stay more competitive, avail opportunities and avoid pitfalls.

The KCG has not imposed any methods of centralization over its associate and group companies. Though the different companies share some of the core values of KCG like professionalism, meritocracy, integrity, they have followed different business models that they have been individually pursuing with different degrees of sophistication and rigour based on individual challenges and aspirations.

M.K. Chanrai places a lot of emphasis in nurturing the right manpower in addition to other things to ensure the success in the

KCG business. As has been pointed out earlier, carefully selecting trustworthy employees as well as treating and paying them well goes a long way in guaranteeing the success of a business.[85]

II. MOHAMED MUSTAFA & SAMSSUDDIN CO. PTE. LTD.

No other ethnic Indian is as big a name in the retail sector as Mohamed Mustafa & Samsuddin Co. (MM & S) in Singapore, our next case study. The family business concern had its inception in 1971 and grew and prospered along with Singapore during its most formative years after Independence. Thriving and prospering in a belt that was originally a hub of the South Indian community, the Mustafa family hailed from North Indian province of Uttar Pradesh. Cheaper prices, large range of consumerables from vegetables and watches to electronics and jewellery at the same place, free parking and aroma of Little India in close proximity — all contribute to the success and attraction of Mustafa. The clientele is as diverse and varied as its large range of products, right from middle-aged housewives and elderly folks to young couples with children in the tow to single men and women, either South Asian, Chinese, Malay or Eurasian, both tourists as well as residents. Generally assumed to be an ideal shopping destination for people from the Indian subcontinent, it has had witnessed an increase of its Chinese customers in considerable numbers, so much so that they had to employ Chinese to serve those clients.[86] The price tags and products of daily use appeal to migrant workers, professional executives or rich businessmen alike, and this uniqueness has made it a landmark of Singapore as well as a "not-to-be-missed" tourist destination, and also earned Mustaq Ahmed, the owner and the Managing Director, the 2003 Tourism Entrepreneur of the Year Award[87] by the Singapore Government.

Background

The Mustafa story started with Haji Mohamed Mustafa (1916–2001), the founder of the Mustafa Centre, who had been a farmer in Jaunpur in the eastern region of Uttar Pradesh in India before he set out to seek better fortunes overseas. He had initially gone to Muar in Malaysia in 1950 and sought his living by peddling dumplings and coconut fillings.[88] He came to Singapore two years later in 1952 and began to sell food on a makeshift cart. In 1956, he brought his son, Mustaq to join him after the death of his first wife. Mustaq grew up helping his father in selling tea and bread. However, his enterprising spirit drove him to sell hankerchiefs at fixed prices next to the food stall, which he bought with his own pocket money.[89] Mohamed Mustafa was so inspired with his son's efforts that he decided to shift to retail clothing business. He began selling children's clothes and adult garments in a stall that he set up in 1965[90] and soon added vests and other items as the business prospered. He ultimately established his business in a 500-square feet shop in the Campbell Lane in 1971.[91] Thus was sown the seeds of the globally renowned retail empire.

In 1973, Mustaq Ahmed went on to rent a 900 square feet of shop space along the Serangoon Road and increased the range of his products and services, adding electrical appliances and foreign exchange.[92] Apart from his father, his uncle, Samsuddin had also been a constant participant in their business ventures and growth.

Growth and Progress

The year 1985 was a turning point in Mustaq Ahmad's career. The fast expanding business was apparently disrupted when the government acquired both the shops for the purposes of conservation. Mustaq took a decision that was bold and had far reaching consequences. He rented a space of 12,000 square feet at the Serangoon Plaza[93] to set up his business in 1985. This involved a huge risk as the location of the new shop was a little away from the main centre of activities in Little India. When this attempt became a success, he continued with his expansions. In the meanwhile, he was also buying old shop houses in the Syed Alwi Road. Having bought the entire row of them, he built up his Mustafa Centre with a retail space of 85,000 square feet. The departmental store also housed a 130-room hotel[94] in the top two floors. In 1996, the retail space increased to 160,000 square feet.

Mustaq Ahmad had taken over the reins of the family business completely in his own hands quite early in his career, and both his father and uncle showed complete faith in his business acumen and foresight. His idea of increasing the shop area and acquisitions of land and old shophouses became instantly successful, in spite of the ups and downs of the general economic conditions. In fact, his efforts had edged out the successful business of well-established neighbours like V.K. Kalyanasundaram (VKK), who had succumbed to the retail slump of the mid-1990s decreasing the business area from 25,000 square feet to about 4,800 square feet comprising of two units only.[95] Unfazed by any retail slump or others' downsizing of business, Mustafa rode high on his success and continued to enlarge the size of his business and his shop space. In 1997, he decided to spend around S$25 million in extending the Mustafa Centre by using the plot of land next to it, thus intending to increase the size of the store by another 18,000 square feet.[96] By 1999, Mustafa achieved a turnover of S$260 million with the sales of the jewellery adding another S$70 million.[97]

The new century ushered in more diversifications and additions for the Mustafas. In 2000, the first outlet of Mustafa outside of Singapore, Mustafa Goldmart was opened at Chennai. It was a 8,000 square feet of jewellery shop housed in a 16,000 square feet of building bought over by Mustaq Ahmed.[98] Besides, Mustafa became the only department store in Singapore to remain open round the clock since June 2003.[99] The earlier attempt to open a supermarket and a department store by "Yokoso" in Tanjong Katong Complex in 1983 had not been successful, had to close down by the late 1980s,[100] but for Mustafa, it worked wonders. In 2004, they already had more than 100,000 items in the shopping complex of 150,000 square feet and 1,000 employees. Earlier in the same year, Mustaq received the Tourism Entrepreneur of the Year Award for making Mustafa Centre a major tourist attraction in Singapore.

With the business expanding by leaps and bounds, Mustaq Ahmed sought a further increase in the shop space by about 45,000 square feet in 2004 by converting the existing third and the fourth levels of the Mustafa Hotel in the same premises. The expansion was undertaken at a cost of about $8 million to "boost the range and depth of merchandise it offers".[101] It had earlier opened a warehouse in the Kallang Pudding Road that had been in use for the export and the wholesale distribution business of the company.[102]

More recently, Mustafa has added remittances in its list of amenities to cater to money transfer round the clock to over 1,500 branches of major banks throughout India, as well as DD drawing services to India, Sri Lanka and Bangladesh.[103] This comes in addition to the foreign exchange facilities that it had been providing over the years. The travel related services are provided by Mustafa Air Travel Pte. Ltd., which is situated around the corner at Verdun Road in the same vicinity. This takes care of the air ticketing, hotel accommodation, visa services and also organizing tour packages at competitive prices. In 2009, the Indian High Commission outsourced its passport collection service, and one of the two centres appointed for this service was the Mustafa Air Travel.[104]

The rapid progress of Mustafa had encouraged it to list itself on the Singapore bourse initially. In 1997, Mustaq Ahmed said that they had plans to enlist in the stock exchange by the turn of the century.[105] However, due to reasons unknown, the plan was shelved. When Mustaq was later asked in 2003, at a time when it was making an annual average of $250 million in sales, he said that he would not include it in the future planning of the company.[106] All the expansions that it had gone through had been financed through the company's internal resources and bank financing. Mustaq Ahmed said that they had no plans to tap the public funds for expansion. He is of the opinion that they would rather do it on their own, or borrow from their existing bankers for now.

Mustafa progressed with a complete package of services to cater to the tourism sector, particularly addressing those from the Indian subcontinent, which, however, benefitted one and all across the continents. About 60 per cent of its clientele still remains South Asians. The ready access to food and fancy items, jewellery, money exchange, travel related services and even the facilities of a budget hotel at one point of time — all under the same unit, made it amply clear that Mustafa's progress and diversification was done keeping tourism sector in view. However, Singapore residents, both from the subcontinent and others, benefited from the conveniences as well. In fact, Mustafa's operations manager in 2005, Norrdin Mustafa said on one occasion that they had decided to open for twenty-four hours for the "tourists to have more time to shop at night while they do the sight-seeing in the day. But it turned out that it was mostly the Singaporeans who came to shop after midnight."[107] It may be mentioned that the migrant workers have also benefited greatly from the amenities at Mustafa not only for the supply of the necessities, but also for the familiarity of language and space that it offers within its vicinity. It has also helped a lot of small-level businesses to build up around the area like CD/DVD selling shops, electronics and clothes retailers, restaurants and others. The overwhelming crowd of these workers on a Sunday evening more than justifies the effect of the "Mustafa" factor on them.

Business Model

Receiving the 2003 Tourism Entrepreneur of the Year Award was recognition of Mustaq Ahmed's successful business model that he had built up around the industry. He had made consistent effort to address the needs of the customers, whether migrant workers, executives, rich businessmen or tourists at competitive prices, continuously adding on the range of products and services that has made "Mustafa" a household name. Mr Raymond Lim, Minister of State for Trade and Transport, who visited the store on 26 September 2003, said that "one attribute of a successful small and medium-sized enterprise is to be customer-centric, and Mustafa Centre is a good example of that".[108]

Mustafa offers a large range of around 200,000 items at extremely competitive prices with a profit margin of, according to some, around 10 to 15 per cent, and encashes on the huge turnover. Though Mustaq Ahmed had continued to take steps towards innovations and improvisations, the basic principles remain the same like the volume driven business at comparatively cheaper fixed prices. Another policy had been to own and acquire premises rather than rent them. Referring to this policy, Mustaq had once said, "our other ideas might change but we will never change our motto to build and own".[109] He also attributes his success to listening and responding to the customer's wants and necessities. In his own words: "We carry out customer surveys regularly and try to find out what consumers would like to have in our store and we will provide them at the best value."[110] At the same time, they have maintained a very traditional outlook with minimum investments on ornamental display of products or advertisements. In fact, the advertisement campaign is done by the word-of-mouth by its customers across the borders.

Another aspect of Mustafa's business strategy is that of sourcing and purchasing. They have managed to procure goods directly from the sources across the globe. It has successfully cut down the distribution middlemen, which has enabled it to keep its prices low and ensure to the customers the best value for money. "Its purchasing network includes Malaysia, Indonesia, Thailand and Hong Kong."[111] It also imports goods from Britain, United States and Japan.[112] However, keeping prices low puts a pressure to sell the large volumes intended to make substantial profit, which in the case of Mustafa, has been quite successful. Besides, Mustafa offers a wide range of Indian products, which very few other retailers have opted for, and has been able to draw in both the residents as well as the tourists interested in these products. This aspect has especially paid off keeping in view of the fact that Indians have been the second biggest spenders in Singapore after the South Africans.[113] Indians also account for 60 per cent of the consumer base at Mustafa, which makes the business of India-centric products all the more lucrative.

Looking Forward

When once asked about the name of his favourite store, Mustaq Ahmed had mentioned it to be Marks & Spencer because of their ability to control both the costs and quality and create their own in-house brands in a way that draws customers' loyalty towards its products.[114] "At the same time", according to Mustaq, "they have a limited number of shops, so they keep costs down and there's enough to go on to make a profit."[115]

Mustafa has been able to create the brand loyalty in its own way. Their efforts to beat competition and be ahead of it, has often been achieved to a considerable extent, but, according to some consumers, at the cost of the quality sometimes. There have also been apprehensions of safety hazards within the complex due to overcrowding of both consumers and consumerables on display. However, that has not made the shoppers relent from thronging into the area, who have had little doubts about the range of services available in relation to the prices elsewhere in the market.

III. CHEMOIL ENERGY LTD.[116]

The founding father of Chemoil Energy Limited, the late Robert Viswanathan Chandran started his company in the U.S. and later moved to Singapore. Chandran's story witnessed an incredible growth graph within a span of only a few decades, and figured amongst the Forbes list of top forty companies in Singapore in 2007.[117] In fact, he had been among the top privately owned companies in the U.S. by 1991. His remarkable growth in entrepreneurship also earned him the Ernst & Young "Entrepreneur of the Year" award (Singapore) for Oil and Gas in November 2007.

Background

Robert Chandran was born in 1950 at Mumbai to a chemist in a detergent factory, who later got involved in his in-laws' paper distribution business and moved to Coimbatore, Tamil Nadu.

Chandran's initial apprenticeship in business was started by helping his father, and the older Chandran's rigid strictures and rebukes left him quite disappointed about the ways of business.[118] His initial aspirations to become a doctor was unsuccessful; instead he earned a master's degree in Chemistry. He left India for the Asian Institute of Management (AIM) in Manila after his mother's demise in 1972, where he studied, worked and later married Vivian, an American of Filipino descent, and moved to the United States.

Chandran started his career as a professional in a chemical trading company at Manila after graduating from the AIM there and quickly rose under the guidance of the Company's Chairman, Antonio Garcia. He, however, migrated to California soon after in 1976, where he found a job with the affiliate of his Manila employer, sourcing chemicals and sending it back to the Philippines.[119]

The story of how Robert Chandran stepped into business is quite a dramatic one. Actually, he had also a passion for teaching, as Dr Joshua Kuma[120] recalls. He had first met Robert Chandran when he came to give a lecture at the National University of Singapore (NUS) where he had been a student, and soon became close to each other with commonalities in ancestry. In Dr Joshua's words, "He always used to tell us that unfortunately he became a businessman, otherwise he would have been a teacher."[121] In fact, while he was working for Garcia in the Philippines, he was also teaching part-time at a girls' college where he had met his future wife.[122] However, destiny had planned otherwise. While in the United States, he had borrowed $10,000 from his mother-in-law to make a down payment of a house in San Mateo and perhaps then realized how lucrative and easy it was to invest in properties in America. Thus, he began with a side business in properties over the weekends, the stepping stone to his world of wealth and fame, and soon co-owned 740 apartments by 1981 and became a millionaire.[123] He became a U.S. citizen in the same year and also established his own company Chemoil to supply chemicals and marine fuel. He soon found his niche in marine fuel; Chemoil Corporation was reorganized in 1982, and the business expanded throughout the 1980s to the U.S. Gulf Coast, East Coast and the West Coast,[124] and by 1991, it became one of the biggest private owned companies in the U.S. making it to the Forbes list of top companies with a revenue of $482 million.[125]

Growth and Progress

Chemoil was faced with a temporary crisis around 1993, when the shipping industry went through a period of slump, the banks refused to invest and he had to close many of the overseas offices and restructure and refinance his set-up, a phase that he described as a "nightmare".[126] But he managed to wade through the crisis and emerged with a more professional approach through the partnership of Itochu Corporation of Japan, a global trading company and a long-time customer of Chemoil, which proved to be a turning point in his career.

In partnering with Itochu in 1997,[127] Chemoil garnered the backing of a company that gave him access to global markets and easy credit facilities. Junji Tanuichi of Itochu saw to the purchase of 50 per cent stakes in the company, and later became its Chairman, a position that he held till 2006. Chemoil thereafter, started on a spree of global acquisitions and expansions, and has never looked back. It spread its wings to the Asian fuel market and the South American market, moved the headquarters to Singapore and ultimately listed the company in 2006. The major achievements and milestones of the company are listed in Table 5.2.

Relocating himself and the company to Singapore was a significant turn in Robert Chandran's career. His calculated vision and quest for new markets and bases in Asia brought him to the

Table 5.2
Some Milestones in the Growth of Chemoil

Year	Acquisitions and Expansions
1981	Commencement of business at San Francisco
1982	Chemoil Corporation was reorganized.
1986	Expansion into Houston and New York Gulf Coast operations started
1997	New partnership with Itochu Corporation of Japan
1998	Acquired Long Beach Marine Terminal and pipelines in California Acquisition of 50 per cent of Allround Fuel Trading B.V. making inroads into the ARA market
2000	Expanded into Singapore market through Chemoil-ITC Acquired 25 per cent stake in Galaxy Energy Group Ltd. Opened the Mediterranean and the Black Sea trade
2003	Chemoil entered the South American market when Chemoil Latin America, Inc. opened the key bunkering port of Panama.
2004	IPC (USA) Inc., associate of Chemoil, expanded into trading, marketing, sale of gasoline and jet fuel in the United States and South America.
2005	Chemoil International Pte. Ltd. was headquartered in Singapore.
2006	Construction of Chemoil Helios Terminal started in 15 June at a cost of US$120 million. Chemoil went public on 14 December on the Main Board of the Singapore Exchange Securities Trading Limited ("the SGX-ST"). Remaining acquisition of 50 per cent interest in All Round Fuel Trading. Chemoil B.V. now became Chemoil Europe B.V.
2007	Chemoil purchased a very large crude carrier (VLCC) tanker.
2008	Acquisition of 34,000 cubic metre storage terminal at Batanga, Philippines Completed expansion of Carson Terminal in the Los Angeles area Expanded to over 94,000 cubic metres of capacity in the GPS Chemoil Terminal in the Middle East

Sources: Chemoil Energy Limited, 2006 Annual Report, Chemoil Energy Limited, 2008 Annual Report, <http://www.chemoil.com/> (accessed 29 May 2009); Wayne Arnold, "Singapore's 40 Richest: Riding the Waves", 9 March 2007, <http://www.forbes.com/global/2007/0903/044_print.html> (accessed 29 May 2009).

city-state of which he eventually became a citizen. "I'm at a stage in life where I can live anywhere, I suppose; I want to live in Asia", he had said.[128] The advantages that Singapore provided in terms of its entrepot facilities, taxation policy, location, infrastructure, and the business environment attracted not only the MNCs but a lot many "small and middle-sized global players", as the Finance Minister had pointed out in his Budget Speech in 2007.[129] Referring to Robert Chandran in his speech he had said:

> ... He had listened to PM talk on TV about Singapore being a place with 'Asian values but Western conveniences'. He explored further, looked around, and eventually decided to move his family and company to Singapore. It is a marine fuel company, Chemoil. In fact he has now taken up Singapore citizenship ...[130]

Chandran's coming to Asia coincided with the timing of the Asian economic resurgence, especially for the two Asian giants, China and India and offered immense opportunities that he could capitalize on. "My view", he said, "is that opportunities are here. It's in China, it's in Vietnam, it's in India. ... this is an ideal place to be ..."[131] Singapore provided with just the right choice to establish his foothold here with the entrepot facilities and big opportunities for bunkering and other activities and avenues of the marine industry. It also provided him with the opportunity to be closer to his original homeland and a conducive living environment for his family.

One of the milestones conceived and achieved by Robert Chandran was the construction of the "Chemoil Helios Terminal" at Jurong Island in Singapore, which was started in 2006 at the cost of $120 million and completed at the beginning of 2008. This state-of-the-art facility terminal houses a very large crude carrier (VLCC) jetty which can accommodate up to 320,000 dead weight tones and can empty out a VLCC in almost twenty-four hours' time. The Chemoil jetty provides a facility which can accommodate two *Suezmaxes* or six smaller tankers at any one period of time; and has eighteen storage tanks with a total capacity of 448,000 cubic metres. This is the Company's largest storage terminal covering a land area of 16.97 hectares.[132] This $19 million investment, which increased to the present valuation of $300 million was, according to Dr Joshua Kuma, received with scepticism from the management initially, so much so that Bob Chandran started with the initial investments from his own privately held company, as he had the "confidence, passion and foresight"[133] about the task he had undertaken. However, the potentials of the investment was soon realized, and soon brought under the Chemoil Group. With "Helios", the Company made its presence in the top four of the world's oil ports along with Rotterdam, the U.S. Gulf and Fuzairah.[134]

The "Helios" facility has proved to be a win-win situation for both the Company as well as Singapore, which is the world's largest bunkering port and occupies a geostrategic position of tremendous importance as the centre of a network of commercial routes in Asia. It has complemented the state's initiatives to develop its storage capacities and helped retain the position of one of the premiere global maritime destinations. It has also been able to generate a lot of job opportunities for Singapore as well.

The Company that emerged as one of the largest and leading integrated suppliers of marine fuel products in the world, Chemoil International Pte. Ltd., is based in Singapore and spread out across the globe along with a network of branch offices, affiliates and partner companies. Chemoil Energy Limited manages the different arms of the supply chain distributing network of the business through its various wholly or partially owned subsidiary companies.[135] The "corporate offices are located in Hong Kong, San Francisco, Singapore, Rotterdam, Panama and Monaco", ... and the service centres are situated in "Los Angeles, New York, Houston, Singapore, Panama, the ARA region, and ... Fuzairah".[136] The Company caters to a "diverse group of ocean-going ship operators, international container and tanker fleets, marine fuel traders and other customers".[137] Chemoil, at present, owns four vessels, including barges and charter tankers for the delivery of the marine fuel. The shipping services were initially provided by Link Marine but later acquired by Chemoil in 2007.[138] Among the most prominent of the customers are A.P. Moller-Maersk A/S, Evergreen Marine Corp, American President Lines Ltd., Yang Ming Marine Transport Corp., World Fuel Services Corporation and others. They also market jet fuel to the commercial airlines of the U.S. through their associate company IPC (USA) and sell unbranded diesel oil and gasoline to retail customers and industrial users.[139] Chemoil faces considerable competition too from the other major global oil giants, government-owned supply companies, independents and traders, but has still risen up the ladder of progress non-stop due to efficient management and integration of its supply chain logistics and distribution network.

Quite different from his general line of enterprises, Robert Chandran had set up the business of coconut products in the Philippines. He started by acquiring a small coconut farm, which gradually grew into a very big business supplying products all over the world.[140] Franklin Baker, the privately held coconut product-maker, has been inherited by Vivian Chandran, his wife, after his death, who is at present the Chairman of the Company. Earlier in his business career, he had also started a software company to deliver integrated solutions for successful projects of Chemoil, which later continued outsourcing for many other clients and grew into a listed company.

Business Model

The primary objective of Chemoil has been to integrate the physical supply of the marine fuel products through different stages beginning from the sourcing and shipping to the storage and blending according to the specifications and demand of the customers, thus adding value to every stage in the distribution process. Each of these stages like shipping and storage is mostly done in-house to cater to the different needs at different locations around the globe. Bob Chandran had a knack of incorporating and acquiring the associate arms of the business, whether it was shipping or software applications for the company, for a smooth flow of supply chain distribution. One example of such an initiative was his involvement in setting up the computer outsourcing company, Calsoft in Chennai in 1992,[141] which despite being a separate entity, helped to deliver integrated solutions for successful projects for Chemoil,[142] thus enabling the company to extract margins through the integrated business model. By 2007, 67.71 per cent stakes of the California Software Co. Ltd. was held by Kemoil Ltd., the Hong Kong-based investment company of Chemoil.[143]

Efficient sourcing has been another strong point of the company, which is done by buying fuel at competitive prices and capitalizing on the regional price differences.[144] According to the company's *Annual Report 2006*, 35 per cent of their raw materials were sourced from Latin America, 31 per cent from Europe and Russia, 31 per cent from North America, 9 per cent from Asia and only 2 per cent from the Middle East.[145] The company also uses hard cash to buy fuels and cost price is usually the lowest when paid by cash.[146] The innumerable storage capacities provided at various terminals across the globe enable efficient storage facilities to buy the oil when the prices are low and sell it at a lucrative opportunity, thus generating maximum profits in the process. The other determinants of the Company's successful business model rest on a three-dimensional business strategy of markets, products and supply chain.

Chemoil had persistently ventured into newer markets ever since its inception. Starting from the United States, it moved to Europe, Middle East, South America and Asia. It was in fact, a very timely move to have established itself in one of the emerging hot spots of business activities, that is, Asia, and relocating to Singapore, which provided the right facilities and environment for further expansion in the region. At the same time, they went on increasing the number of products from marine fuel to jet fuel and environment friendly energy, gasoline and diesel. In parallel to the product portfolio expansion, Robert Chandran was keen to enhance the cost advantage by investing in terminals, storage capacity, shipping, barging and even software facilities, the assets intimately associated with their core business. Helios in Singapore is the biggest terminal owned by the enterprise till date. Thus, controlling over products, markets as well as supply

Table 5.3
Profit Figures of Chemoil

Year	Net Profit After Tax (USD million)
2005	49.51
2006	57.85
2007	30.32
2008	46.20

Source: "Summary Consolidated Income Statements", <http://www.chemoil.com/investors/FinancialSummary.asp> (accessed 9 September 2009).

chain distribution network was a strategic move to make use of the maximum cost-benefit opportunities as well as emerge as one of the top most global players in the business.

Through its effective business strategies and efficient management skills and proven track record, Chemoil has evolved to create a brand value of its own and thus has been able to carve its own niche in the global market. This has helped it to enhance itself into an attractive business potential for investors and further growth.

Looking Forward

In its incredible speed of growth and success, Chemoil had to come to terms with a rude shock when the dynamic entrepreneur and the founding father, Robert Chandran died in a helicopter crash on 7 January 2008. In spite of the immeasurable loss of its leader and the man with a great vision, it did not in any way refrain its wings from spreading further. Chandran had once said, "I'm driving a Ferrari at 180 miles an hour or 200 miles an hour ... Take my eye out and this car will hit the wall."[147] However, the able management and the Board of Directors did not let the Chemoil Ferrari "hit the wall". Though there were initial problems with the share prices plummeting (it fell 8 cents or 16 per cent[148]) and the general public's confidence appearing shaky on the future of the Company, Chemoil had consolidated itself within a year under the new CEO and Chief Executive, Clyde Michael Bandy, who had served as the independent Director of the Company since 2006 and had taken over the reins after Chandran's demise[149] to carry on with the founder's vision and expansion. "As part of our business growth strategy, there's always three or four or five targets on our radar screen, and this year is no different", Bandy said in a news conference after the company reports of

2008 were released.[150] They had completed the expansion of the Carson Terminal in the Los Angeles area by 2008 and are in the process of ongoing construction of the GPS Terminal at Fuzairah in the Middle East aiming to raise the capacity to 650,000 cubic metres.[151] Chemoil has also acquired the 34,000 cubic metre storage terminal at Batangas in the Philippines in 2008, and is in the process of expanding the Rotterdam Terminal through their associated company, Burando Holding BV, that is jointly owned by a European oil company.[152]

Chemoil has also expanded to the Indian market. With the joint venture with the Adani Group, it is engaged in bunkering at the Mundra port in Western India, which accounts for more than 22 per cent of the Indian maritime cargo traffic, and is expected to cross the 30 per cent mark by 2011–12.[153] It has expansion plans also for other Indian ports like Chennai and Mumbai.[154]

It was the vision of Robert Chandran that strove Chemoil to where it stands at present. In spite of initiating a large number of ventures around the globe, he entrusted most of their management and control in professional hands, which showed his foresight and trust that he had in the managerial body. This was, perhaps, one of the strong reasons for Chemoil to successfully tide over the temporary crisis and bounce back to the rails soon after the sudden shock of the patron's demise. His entrepreneurial vision could be best summarized in his own words:

> If you want to build a global company, you need to relinquish control. You have to get people to do things for you. And that's the problem — many entrepreneurs just don't. Then they come to a point when they don't grow. So they get bored and just sell their businesses.[155]

Robert Chandran's vision, foresight and the ability to turn difficult situations into opportunities have gone a long way in ensuring the growth of Chemoil. His objective of donning the presence of Chemoil in all major ports and upcoming markets have been carried on with due enthusiasm by the company enabling it to secure a bright future for the Energy Group.

IV. CONCLUSION

The three case studies are unique in their own way, yet represent a community that had been a minority, but significantly visible. Since the three cases are situated at different phases of Singapore's history and bear continuity to the contemporary period, they are, in a way, representative of the adaptability and the diversifications of the Indian business communities not only in the different phases, but also in different sectors. They have been successful examples of efficient sourcing, value addition to their products and integration in the supply chain logistics. Though majority in the community had been participating in the trading sector and most of them have been family business concerns, the successful ventures have had imbibed considerable degree of professionalism and have also diversified into different sectors. Our case studies have had the regular characteristics of the Indian business communities, yet each of them bore the distinction of standing apart from the rest, so much so that all the three figured among the biggest names in business in Singapore.

Notes

1. "Group Profile", <http://www.chanrai.com/groupprofile> (accessed 25 June 2009).
2. Geoff Hiscock, *India's Global Wealth Club: The Stunning Rise of its Billionaires and the Secrets of their Success* (Singapore: John Wiley & Sons (Asia) Pte. Ltd., 2008), p. 204.
3. Hyderabad was then a part of the Indian subcontinent, but came under Pakistan after the Partition of 1947.

4. "Chanrai started trade in handlooms in 1860", *Straits Times*, 31 May 1965.

5. "Chanrai's Centenary: 1860–1960", Straits Times Special Feature, *Straits Times*, 12 October 1960.

6. The *Sindhworkies* have been discussed in more details in the first chapter.

7. Claude Markovits, *The Global World of Indian Merchants, 1750–1947: Traders of Sindh from Bukhara to Panama*, Cambridge Studies in Indian History and Society (Cambridge: Cambridge University Press, 2000), p. 283.

8. Ibid.

9. "100 years of J.T. Chanrai", *Centenary Souvenir*, Chanrai's Group of Organisations, 1960, p. 2. Courtesy: N.G. Chanrai, Director, Kewalram Chanrai Group.

10. "Chanrai's Centenary: 1860–1960", op. cit.; *Centenary Souvenir*, ibid.

11. "100 years of J.T. Chanrai", *Centenary Souvenir*, op. cit., p. 2.

12. The Malta concern, which they took over from Mr Titu, a Sindhi businessman, was the first in the chain of stores that they later opened in Spanish Morocco, Panama, West Africa, Canary Islands and South America. "Chanrai started trade in handlooms in 1860", op. cit.

13. Ibid.; *Centenary Souvenir*, op. cit., p. 3.

14. "Chanrai's Centenary: 1860–1960", op. cit.

15. *Centenary Souvenir*, op. cit., p. 4.

16. Ibid.; "Chanrai's Centenary: 1860–1960", op. cit.

17. *Centenary Souvenir*, op. cit., p. 5.

18. "Chanrai's Centenary: 1860–1960", op. cit.; "Chanrai started trade in handlooms in 1860", op. cit.

19. "Chanrai's Centenary: 1860–1960", op. cit.

20. Ibid.

21. Ibid.; *Centenary Souvenir*, op. cit., p. 7.

22. *Centenary Souvenir*, op. cit., p. 7.

23. "About us", Kewalram Chanrai Group, <http://www.chanrai.com/history> (accessed 23 May 2009).

24. Tan Sung, "A behind-the-scenes mover takes over the helm at Indian Chamber", *Straits Times*, 18 April 1992.

25. Geoff Hiscock, *India's Global Wealth Club*, op. cit., p. 203.

26. Madhu Madan et al., "An Octogenarian who Values Honesty & Fair Play: Mr. M.K. Chanrai", in *Singapore Indian Entrepreneurs, Dreams to Reality* (Singapore: Singapore Indian Chamber of Commerce and Industry, 2004), p. 89.

27. "Africa Group", <http://www.chanrai.com/africagroup> (accessed 24 May 2009).

28. "Pt Kewalram Indonesia", <http://www.chanrai.com/indonesia> (accessed 25 June 2009).

29. Ibid.

30. "The Kewalram-Chanrai group: From wholesale trading to real estate", *Straits Times*, 3 April 1982.

31. "Charting Our Success", Milestone panels to celebrate the 150th Anniversary of the Chanrai Group, 2010. Courtesy: N.G. Chanrai, Director, Kewalram Chanrai Group.

32. "Africa Group", <http://www.chanrai.com/africagroup> (accessed 25 June 2005).

33. Ibid.

34. Ibid.

35. "Olam" is a Hebrew word which meant "transcending boundaries". In the words of Sunny Verghese, the Group MD and CEO, "when we set up the company, we wanted to choose a name that was fairly unique, that would symbolise what we were trying to do ... And it was easy for us to register that name in multiple jurisdictions because it was unique and unusual"; interview with Sunny Verghese, 7 July 2009.

36. "Heritage", <http://www.olamonline.com/aboutus/heritage.asp> (accessed 25 June 2009).

37. "Simply outstanding", *Business Times*, Singapore, 12 March 2007.

38. "Heritage", <http://www.olamonline.com/aboutus/heritage.asp> (accessed 25 June 2009).

39. Ibid.
40. "Olam International Limited: History", *Datamonitor Company Profiles*, 19 August 2008.
41. The Group MD and CEO of Olam, Sunny Verghese said this in an interview with *The Edge*. Rosana Gulzar, "Corporate: Olam taps commodity play appetite", *The Edge*, Singapore, 31 January 2005.
42. Ibid.
43. "Olam Interational Limited: Key Employees and Biographies", *Datamonitor Company Profiles*, 19 August 2008.
44. Interview with Sunny Verghese by the author on 7 July 2009.
45. Ibid.
46. Ibid.
47. Rosana Gulzar, "Corporate: Olam taps commodity play appetite", op. cit.
48. "Simply Outstanding", *Business Times*, 12 March 2007.
49. Case Study prepared by David E. Bell and Mary Shelman, "Olam International", Harvard Business School, 16 December 2008.
50. Interview with Sunny Verghese, op. cit.
51. Ibid.
52. "Redington", <http://www.chanrai.com/redington> (accessed 26 June 2009).
53. Ibid.
54. "History: Redington Group", <http://www.redingtonindia.com/history.asp> (accessed 26 June 2009).
55. Ibid.
56. "Building Professional Management", Milestone panels to celebrate the 150th Anniversary of the Chanrai Group, 2010, op. cit.
57. "EcoProcessors", <http://www.chanrai.com/ecoprocessors> (accessed 26 June 2009).
58. Ibid.
59. "Building Professional Management", op. cit.
60. "Kewalram House: First in a New Generation of Ultra-modern Industrial Developments", *Straits Times*, 3 April 1982.

61. Ibid.
62. "Kewalram Group to build $163m KL office block", *Straits Times*, 24 March 1993.
63. "Kewalram Chanrai launches RM80m apartment project", *Business Times*, 12 March 1997.
64. "Kewalram Group, Filipino firms to build towers in FCC", *Businessworld*, 19 December 1996.
65. Ibid.
66. Tuminah Sapawi, "Blood is Thicker in Business", *Straits Times*, 21 December 1992.
67. Sylvia Wong, "Indian Chamber to Help Members Tackle Succession", *Business Times*, 17 September 1992.
68. Tuminah Sapawi, "Blood is Thicker in Business", op. cit.
69. Ibid.
70. Interview with Sunny Verghese, op. cit.
71. "Building Professional Management", op. cit.
72. Interview with N.G. Chanrai, the KCG Director on 10 September 2009.
73. *Singapore Indian Entrepreneurs*, op. cit., p. 91.
74. "The SICCI-DBS Singapore India Business Awards 2007", in *SICCInsights 83rd Anniversary Special*, a publication of the Singapore Indian Chamber of Commerce and Industry, vol. 4, November 2007.
75. "Philanthropy", Milestone panels to celebrate the 150th Anniversary of the Chanrai Group, op. cit.
76. Ibid.
77. Tan Sung, "A behind-the-scenes mover takes over the helm at Indian Chamber", *Straits Times*, 18 April 1992. The group generated an annual turnover of US$80 million, out of which 70 per cent came from trading.
78. Ibid.
79. Ibid.
80. "Simply Outstanding", *Business Times*, 12 March 2007.
81. Conversation with Sunny Verghese, op. cit.

82. "An Octogenarian who Values Honesty & Fair Play: Mr. M.K. Chanrai", in *Singapore Indian Entrepreneurs*, op. cit., p. 90. R. Jayachandran has been a member of the Board since 1992. He is a qualified Chartered accountant and a business administration graduate from the Harvard University, *Datamonitor Company Profiles*, 19 August 2008.

83. *Singapore Indian Entrepreneurs*, ibid.

84. Ibid.

85. Ibid., p. 91.

86. The increase in the number of tourists from China visiting Mustafa Centre had driven them to employ thirty Chinese-speaking staff in 1998. Ben Dolven, "Retailing: Shoppers' Paradise: A Singapore store's winning strategy: source widely, price low", *Far Eastern Economic Review*, 3 September 1998.

87. "Mustafa Centre's owner Mustaq Ahmed Wins Tourism Entrepreneur of the Year Award", *Channel NewsAsia*, 25 March 2004.

88. Karl Ho, "Big Man in Little India", *Straits Times*, 29 July 2001; Nureza Ahmad, "Mohamed Mustafa and Samsudin Co Pte Ltd.", *singaporeinfopedia*, National Library Board, 23 March 2004, <http://infopedia.nl.sg/articles/SIP_442_2005-02-03.html> (accessed 30 June 2009).

89. Ibid.

90. Kingshuk Nag, "Mustafa all set to enter India", *Times of India*, 30 June 1999.

91. Karl Ho, "Big man in Little India", op. cit.

92. "The Man who Built Mustafa Centre", *Business Times*, Singapore, 30 November 1996.

93. "The Man who Built Mustafa Centre", op. cit.

94. Ibid.

95. Rohaniah Saini, "It's Boom Time for Little India Retailer", *Straits Times*, 8 November 1995.

96. Kalpana Rashiwala, "Mustafa to spend S$25m on Store Expansion", *Straits Times*, 10 December 1997.

97. Kingshuk Nag, "Mustafa All Set to Enter India", *Times of India*, 30 June 1999.

98. Nureza Ahmed, "Mohamed Mustafa and Samsudin Co. Pte. Ltd.", op. cit.

99. "Late-night Shoppers Throng 24-hour Mustafa Centre", *Straits Times*, 6 March 2005.

100. Arti Mulchand, "24-hour Shopping comes to Mustafa's", *Straits Times*, 11 June 2003.

101. Kalpana Rashiwala, "Mustafa Expands Shopping Space by 50,000 sq ft", *Business Times*, 13 August 2004.

102. Ibid.

103. "Mustafa Online", <http://www.mustafa.com.sg/index.asp> (accessed 4 July 2009).

104. "India Outsources Passport Collection", *Today*, 20 January 2009. The two centres appointed by the Indian High Commission are "Quoprro Global Services Pte Ltd." and "Mustafa Air Travel".

105. Kalpana Rashiwala, "Mustafa to Spend S$25m on Store Expansion", *Straits Times*, 10 December 1997.

106. Azhar Khalid, "$250m Annual Sales but no Plans for Mustafa Centre to go Public", *Straits Times*, 27 September 2003.

107. "Late-night Shoppers Throng 24-hour Mustafa Centre", *Straits Times*, 6 March 2005.

108. Azhar Khalid, "$250m Annual Sales but no Plans for Mustafa Centre to go Public", op. cit.

109. S. Tsering Bhalla, "Megastore for India, from Singapore's Little India", *Straits Times*, 28 June 1997.

110. Azhar Khalid, "$250m Annual Sales but no Plans for Mustafa Centre to go Public", op. cit.

111. Quoted from the remarks of Raymond Lim, Minister for Trade and Industry & Foreign Affairs, on his visits to Mohamed Mustafa & Samsuddin Co. Pte. Ltd. and Jumain Sataysfaction Pte. Ltd. on 26 September 2003, <http://www.spring.gov.sg/newsarchive/news/speeches/03_09_26.html> (accessed 30 June 2009).

112. Kalpana Rashiwala, "Mustafa to spend S$25m on store expansion", *Straits Times*, 10 December 1997.

113. Indians had spent an average of S$894 in 1996, second to the South Africans who had spent an average of S$918 in the same year. S. Tsering Bhalla, "Megastore for India", op. cit.

114. "The Man who Built Mustafa Centre", *Business Times*, 30 November 1996.

115. Ibid.

116. The timeline in this case study has been restricted to the beginning of June 2009 and do not take into account the structural changes that have taken place after that. I am grateful to Mrs Vivian Chandran for her kind comments and feedback on the case study.

117. Wayne Arnold, "Singapore's 40 Richest: Riding the Waves", 9 March 2007, <http://www.forbes.com/global/2007/0903/044_print.html> (accessed 29 May 2009).

118. Ibid.

119. Wayne Arnold, "Singapore's 40 Richest: Riding the Waves", 9 March 2007, <http://www.forbes.com/global/2007/0903/044_print.html> (accessed 29 May 2009).

120. Dr Joshua Kuma is the Director (Operations) at the Minerals, Metals and Materials Technology Centre (M3TC) at the Faculty of Engineering, National University of Singapore. He has also been the Corporate & Business Advisor to Chemoil International Pte. Ltd.

121. Interview with Dr Joshua Kuma by the author on 4 June 2009.

122. Wayne Arnold, op. cit.

123. Ibid.

124. "Corporate History", *Chemoil Energy Limited, 2006 Annual Report*, p. 6.

125. Wayne Arnold, op. cit.

126. Ibid.

127. "Corporate History", op. cit.

128. Wayne Arnold, op. cit.

129. "World is Coming to Singapore", Budget Speech 2007 of Tharman Shanmugharatnam, Finance Minister of Singapore, <http://www.mof.gov.sg/budget_2007/budget_speech/subsection4.1.html> (accessed 10 June 2009).

130. Ibid.

131. CNBC's Christine Tan in conversation with Bob Chandran, "Managing Asia on CNBC Podcast: Bob Chandran episode", 7 September 2007, <http://www.podcastdirectory.com/podshows/1890890> (accessed 12 June 2009).

132. "Helios Virtual Tour", <http://www.chemoil.com/default.asp> (accessed 13 June 2009).

133. Interview with Dr Joshua Kuma by the author on 4 June 2009.

134. "Helios Virtual Tour", op. cit.

135. In early 2008, the Company announced addition of new subsidiaries namely Chemoil Middle East DMCC (UAE), George Sea Shipping Corporation Ltd. (Marchall Islands), Cypress Point Pte. Ltd. (Singapore), Saral Shipping Pte. Ltd. (Singapore), and others. "Chemoil Energy Limited Announces Addition of New Subsidiaries", Reuters India, 25 February 2008, <http://in.reuters.com/money/quotes/keyDevelopments?symbol=CHEL.SI&pn=2> (accessed 14 June 2009).

136. *Chemoil Energy Limited, 2006 Annual Report*, p. 18.

137. Ibid.

138. Seng Li Peng, "Chemoil to Expand Fuel Supply to Indian Ports", *Reuters*, 4 June 2009, <http://www.reuters.com/article/GlobalEnergy09/idUSTRE5534B120090604> (accessed 12 June 2009).

139. *2006 Annual Report*, op. cit., pp. 18–19.

140. Ibid.

141. "About us", <http://www.calsoftgroup.com/aboutus/history.html> (accessed 13 June 2009).

142. Interview with Joshua Kuma; op. cit.

143. "Chemoil Energy Limited Unit to acquire California Software Co. Ltd.", Reuters, 21 August 2007, <http://in.reuters.com/money/

quotes/keyDevelopments?symbol=CHEL.SI&pn=3> (accessed 14 June 2009).

144. Interview with Joshua Kuma, op. cit.; *2006 Annual Report*, op. cit., p. 20.

145. *Chemoil Energy Limited, 2006 Annual Report*, p. 19.

146. Interview with Joshua Kuma, op. cit.

147. Christine Tan in conversation with Bob Chandran, op. cit.

148. Sophie Tan and Nesa Subrahmaniyan, "Chemoil Shares Fall after Chief Executive's Death", 8 January 2008, <http://www.bloomberg.com/apps/news?pid=20601087&sid=aYhaKxnO.fZg&refer=home> (accessed 14 June 2009).

149. "Singapore-listed Chemoil Appoints New CEO", Reuters, 13 January 2008, <http://www.reuters.com/article/rbssEnergyNews/idUSSGC00160220080113> (accessed 29 May 2009); "Chemoil appoints new CEO", *Asiaone News*, 14 January 2008, <http://www.asiaone.com/News/Latest%2BNews/Business/Story/A1Story20080114-44885.html> (accessed 14 June 2009).

150. Jennifer Tan, "Chemoil CEO says Eyes Acquisitions, New Markets", Media Monitoring, *Huntington Communications*, 26 February 2009.

151. *Delivering the Power, Chemoil Energy Limited, 2008 Annual Report*, p. 25.

152. Ibid.

153. Seng Li Peng, "Chemoil to Expand Fuel Supply to Indian Ports", *Reuters*, 4 June 2009, <http://www.reuters.com/article/GlobalEnergy09/idUSTRE5534B120090604> (accessed 12 June 2009).

154. Ibid.

155. Chan Chao Peh, "Managing with Passion", *The Edge*, Singapore, 26 February 2007.

CONCLUSION:
SURGING FORWARD

The changing historical trajectories of Singapore have had enormous influence on the growth and development of the Indian business communities in the city-state, both from economic and sociological perspectives. In the course of their ascent in the development ladder, the economies of Southeast Asia witnessed shifts in growth paradigms with increased globalization of capital, rapid transnational mobilization of human resources as well as the new requirements of the contemporary knowledge-based economy. Though with different parameters and backed by increasing interest of the Indian Government in connecting with the successful overseas Indians, the new age has initiated the re-emergence of inter-firm and intra-firm linkages as in the colonial diasporic networks, thus setting the scene for powerful economic synergies between different Indian ethnic settlements in Southeast Asia and the Indian subcontinent.

In the light of the new age developments and the technological revolution, conventional concepts of communities and networks have been seriously challenged. The corporatization of business that has emerged at large among the Indian business community is much diffused from the nuances of caste, region, sect or religion that had earlier bonded business and trade so closely with financial ties and product markets. What has also emerged at present are the business networking activities that are based more on economic considerations irrespective of geographical locations and interpersonal relationships with a much wider scope of activity coordination. This has helped form real and virtual or imaginative communities based on professions, services, products, alumni bodies or shared neighbourhood spaces for business transactions. These have also emerged as overlaps between social organizations and business networks that are neither linguistically based nor with typical regional flavours. Yet, a certain sense of a community prevails, with an essence of ethnicity, in a mixture of different interest groups. Thus, the Indian, Malay and Chinese Chambers of Commerce in Singapore represent to a large extent, the business interests of different communities and participate actively in the shaping and restructuring policies in the city-state.

In the present context of study, one might also perceive the inter-ethnic business relationships between the Indian and Chinese communities in the Singaporean experience. The Chinese have been the largest racial component of the nation state and dominant actors in the political, cultural and economic systems in the administration. Their relationship with the Indian communities has largely been perceived as a relation between the demographic majority and a minority. It might be relevant to discuss the negotiation of space and identification of business interests of both the ethnicities, keeping in view the mindset of profitability as a primary interest of any business initiative irrespective of race, language or creed, as elsewhere in the world. However, geopolitics and genealogy are also factors in determining the degree to which different ethnic groups have interacted over time.

The Chinese communities of Southeast Asia, or *Nanyang*[1] as they have been called, have very often been incorrectly regarded, just as their Indian counterparts, as a homogeneous community.

Very much like the ethnic Indians, the *hua qiao*[2] not only belonged to different regions of China, but also spoke different languages and had unique characteristics of their respective regions. Both these communities formed a large part of the labouring masses in the nineteenth and the early twentieth century migrating from the southern coastal regions of their respective countries. A comparative socio-linguistic research project merits the attention of scholars, but requires a different context of study. What may be noted, however, is that both these groups were multidimensional in their own rights with a kind of homogeneity imposed by their respective connections with two of the most distinguished civilizations of the world.

In the operation of market forces, the interactions between the business interests of the two groups were, traditionally speaking, not overtly competitive, but, in fact, accommodative to a large extent, except for certain participants in the retail sectors and very small competing businesses like the corner shops and the like. This was not due to the intimidating effect of sheer majority in numbers of one community over the other, but due to their participation in different sectors of business activities. These two communities had been active participants in the "spice trade" networks of much earlier times, which extended from the Pacific in the East to the Mediterranean in the West, the Southeast Asian region being the main theatre of the commercial activities. Colonial capitalism reshuffled many established norms, yet the interactions persisted with changed permutations and new combinations with the Europeans. This produced diversifications of the two communities and their participation in different sectors of business activities. Whereas the Chinese entrepreneurial community emerged as big names in the Southeast Asian economies in banking, shipping, insurance, plantations, agro-business, real estate and others,[3] Indians, to a large extent, remained as a trading community until recently. If the ethnic Indian businessmen happened to diversify, which they did to a considerable extent in the post-colonial phase, they preferred to choose a destination abroad, which was cost-effective and offered a bigger market. Being participants in the trading sector for generations and with their consequent exposure to different global markets, such transnational ventures are not surprising given their knowledge of market characteristics and price variations of different regions. In fact, true to the essence of trading capabilities, where merchants and businessmen are constantly on the lookout for competitive sourcing avenues as well as profitable markets, the Indian trading community had long been active in the global theatre of commerce in a way that was more progressive than many other business communities.

On the other hand, the accumulation of wealth and entrepreneurial ventures of the ethnic Chinese had been quite remarkable. They were successful in filling the economic void created by the departure of the colonialists[4] and consequently strengthened their economic status. They successfully modernized and at the same time, preserved the elements of tradition. Thus the terms *guanxi* (links — the basis of relationships), *towkay* (boss) or *kongsi* (company) have been readily entrenched in the lingua franca of the business operations in the region. Ian Rae and Morgen Witzel have quite pertinently observed:

> The Huaqiao business community, despite being, for the most part, modern, efficient, rapid and with huge resources is still largely organised along traditional lines. It shares certain fundamental traits with business in China; equally, some Overseas Chinese businesses are, apart from a little local colour, indistinguishable from comparable concerns in London, New York or Sydney.[5]

The Indians, on the other hand, adapted and reconciled more readily to the colonial notions of the market exchanges, though the essence of distinct ethnic identities remained to some extent, as has already been discussed in the preceding chapters. Thus, the transition and progress of both the diasporic business communities shaped up distinctly and differently in Singapore as in the Southeast Asian region more broadly. What might be noted in this context is that the overseas Chinese were more closely associated with the Chinese Government and investments in China than was the case with the overseas Indians' relations with the Indian Government until recently, when Indian policy-makers turned their focus to the twenty million overseas Indians scattered all over the globe, perhaps drawing lessons from the effective accommodative approach of the Chinese policy.[6]

It is interesting to note that the language of the market interactions was "Bazaar Malay" and not English, as one would have thought would be, even as late as the 1950s and the 1960s.[7] English language came to be more popular only at a later stage. Chinese and Indian businessmen as also the European planters (during colonial times) picked up the "Bazaar Malay", which could be learnt easily.[8] The Indian communities, as has been discussed by R.A. Brown,[9] were indispensible players in the inland distribution network. The items of the trade were decided by colonial imperatives, which determined points of business contacts in the entrepot areas like Singapore and other port cities. Nothing better exemplifies this than the Sindhi business network throughout Southeast Asia.

Intense competition between the two ethnic business communities has not been a characteristic feature in the Singaporean economy at any point of time. Since 1965, as has been mentioned earlier, many of the Indian businessmen sought entrepreneurial avenues abroad, both within and beyond the periphery of Southeast Asian waters. One could, therefore, argue that a certain lack of communication and interest in business cooperation between the two ethnic groups prevailed until very recently. What had been notable previously was the absence of any joint ventures or collaborations cutting across ethnic lines. It is only in the present economic scenario of rapid globalization, when the significance and magnitude of the manufacturing sector has been overhauled by the service sector and the knowledge economy, that an assimilation of approaches has been witnessed. Bigger business ventures include the traditional KCG and the more recently founded KSP holdings (refer to Chapter 3), have among their managerial team and Board of Directors Chinese professionals or entrepreneurs, thus changing the paradigm of traditional business principles and systems. A recent SICCI initiative of organizing Mandarin classes for its members and others reveals the building up of a greater interest in cross-community interactions. This phenomenon, added to the India-China growth trajectory, might be significant in terms of bringing the nations closer to each other with Singapore playing an important role in the dialogue. This in turn might accrue advantages to the progress and economic transition of the Asian region as a whole.

Some of the most serious challenges faced by both the Chinese and the Indian business communities are the issues dealing with leadership and managing inheritance for families with substantial wealth. The social and kinship networks between the owners and the employees that have played an influential role in Chinese businesses have been similar in certain respects to the traditional patterns of Indian family business concerns as well. Since families have significantly dominated and controlled a large number of the corporations in the region, the question of family businesses and their survival has inevitably reflected on the progress of the ethnic business communities. Family feuds and inept management of wealth as well as inability to provide cost-effective solutions, swift response to customers' demands or appropriate planning of new investments have been some of the most pertinent challenges in the face of competition with the multinationals in the increasingly globalized economic arena. Several studies have been conducted to examine the patterns of Chinese family businesses — whether they have been increasingly adapting to "professionally managed family-ruled" business practice[10] or have successfully made the transition to multinational enterprises.[11] However, similar studies are lacking for the exploration of the ethnic Indian business communities in the region, leaving ample scope for a comparative analysis in the survival tactics and development of the family business concerns of the two communities. If on the one hand, there has been a successful inheritance and management of family business for about one-and-a-half centuries like in the case of the KCG, as has been discussed in one of the case studies (see Chapter 5), there are also less successful inheritance and managerial examples like the P. Govindasamy Pillai (PGP) family business that started almost eighty years ago as a small shop and enlarged into a million dollar business in Singapore that breathed its last after its component firms were shut down recently after lying dormant for a decade.[12] Ramachandran, the eldest son of the patriarch, had been a prominent figure in the business and social circles of Singapore, as has been mentioned earlier. He was also the youngest President of the SICCI at the age of thirty-four in 1966[13] who made significant contributions to the development of the Indian Chamber.

    In the extremely competitive market scenario in contemporary times greater degree of professionalism and corporate governance may be desirable for the Indian business entities to progress and prosper. Corporate governance has the advantages of conjunction of mind and skills where the decision-making is a consultative process and the continuity of decisions and consequences are the joint responsibilities of the management. Delegation of authority can come with proper checks and balances to prevent its misuse and the progress of the decisions taken can be monitored to see if the overall corporate objectives have been achieved. In an individual business entity, decision-making rests with one or two persons and professional talent pool is limited. Family business entities, which are what most of the Indian business firms are, face this limitation where the delegation of responsibility and authority is restricted and depends solely on the attitude and the aptitude of the owner. Profitable growth for a firm is also achieved when the boundaries of the core business are expanded to its adjacent space and a formula for profitability is achieved. This would require a broader vision and a global mindset apart from the willingness to expand and prosper. It would also demand certain risk-taking capacity. The successful formula then derived should be repeated along with taking advantage of the learning curve effects.[14]

Ethnic Indian business also faced great difficulties in matters of trade finance. Indians traders, in their ventures in the unchartered waters of lesser known geographical terrains, and making most of the unexploited resources and contacts, required a substantial amount of risk capital to be invested in the business. The banks in Singapore have usually been conservative in their approach and have preferred to support and finance the asset-based businesses, a sector in which most of the Chinese were involved in the region. Thus, the Chinese business received an advantage over the Indian business communities in matters of raising capital and finance locally.

It might be interesting to consider a comparison between Singaporean Indian business concerns and those that have originated on the Indian soil. In the face of a recent surge in relations between the businessmen from the subcontinent and their diasporic counterparts in Singapore, and the consequent intermingling of the two on a common ground, it might be of significance to glance at the relationship of the business structures and operations in perspectives of two offshoots of identical genealogies. According to Helen B. Lamb, the growth pattern of the Indian enterprise reflects "the gradual emergence of industrial enterprise from a background of highly developed commercial capitalism having roots deep in the past".[15] Indian entrepreneurship was primarily rooted in the legacies of caste, clan and other social demarcations, as these concepts were historically based on occupational structures. The *vaisya* or the trading caste in that context had more ready access and skills to finance and enterprise both from the perspectives of heredity and business acumen as well as dominant ethnic networks. During the colonial period, the managing agency system initiated growth for many middlemen who could accumulate wealth and invest prudently in the "colonial industrialization" process that was ushered in the twentieth century. These businessmen predominantly engaged themselves in speculative trade.[16] There were also attempts to reverse the process of "de-industrialization" through nationalistic endeavours in sporadic setting up of enterprises, which also initiated the process of dilution of caste strictures related to it. Based on these foundations, the private sector big corporate groups that emerged in the post-independence period were patriarchal institutions, both ownership and management mostly resting within the family. They flourished and operated within the periphery of the huge domestic market of the subcontinent keeping in tune with the national policies of protectionism, and relentlessly involved in nexus with the political forces, well manifested in the interactions with the "license-raj" that prevailed — the inevitable legacy of the British bureaucracy that had persisted within the Indian administrative system.

The reversal of the protectionist economic policies since the 1990s through the liberalizing and opening up of the Indian economy, coupled with the realization of the human resource potential of the country accelerated the global growth of the Indian technology and service sectors. This change of mindset has prompted many entrepreneurs to reorient their expansive policies and venture abroad, both in service as well as manufacturing sectors, which ushered in a new chapter of growth in Asia and the world, the like of which could not have been envisaged in the 1970s or the 1980s of the past century.

The ethnic Indian trading community in Singapore, on the other hand, has had to contend with the forces of the global market right from the beginning of the post-independence era. Tables had started turning since the induction and participation of the MNEs and the GLCs in the economic system of the country when the traditional business communities, whether Indian or Chinese, began to lose out in the competition. Ethnic business concerns also lost ambitious and efficient manpower to the MNCs and GLCs who offered better wages and more professional work environment. Some revival from the 1980s onwards was witnessed when the Government began to take steps to promote the SMEs. However, modernized and technically advanced businesses, in some cases, also provided the inducement to upgrade traditional concerns.

The ethnic network links with their homeland regions in India had been mostly broken in the post-colonial era in separate political entities. In addition, it had all altered the colonial market patterns and products, and the small size of the domestic market was also a serious challenge. The survival and progress of these communities have already been discussed in detail in the second chapter. What might be important to mention here is the difference in the growth patterns of these business entities, which had to diversify and compete globally and look beyond the nation's territory to expand further, in contrast to their domestic market-oriented Indian counterparts. Only a few, however, emerged as global players, with the rest remaining content with small and middle-level trading activities. Many have managed to move up the value chain, for others it is still competing among one another for thin margins. There are some who want to venture into new areas, but are not decisive about what can be done professionally and technically; others have the professional knowledge, but lack adequate capital.

The entry of the new Indian migrants in the recent decades has resulted in a reshuffle of the ethnic Indian participation in different economic sectors. It has also motivated modifications and adjustments in the traditional mindset regarding the business activities in Singapore. Also decades of communication gap between the two groups has resulted in a lack of awareness of each other, which has posed a major challenge in interactions and coordination of interests between them. According to Vijay Iyenger, "The difference (between the two communities) would be in terms of diversity of reach. The older community who were in Singapore doing business were using Singapore as an entrepot ... Now, they are using Singapore because of its connectivity, whether it is shipping, or ease of doing business."[17] However, the differences are much more complex. One might argue that there is an ardent need for a change in the traditional mindset of the local Indian businessmen. Corporatization of family firms, globalization of operations to non-traditional markets and moving away from sectors of traditional trading could help in transforming the general mindset. At the same time there is a need for development of better understanding of local factors in the business world. The dearth of scholarship and research on successful business models, sustainability issues and inter-generational changes are some of the factors that account for the void in the communication amongst the business fraternity. However, the same cultural roots and similar customs and traditions, together with encouragement of platforms of networking and intermingling would be significant steps to help induce the synergies and overcome the transitional phase of restrained interactions. In the words of Inderjit Singh, Member of Parliament in Singapore, "I feel if we can bring both groups together, we have a good platform to allow everyone to succeed and benefit from each others' network. We have yet to see closer integration and interaction among the two groups."[18]

The Singapore Indian Chamber of Commerce and Industry, having emerged as the most important of the business organizations among the ethnic Indian communities in Singapore, has often been given the unintentional responsibility of acting as an umbrella organization to incorporate varied interest groups. The expectations may be justified going by its long history of active interactions with the government at different periods of history and its spokesmanship for the different groups. However, it faces the challenges of assimilating diversified business interests both from the perspectives of varied regional identification that is, from the northern and the southern regions of the subcontinent; as well as differences between the local entrepreneurs and the new migrants. The challenges are formidable indeed, keeping in view the changing mindset of the community, both in terms of changing business sectors as well as perceptions of economic and social dimensions. In addition, in order to sustain itself as a significant business organization which has relevance to the bigger Singaporean community, SICCI has had to develop distinct policy initiatives which serve the larger economic interests of the nation. Starting with its efforts on the ASEAN-CCI initiatives way back in 1978, and its recent subsidiary arm, "EDC@SICCI", it has been working with government agencies like SPRING Singapore, International Enterprise (IE) Singapore, Economic Development Board (EDB), Infocomm Development Authority of Singapore (IDA), and others. Besides, as we have seen earlier, it has been instrumental in providing platforms for dialogue between the Singapore and the Indian Governments, as well as other Indian Chambers of Commerce or business delegations from India. The task of engaging economic partnerships and collaborations, a mission that SICCI has been fruitfully involved in, has been further accelerated by facilitating such networking through the prism of diasporic connectivity in the region. One such significant step had been taken by the Chamber in organizing and hosting the PBD Conference in Singapore in 2008 along with the Ministry of Overseas Indian Affairs (MOIA), India, but much remains to be done. It could assume the role of a "pilot vessel" in steering Indian entrepreneurship to the relatively unchartered waters of Southeast Asia, benefitting the nation of Singapore and consolidating the diasporic communities of the region at the same time.

When Gunnar Myrdal penned his *Asian Drama*,[19] he gave it the subtitle of *An Inquiry into the Poverty of Nations*. That was back in 1968, when the post-colonial journey had just begun for many of the Asian nations reeling under the myriads of experimental constructiveness. Little did Myrdal envisage the changes of the post-Cold War era into the twenty-first century, when the poverty-stricken, corrupt nations could have managed to attract the attention of the entire world, replacing the Euro-centric notions with Asian paradigms. The rise of Asia and awareness of its historicity has brought about a new consciousness, which has generated a spirit of optimism and success for the present generation and helped to bind them into a kind of globalized regionalism, which would comprise again a different and detailed study in its own right.

In the refashioning of the Indian identity in the Southeast Asian region, and in the optimism of global economic resurgence for the subcontinent, one perhaps tends to underestimate the participation of Indians in the reshuffling of economic structures at different periods of time. If "power has, to a degree, been a geographical concept, shaped by the ability to route exports and imports", as has been opined by Michael B. Miller,[20] and has helped in the production and control of "modern wealth and productive capacity",[21] that power, through the prism of economic interactions, has also been greatly instrumental in promoting the intra-Asian cultural and ideological exchanges across the Indian Ocean through the ages. Unravelling the historicity of some of these encounters and their long-term implications will help to redefine the structure of the growth trajectory in the contemporary setting and of endeavours in the future.

Notes

1. *Nanyang*, literally meaning "south ocean" in Chinese, is what the Chinese consider as the area between the south of China and north of Australia and the ocean space between the Indian Ocean in the west and the Pacific in the east.

2. *Hua qiao* was a term used for "overseas Chinese". It has recently been modified to *huaren* (ethnic Chinese) or *huayi* (Chinese descent) denoting greater diasporic ties with the homeland. Leo Suryadinata, *Understanding the Ethnic Chinese in Southeast Asia* (Singapore: Institute of Southeast Asian Studies, 2007), p. 56.

3. Ibid., refer to the table on the leading tycoons of Singapore as recent as in 1995, p. 40.

4. Ibid., p. 79.

5. Ian Rae and Morgen Witzel, *The Overseas Chinese of South East Asia* (Houndmills, Basingstoke, Hampshire, New York: Palgrave Macmillan, 2008), p. 78.

6. Wang Gungwu, "India and Indians in East Asia: An Overview", in *Rising India and Indian Communities in Southeast Asia*, edited by K. Kesavapany et al. (Singapore: Institute of Southeast Asian Studies, 2008), pp. 4–5.

7. This has been revealed by many businessmen, who have had market interactions during that age, during the course of their conversations with the author.

8. Rae and Witzel, *The Overseas Chinese of South East Asia*, op. cit., pp. 83–84.

9. Rajeswary Ampalavanar Brown, *Capital and Entrepreneurship in South-East Asia* (Houndmills, Basingstoke, Hampshire and London: The Macmillan Press Ltd. and New York, St. Martin's Press, INC., 1994).

10. Lai Si Tsui-Auch, "The Professionally Managed Family Ruled Enterprise: Ethnic Chinese Business in Singapore", *Journal of Management Studies* 41, no. 4 (June 2004): 693–723.

11. Wee-Liang Tan and Siew Tong Fock, "Coping with Growth Transitions: The Case of Chinese Family Businesses in Singapore", *Family Business Review* 14, no. 2 (2001): 123–39.

12. K.C. Vijayan, "End of an Era for Iconic PGP Family Business", *Straits Times*, 22 June 2009.

13. Ibid.

14. "Repeatability Allows the Company to Systematize the Growth"; Chris Zook and James Allen, "Growth Outside the Core", *Harvard Business Review*, December 2003, p. 2.

15. Helen B. Lamb, "The Indian Business Communities and the Evolution of an Industrialist Class", *Pacific Affairs* 28, no. 2 (June 1955): 102.

16. Asim Chaudhuri, "Conglomerate Big Business Groups in India: Some Traits of Tycoon Capitalism", *Social Scientist* 8, no. 7 (February 1980): 38–51.

17. Interview with Vijay Iyenger, MD of Agrocorp International Pte. Ltd. and also the former Chairman of SICCI on 19 January 2009.
18. Inderjit Singh, Member of Parliament, Singapore, in answers to a questionnaire prepared by the author, 4 July 2008.
19. Gunnar Myrdal, *Asian Drama: An Inquiry into the Poverty of Nations* (London: Penguin Books, 1968).
20. Michael B. Miller, "The Business Trip: Maritime Networks in the Twentieth Century", *The Business History Review* 77, no. 1 (Spring 2003): 2.
21. Ibid.

APPENDICES

Appendix I

Top Singapore's Exports to India

SL No	HS CODE	DESCRIPTION	YEAR								
			IN US$ MILLIONS								
			2000–01	2001–02	2002–03	2003–04	2004–05	2005–06	2006–07	2007–08
1	27	mineral fuels, mineral oils and products of their distillation; bituminous substances; mineral waxes	5.54	14.52	9.42	5.29	10.54	15.68	1099.77	2652.63
2	29	organic chemicals	113.43	131.69	112.59	186.54	359.39	412.65	548.99	642.69
3	32	tanning or dyeing extracts; tanning and their deri dyes, pigments and other colouring matter, paints and ver; putty and other mastics; inks	7.27	8.83	11.72	12.72	21.47	24.55	28.64	32.93
4	38	miscellaneous chemical products	20.85	27.36	22.30	33.25	34.99	42.87	60.35	69.6
5	39	plastic and articles thereof	39.74	56.11	52.92	81.07	107.49	122.40	135.76	199.92
6	40	rubber and articles thereof	9.82	9.69	8.68	10.51	16.23	17.74	21.48	24.40
7	48	paper and paperboard; articles of paper pulp or of paperboard	16.25	17.68	6.46	4.66	9.56	4.62	5.27	15.52
8	49	printed books, newspapers, pictures and other products of printing industry, manuscripts, typescripts and plans	75.00	105.06	82.29	133.13	175.53	258.38	317.79	303.18

Sl	HS	Product								
9	71	natural or cultured pearls, precious or semi-precious stones, pre-metals, clad with pre-metals and articles thereof; immitation jewellery; coins	41.64	13.24	22.19	24.86	39.46	19.66	17.63	35.62
10	72	iron and steel	23.61	29.95	25.42	44.50	65.70	54.31	78.40	95.92
	73	articles of iron and steel	9.92	13.55	18.80	22.04	32.87	51.02	66.73	76.63
11	84	nuclear reactors, boilers, machinery and mechanical appliances; parts thereof	475.30	372.94	418.07	575.62	778.72	1014.73	1229.05	1621.76
12	85	electrical machinery and equipment and parts thereof; sound recorders and reproducers, television image and sound recorders and reproducers and parts	346.67	277.42	305.16	432.65	528.72	657.39	955.42	932.32
13	88	aircraft, spacecraft and parts thereof	11.41	9.44	100.66	95.11	46.12	131.44	115.63	125.44
14	89	ships, boats and floating structures	33.80	19.71	70.42	219.45	173.01	216.61	195.21	702.11
15	90	optical, photographic cinematographic measuring, checking precision, medical or surgical intst and appratus parts and accessories thereof	58.51	53.07	68.32	82.88	110.87	144.17	183.28	266.8
		Total of top export products from Singapore to India	1288.76	1160.26	1335.42	1964.28	2510.67	3188.22	5059.40	7797.47
		Total Singapore exports to India	1463.91	1304.09	1434.81	2085.37	2651.4	3353.77	5485.26	117.64
		Exchange rate of 1 US$ to Indian RS.	45.6844	47.6919	48.3953	45.9516	44.9315	44.2735	45.2849	40.2607

Top India's Exports to Singapore

SL No	HS CODE	DESCRIPTION	YEAR								
			2000–01	2001–02	2002–03	2003–04	2004–05	2005–06	2006–07	2007–08	
			IN US$ MILLIONS								
1	3	fish and crustaceans, molluscs and other aquatic invertabrates	17.42	17.82	16.3	15.82	20.58	18.90	25.40	25.86
2	8	edible fruits and nuts; peel or citrus fruits or melons	6.27	5.87	5.01	4.63	5.63	7.68	6.71	7.83
3	9	coffee, tea, mate and spices	7.96	6.10	5.80	5.94	6.84	5.44	11.14	20.75
4	10	cereals	9.12	17.85	19.73	11.48	9.52	15.11	14.23	20.59
5	12	oil seeds and olea fruits; misc grains, seeds and fruits; industrial or medicinal plants; straw and fodder	7.43	4.36	4.82	4.88	8.75	7.91	8.77	9.45
6	23	residue and waste from the food industrial; prepared animal fodder	75.91	71.93	23.24	45.22	46.72	75.00	35.09	19.50
7	24	tobacco and manufactured tobacco substitute	7.56	8.06	8.82	9.15	9.39	9.26	15.39	9.28
8	25	salt; sulphur; earths and stones; plastering materials, lime and cement	6.00	4.61	3.46	3.31	2.45	3.86	34.13	3.03
9	27	mineral fuels, mineral oils and products of their distillation; bituminous substances; mineral waxes	0.05	0.31	309.64	914.32	1874.69	2198.30	3380.90	4022.97

10	organic chemicals	47.18	40.21	47.79	42.99	135.13	213.65	200.88	211.20
11	pharmaceutical products	10.82	12.37	15.00	17.18	17.41	13.81	12.31	22.32
12	tanning or dyeing extracts; tanning and their deri dyes, pigments and other colouring matter; paints and ver; putty and other mastics; inks	14.73	11.78	13.05	21.62	16.82	17.64	18.99	20.87
13	essential oils and resinoids; perfumery, cosmetics or toiletaries	8.38	4.51	5.65	6.97	8.21	13.23	16.93	25.95
14	miscellaneous chemical products	11.79	17.41	19.13	27.61	35.75	42.50	22.13	27.88
15	plastic and articles thereof	14.55	6.83	8.10	8.98	22.14	22.75	24.24	31.45
16	rubber and articles thereof	9.02	7.30	9.30	24.97	11.36	12.38	13.86	14.48
17	silk	8.36	9.71	9.74	13.63	14.20	10.99	7.12	6.76
18	cotton	26.29	15.48	14.26	17.40	16.62	14.23	12.08	15.52
19	manmade filaments	10.30	18.03	54.59	58.49	38.73	18.41	12.25	21.66
20	articles of apparel and clothing accessories, knitted or corcheted	10.95	7.86	13.64	10.96	10.34	13.37	14.85	20.12
21	articles of apparel and clothing accessories, not knitted or corcheted	26.2	21.89	30.68	31.01	30.18	30.19	38.73	30.59
22	natural or cultured pearls, precious or semi-precious stones, pre-metals, clad with pre-metals and articles thereof, immitation jewellery; coins	121.51	123.57	259.78	195.38	567.76	1246.02	152.76	218.62

continued on next page

SL No	HS CODE	DESCRIPTION	YEAR							
			IN US$ MILLIONS							
			2000–01	2001–02	2002–03	2003–04	2004–05	2005–06	2006–07	2007–08
23	72	iron and steel	18.95	7.13	17.35	30.54	41.71	45.82	24.17	27.81
24	73	articles of iron and steel	17.05	22.73	29.02	38.49	42.40	45.18	57.92	66.37
25	74	copper and articles thereof	7.48	2.84	3.32	11.2	49.74	64.86	187.67	148.31
26	76	aluminium and articles thereof	82.50	108.72	91.28	49.77	94.28	108.36	198.60	221.49
27	84	nuclear reactors, boilers, machinery and mechanical appliances; parts thereof	46.16	76.43	70.38	90.05	190.97	151.83	216.93	238.65
28	85	electrical machinery and equipment and parts thereof; sound recorders and reproducers, television image and sound recorders and reproducers and parts	114.53	103.39	123.46	111.89	127.61	162.63	228.57	265.01
29	89	ships, boats and floating structures	8.06	0.09	1.08	24.24	143.34	447.14	329.64	535.40
30	90	optical, photographic cinematographic measuring, checking precision, medical or surgical intst and appratus parts and accessories thereof	9.62	14.66	17.95	31.18	49.92	53.06	67.05	98.99
31	99	miscellaneous goods	20.11	100.30	59.1	120.53	208.28	128.58	468.87	458.41
		Total of top export products from India to Singapore	782.26	870.15	1310.47	1999.83	3857.47	5218.09	5858.31	6867.12
		Total India's exports to Singapore	877.11	972.31	1421.58	2124.83	4000.61	5425.29	6064.19	7367.54
		Exchange rate of 1 US$ to Indian RS	45.6844	47.6919	48.3953	45.9516	44.9315	44.2735	45.2849	40.2607

Source: Based on "Export: Country-wise all commodities", Export Import Data Bank, Department of Commerce, Government of India, 29 December 2008, <http://commerce.nic.in/eidb/ecntcom.asp> (accessed 29 December 2008).

Appendix II

Chanrai Family Geneology

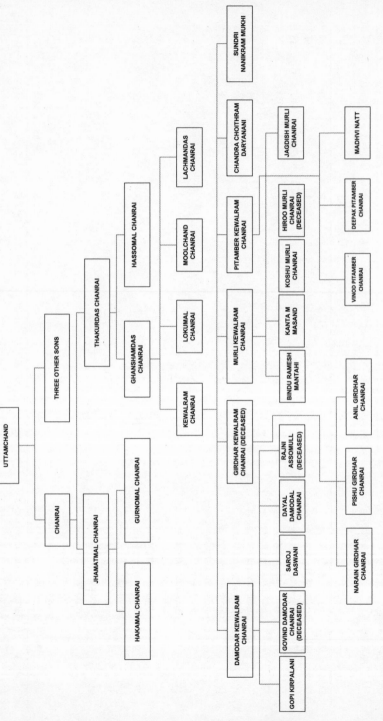

Source: N.G. Chanrai, Director, Kewalram Chanrai Group.

SELECT BIBLIOGRAPHY

Official Records

Company Information, Products and Services. Singapore: Kompass South East Asia Ltd., Singapore, 2008.

Directory on Malaya, 1927–29, 1931–37, containing fullest information of Straits Settlements, Federated Malay States [and] Unfederated Malay States. Singapore: Lithographers Ltd., 1927–37.

General Household Survey 2005: Socio-demographic and Economic Characteristics. Singapore: Department of Statistics, 2006.

Jarman, Robert L., ed. *Annual Reports of the Straits Settlements, 1855–1941*. Slough, U.K.: Archive Editions, 1998.

Leow Bee Geok. *Census of Population 2000: Demographic Characteristics*. Statistical Release 1. Singapore: Department of Statistics, Ministry of Trade and Industry, 2001.

Malayan Union. *Advisory Council Proceedings*. British Military Administration, November 1945–March 1946.

Report of the High Level Committee on the Indian Diaspora. New Delhi, India: Indian Council for World Affairs, Ministry of External Affairs, December 2001.

Singapore Legislative Council. *Proceedings of the Legislative Council: Colony of Singapore*. Singapore: Government Printing Office, 1948–55.

Straits Settlements. *Circulars in force on 1st January, 1936*. Singapore: Government Printing Office, 1936.

Straits Settlements Government Gazettes. Singapore: Mission Press, 1858–1942.

Straits Settlements, Trade Commission. *Report of the Commission appointed by His Excellency the Governor of the Straits Settlements to enquire into and report on the trade of the colony, 1933–1934.* Singapore Government, 1934.

Directories

SICCI's Membership Directory, 2007–2008. Singapore: Singapore Indian Chamber of Commerce and Industry, 2008.

Singapore Small Business Directory, <http://www.sgsmallbiz.com/chutney-cafe-link-2188.html> (accessed 7 April 2009).

Times Business Directory of Singapore. 128th ed. Singapore: Marshall Cavendish Business Information Private Limited, 2009.

Oral History Recordings

Behramgore Ratanshaw Vakil. Oral History Recordings. Accession no. 000297. National Archives of Singapore.

Jaswant Singh Bajaj. Oral History Recordings. Accession no. 000167. National Archives of Singapore.

Jumabhoy, Rajabali. Oral History Recordings. Accession no. 000074. National Archives of Singapore.

Kothari, Girishchandra. Oral History Recordings. Accession no. A000549. National Archives of Singapore.

Melwani, Bhagwan H. Oral History Recordings. Accession no. 000146. National Archives of Singapore.

Muthuvellu, Arumuga. Oral History Recordings (in Tamil). Accession no. A001175/04, Reel no. 3. National Archives of Singapore.

Nair, Karunakaran. Oral History Recordings (in Tamil). Accession no. 001177. National Archives of Singapore.

Nomanbhoy, Moez. Oral History Recordings. Accession no. 000823. National Archives of Singapore.

Paramanayagam, Muthiahpillai. Oral History Recordings (in Tamil). Accession no. B001285. National Archives of Singapore.

M. Ramachandra. Oral History Recordings (in Tamil). Accession no. 001122. National Archives of Singapore.

Rutton Patel. Oral History Recordings. Accession no. 000302. National Archives of Singapore.

Shah, Devji Gopaldas. Oral History Recordings. Accession no. A000796. National Archives of Singapore.

Shah, Kantilal Jamnadas. Oral History Recordings. Accession no. 000094. National Archives of Singapore.

Rethnavelu Suppiah. Oral History Recordings (in Tamil). Accession no. 001161/03, Reel no. 1. National Archives of Singapore.

Reports and Publications of the Chambers of Commerce

Archival materials (unpublished) of the Sindhi Merchants Association.

Inauguration of the SICCI Building & Launch of EDC@SICCI. Singapore: Singapore Indian Chamber of Commerce and Industry, 8 March 2008.

India-ASEAN Partnership Agenda. Confederation of Indian Industry, 2008.

Nattukottai Chamber of Commerce. *Annual Report for 1989* (in Tamil).

Post-Conference Review. *PBD Singapore: Towards a Dynamic Diaspora*, 9–11 October 2008. Singapore Indian Chamber of Commerce and Industry (SICCI), Ministry of Overseas Indian Affairs, New Delhi (MOIA), Confederation of Indian Industries (CII), 2008.

Puru Shotam, Nirmala. "A monograph commemorating the 60th anniversary of the Singapore Indian Chamber of Commerce". Singapore: Singapore Indian Chamber of Commerce and Industry, unpublished, 1985.

Sindhi Association. *Fourteenth International Sindhi Sammelan.* Commemorative booklet. Singapore, 27–29 July 2007.

Singapore Indian Chamber of Commerce and Industry (SICCI). *Fortieth Anniversary Souvenir Programme.* 17 November 1977.

———. *Sixtieth Anniversary Memento.* 3 December 1985.

———. *Trading with Singapore, Special 60th Anniversary Issue of the SICCI.* Singapore: SICCI, 1986.

———. *SICCI's 80th Anniversary volume, 1924–2004.* Singapore: SICCI, 2004.

———. *SICCI's Membership Directory, 2007–2008.* Singapore: SICCI, 2008.

———. *Annual Reports, 2004–2005; 2005–2006; 2007–2008; 2008–2009.* Singapore: SICCI, various years.

———. *Report for the Year 1936, 1937, 1946, 1947, 1948, 1949, 1950, 1951, 1952, 1953, 1954, 1955, 1956, 1957, 1958, 1966.* Singapore: SICCI, various years.

Singapore: Your Business Partner for India, 2005/2006. Singapore: FICCI, East & Asia Pacific Trade & Industry Publications Pte. Ltd., 2006.

"Trade Bulletins issued by the Indian Chamber of Commerce", 1947, 1948 (for members only). Unpublished.

Newspapers and Periodicals

Business Times
Business World
Dow Jones International News
Entrepolis Daily
Far Eastern Economic Review

India News (a monthly newsletter published by the High
    Commission of India, Singapore)
India Se
Overseas Indian (e-magazine of MOIA)
New Nation
Tamil Murasu (in Tamil)
The Edge, Singapore
The *Malay Mail*
The *Straits Times*
The *Times of India*
Today

Books

Abraham, Meera. *Two Medieval Merchant Guilds of South India*. South
    Asian Studies, No. XVIII. New Delhi: Manohar, 1988.
Acharya, Amitav. *Singapore's Foreign Policy: The Search for Regional
    Order*. Singapore: World Scientific Publishing Co. Pte. Ltd.,
    2008.
Alatas, Syed Farid. *Notes on Various Theories Regarding the
    Islamization of the Malay Indonesia Archipelago*. Kuala Lumpur:
    Dewan Bahasa and Pustaka, 1969.
Amapalavanar, Rajeshwary. *The Indian Minority and Political Change
    in Malaya, 1945–1957*. Kuala Lumpur: Oxford University
    Press, 1981.
Anderson, Colin et al., ed. *Singapore 30: A Portfolio of Singapore's
    Leading Companies*. Singapore: Springham Anderson Design
    Pte. Ltd., 1995.
Anstey, Vera. *The Economic Development of India*. London, reprinted
    in 1957.
Arasaratnam, Sinnappah. *Indians in Malaya and Singapore*. London:
    Oxford University Press, 1970.
———. *Islamic Merchant Communities of the Indian Sub-continent*

in Southeast Asia. Kuala Lumpur: University of Malaya, 1989.

————. *Maritime Trade, Society and European Influence in Southern Asia, 1600–1800*. Collected Studies Series. Hampshire, Vermont, Variorum: Ashgate Publishing Limited, 1995.

Barman, Amrit. *India Fever: The Indian Professional in Singapore*. Book Series 2. Singapore: Singapore Indian Association, 2009.

Barr, Michael D. *Constructing Singapore: Elitism, Ethnicity and the Nation-building Project*. Copenhagen: NIAS Press, 2008.

Bharadwaj, P. *Sindhis Through the Ages*. Hong Kong: World Publishing Company, 1988.

Boivin, Michel. *Sindh through History and Representations: French Contributions to Sindhi Studies*. Karachi: Oxford University Press, 2008.

Bose, Sisir K. and Bose Sugata, eds. *Chalo Delhi: Writings and Speeches, 1943–1945/Subhas Chandra Bose*. Calcutta: Netaji Research Bureau and Delhi, Permanent Black, 2007.

Bose, Sugata. *A Hundred Horizons: The Indian Ocean in the Age of Global Empire*. Cambridge, Massachusetts, London: Harvard University Press, 2006.

Bowman, Larry W. and Ian Clark, eds. *The Indian Ocean in Global Politics*. Boulder, Colorado: Westview Press, 1981.

Brown, Ian. *Economic Change in South-East Asia, c.1830–1980*. New York: Oxford University Press, 1997.

Brown, Rajeswary Ampalavanar. *Capital and Entrepreneurship in South-East Asia*. Houndmills, Basingstoke, Hampshire and London: The Macmillan Press Ltd. and New York, St. Martin's Press, INC., 1994.

Buckley, Charles Burton. *An Anecdotal History of Old Times in Singapore, 1819–1867*. Kuala Lumpur: University of Malaya Press, first published in 1902, reprinted in 1965.

Chan Heng Kong. *Singapore's Political Economy: A Case Study of Social Costs in a Market Economy*. Melbourne: Universal Books, 2005.

Chaudhuri, K.N. *Trade and Civilisation in the Indian Ocean: An Economic History from the Rise of Islam to 1750*. Cambridge, London, New York, New Rochelle, Melbourne, Sydney: Cambridge University Press, 1985.

Chen, Jerome and Nicholas Tarling, eds. *Studies in the Social History of China and Southeast Asia: Essays in Memory of Victor Purcell*. Cambridge, England: Cambridge University Press, 1970.

Chen, Peter S.J., ed. *Singapore: Development Policies and Trends*. Singapore: Oxford University Press, 1983.

Chong Li Choy. *Multinational Business and National Development: Transfer of Managerial Knowhow to Singapore*. Issued under the auspices of ISEAS, Maruzen Asia, 1983.

Christie, Clive J. *A Modern History of South East Asia: Decolonization, Nationalism and Separatism*. London, New York: I.B. Tauris & Co. Ltd. and Singapore, Institute of Southeast Asian Studies, 1996.

Clammer, John. *Race and State in Independent Singapore, 1965–1990: The Cultural Politics of Pluralism in a Multi-ethnic Society*. Aldershot, Brookfield: Ashgate Publishing Ltd., 1998.

———. *Diaspora and Identity: The Sociology of Culture in Southeast Asia*. Subang Jaya: Pelanduk Publications, 2002.

Cowdhury, A. and C. Kirkpatrick. *Industrial Restructuring in a Newly Industrialising Country: The Identification of Priority Industries in Singapore*. U.K.: Department of Economics, University of Manchester 1989.

Dahles, Heidi and Otto Ven den Muijzenberge, eds. *Capital and Knowledge in Asia: Changing Power Relations*. London: Routledge Curzon, 2003.

Dahlman, Carl. *India and the Knowledge Economy: Leveraging Strengths and Opportunities*. The World Bank Institute (WBI) Development Studies. Washington, D.C.: The International Bank for Reconstruction and Development/The World Bank, 2005.

Damodaran, A.K. and U.S. Bajpai, eds. *Indian Foreign Policy: The*

Indira Gandhi Years. London: Sangam Books and New Delhi, Radiant Publishers, 1990.

Damodaran, Harish. *India's New Capitalists: Caste, Business and Industry in a Modern Nation*. New Delhi: Permanent Black, 2006.

David, Maya Khemlani. *The Sindhis of Malaysia: A Socio-Linguistic Study*. London: ASEAN Academic Press, 2001.

Dhoraisingam, Samuel S. *Peranakan Indians of Singapore and Melaka: Indian Babas and Nonyas — Chitty Melaka*. Singapore: Institute of Southeast Asian Studies, 2006.

Dixit, Ramesh. *South East Asia in Indian Policy: Problems of Relationship with a Neighbouring Region*. New Delhi: Radha Publications, 1998.

Drake, P.J. *Currency, Credit and Commerce: Early Growth in Southeast Asia*. Aldershot: Ashgate Publishing, 2004.

Falzon, Mark-Anthony. *Cosmopolitan Connections: The Sindhi Diaspora, 1860–2000*. International Comparative Social Studies. Leiden, Boston: Brill, 2004.

Godfrey, Robert and Samuel Dhoraisingam, eds. *Passage of Indians, 1923–2003*. Singapore: Singapore Indian Association, 2003.

Gomez, Edmund Terence and Michael Hsiao Hsin-Huang, eds. *Chinese Business in Southeast Asia: Contesting Cultural Explanations, Researching Entrepreneurship*. London: Routledge, 2003.

Graham, G.S. *Great Britain in the Indian Ocean: A Study of Maritime Enterprise, 1810–1850*. Oxford: Clarendon Press, 1967.

Hamilton, Gary G. *Asian Business Networks*. Proceedings of the Workshop on Asian Business Networks held from 31 March to 2 April 1998 at the National University of Singapore (NUS). New York: Walter de Gruyter, 1996.

Hiscock, Geoff. *India's Global Wealth Club: The Stunning Rise of its Billionaires and the Secrets of their Success*. Hoboken, N.J.: John Wiley and Sons, 2008.

Ho Khai Leong, ed. *Reforming Corporate Governance in Southeast Asia: Economics, Politics and Regulations*. Singapore: Institute of Southeast Asian Studies, 2005.

Huff, W.G. *The Economic Growth of Singapore: Trade and Development in the Twentieth Century*. Cambridge, New York: Cambridge University Press, 1994.

Jayaram, N. *The Indian Diaspora: Dynamics of Migration*. New Delhi: Sage Publications India Pvt. Ltd., 2004.

Jones, Geoffrey. *Multinationals and Global Capitalism: From the Nineteenth to the Twenty-first Century*. Oxford, New York: Oxford University Press, 2005.

Jumabhoy, Rajabali. *Multiracial Singapore: On to the Nineties*. Revised ed. Singapore: Chopman Publishers, 1990.

Karashima, Noboru, ed. *Ancient and Medieval Commercial Activities in the Indian Ocean: Testimony of Inscriptions and Ceramic-sherds*. Tokyo: Taisho University, 2002.

————, ed. *In Search of Chinese Ceramic-sherds in South India and Sri Lanka*. Tokyo: Taisho University Press, 2004.

Kaur, Amarjit. *International Migration in Malaysia and Singapore since the 1880s: State Policies, Migration Trends and Governance of Migration*. The Fourteenth James C. Jackson Memorial Lecture, 2006. Armidale, New South Wales: University of New England Asia Centre, 2006.

Kaur, Amarjit and Ian Metcalfe, eds. *Mobility, Labour Migration and Border Controls in Asia*. London: Palgrave Macmillan, 2006.

Khilnani, Niranjan M. *New Dimensions of India's Foreign Policy*. New Delhi: Westvill Publishing House, 1995.

Kondapi, C. *Indians Overseas*. New Delhi: Oxford University Press, 1951.

Kudaisya, Medha and Ng Chin-Keong, eds. *Chinese and Indian Business: Historical Antecedents*. Boston: Brill, 2009.

Lai Ah Eng. *Meanings of Multiethnicity: A Case Study of Ethnicity and Ethnic Relations in Singapore*. Kuala Lumpur: Oxford University Press, 1995.

Lal, Brij V. et al., eds. *The Encyclopedia of the Indian Diaspora.* Singapore: Editions Didier Millet in association with the National University of Singapore, 2006.

Lebra, Joyce. *Japanese Trained Armies in Southeast Asia: Independence and Volunteer Forces in World War-II.* Hong Kong: Heinemann, 1977.

———. *Jungle Alliance, Japan and Indian National Army.* Singapore: Donald Moore for Asia Pacific Press, 1971.

Lee Soo Ann. *Industrialisation in Singapore.* Victoria: Longman Australia Pty. Ltd., 1973.

Leifer, Michael. *Singapore's Foreign Policy: Coping with Vulnerability.* London: Routledge, 2000.

———. *Indonesia's Foreign Policy.* London: The Royal Institute of International Affairs, 1983.

Lim Mah Hui. *Ownership and Control of the One Hundred Largest Corporations in Malaysia.* Kuala Lumpur: Oxford University Press, 1981.

Lombard, Denys and Jean Aubin, eds. *Asian Merchants and Businessmen in the Indian Ocean and the China Sea.* New Delhi: Oxford University Press, 2000.

Mackenzie, J.M. *Orientalism: History, Theory and the Arts.* Manchester: Manchester University Press, 1995.

MacLean, Roderick. *A Pattern of Change: The Singapore International Chamber of Commerce from 1837.* Singapore: SICC, Saik Wah Press, 2000.

Madan, Madhu et al. *Singapore Indian Entrepreneurs: Dreams to Reality.* Singapore: Singapore Indian Chamber of Commerce and Industry, 2004.

Majumdar, R.C. *Corporate Life in Ancient India.* 3rd ed. Calcutta: Firma K.L. Mukhopadhyaya, 1969.

———. *Hindu Colonies in the Far East.* 2nd ed. (revised and enlarged). Calcutta: Firma K.L. Mukhopadhyaya, 1973.

Makepeace, Walter et al. *One Hundred Years of Singapore.* Singapore, Oxford, New York: Oxford University Press, 1991.

Markovits, Claude. *The Global World of Indian Merchants, 1750–1947: Traders of Sind from Bukhara to Panama*. Cambridge: Cambridge University Press, 2000.

———. *Merchants, Traders, Entrepreneurs: Indian Business in the Colonial Era*. New Delhi: Permanent Black, 2008.

Mazumdar, Asis Kumar. *South-east Asia in Indian Foreign Policy: A Study of India's Relations with South-east Asian Countries from 1962–1982*. Calcutta: Naya Prokash, 1982.

Mishra, Kashi Prasad. *Studies in Indian Foreign Policy*. Delhi: Vikas Publications, 1969.

Mookerji, Radha Kumud. *Indian Shipping: A History of the Sea-borne Trade and Maritime Activity of the Indians from the Earliest Times*. 2nd ed. London: Orient Longmans, 1957.

Mookherji, Sudhansu Bimal. *Southeast Asia: A Study of Socio-Economic, Political and Cultural Problems and Prospects*. Calcutta: Post-Graduate Book Mart, 1966.

Nanda, B.R., ed. *Indian Foreign Policy: The Nehru Years*. Delhi: Vikas Publishing House, 1976.

Nafziger, E. Wayne. *Entrepreneurship, Equity, and Economic Development*. Contemporary Studies in Economic and Financial Analysis, vol. 53. Greenwich, Connecticut, London: Jai Press Inc., 1986.

Panikkar, K.M. *India and the Indian Ocean: An Essay on the Influence of Sea Power on Indian History*. Bombay: First Indian reprint by George Allen & Unwin (India) Private Limited, 1971.

Pillai, K. Raman. *Indian Foreign Policy in the 1990s*. New Delhi: Sangam Books, 1997.

Pugalenthi Sr. *Indian Pioneers of Singapore*. Singapore: VJ Times International Pte. Ltd., 1998.

Purfield, Catriona and Jerald Schiff, eds. *India Goes Global: Its Expanding Role in the World Economy*. Washington, D.C.: International Monetary Fund, 2006.

PuruShotam, Nirmala Srirekam. *Negotiating Language, Constructing*

Race, Disciplining Difference in Singapore. Berlin, New York: Mouton de Gruyter, 1998.

Rae, Ian and Morgan Witzel. *The Overseas Chinese of Southeast Asia: History, Culture and Business*. Houndmills, Basingstoke, N.Y., Hampshire: Palgrave Macmillan, 2008.

Reeves, Peter and Rajesh Rai, eds. *The South Asian Diaspora: Transnational Networks and Changing Identities*. London, New York: Routledge, 2008.

Reimenschnitter, Andrea and Deborah L. Madsen, eds. *Diasporic Histories: Cultural Archives of Chinese Transnationalism*. Hong Kong: Hong Kong University Press, 2009.

Rohwer, Jim. Asia *Rising: How History's Biggest Middle Class will Change the World*. Singapore: Butterworth-Heinemann Asia, 1995.

Rudner, David West. *Caste and Capitalism in Colonial India: The Nattukottai Chettiars*. Berkeley, Los Angeles, Oxford: University of California Press, 1994.

Sabade, B.R. and M.V. Namjoshi. *Chambers of Commerce and Trade Associations in India*. Poona: Shubhada-Saraswat, 1977.

Sandhu, K.S. *Indians in Malaya: Some Aspects of their Immigration and Settlement (1786–1957)*. London: Cambridge University Press, 1969.

Sandhu, K.S. and A. Mani, eds. *Indian Communities in Southeast Asia*. 2nd ed. Singapore: Institute of Southeast Asian Studies, 2006.

Sankaran, Chitra and S.P. Thinappan, eds. *Tamil in an International Arena 2002: First Step*. The Conference Proceedings. Singapore: NUS Press, 2004.

Sanyal, Sanjeev. *The Indian Renaissance: India's Rise after a Thousand Years of Decline*. Singapore, New Jersey, London: World Scientific Publishing Co. Pte. Ltd., 2008.

Sardesai, D.R. *British Trade and Expansion in South East Asia, 1830–1914*. Bombay: Allied Publishers Private Ltd., 1977.

Sen, Tansen. *Buddhism, Diplomacy and Trade: The Realignment of*

Sino-Indian Relations, 600–1400. Honolulu: University of Hawaii Press, 2003.

Sharma, Kavita A., Adesh Pal, and Tapas Chakrabarti, eds. *Theorizing and Critiquing Indian Diaspora*. Creative New Literatures Series-64. New Delhi: Creative Books, 2004.

Siddique, Sharon and Nirmala Puru Shotam. *Singapore's Little India: Past, Present and Future*. Singapore: Institute of Southeast Asian Studies, 1982.

Singh, Gurmukh. *The Rise of Sikhs Abroad*. New Delhi: Rupa & Co., 2003.

Singh, I.J. Bahadur, ed. *Indians in Southeast Asia*. New Delhi: India International Centre, 1982.

Sinha, Atish and Madhup Mohta, eds. *Indian Foreign Policy: Challenges and Opportunities*. New Delhi: Academic Foundation, 2007.

Tan Tai Yong. *Singapore Khalsa Association*. 2nd ed. Singapore: Published for the Association by Marshall Cavendish International (Asia) Pte. Ltd., 2006.

Tan Tarn How, ed. *Singapore Perspectives 2007: A New Singapore*. Singapore: World Scientific Publishing Co. Pte. Ltd., 2007.

Thapar, Anita Raina. *Sindhi Diaspora in Manila, Hong Kong and Jakarta*. Quezon City: Ateneo de Manila University Press, 2002.

Thapar, Romila. *A History of India: From the Discovery of India to 1526*. Vol. I. London: Penguin Books, 1966.

Tipton, Frank B. *Asian Firms: History, Institutions and Management*. Massachusetts: Edward Elgar Publishing Inc., 2007.

Turnbull, C.M. *A History of Singapore, 1819–1988*. 2nd ed. Singapore: Oxford University Press, 1989.

———. *The Straits Settlements, 1826–67: Indian Presidency to Crown Colony*. London: The Athlone Press, 1972.

Vasil, Raj. *Asianising Singapore: The PAP's Management of Ethnicity*. Singapore: Heinemann Asia, 1995.

Veeramani, A., ed. *Our History in Singapore* (in Tamil). Tenth

Singapore Tamil Youth Conference Proceedings, The Tamil Youth's Club, 1999.

Vella, Walter F., ed. *The Indianized States of Southeast Asia by Coedes*. Honolulu: East West Centre Press, 1968.

Vente, Rolf E. and Peter S.J. Chen, eds. *Culture and Industrialization: An Asian Dilemma*. Institut für Asienkunde (Hamburg, Germany). Singapore, London: Published for the Institute of Asian Affairs by Tata McGraw-Hill, 1980.

Visscher, Sikko. *Business, Ethnicity and State: The Representational Relationship of the Singapore Chinese Chamber of Commerce and the State, 1945–1997*. Amsterdam: Academisch Proefschrift, Vrije Universiteit Amsterdam, 2002.

————. *The Business of Politics and Ethnicity: A History of the Singapore Chinese Chamber of Commerce and Industry*. Singapore: NUS Press and Leiden, International Institute for Asian Studies, 2007.

Walker, Anthony R., ed. *New Place, Old Ways: Essays on Indian Society and Culture in Modern Singapore*. New Delhi: Hindustan Publishing Corporation, 1994.

Walling, R.N. *Singapura Sorrows*. Singapore: Malaya Publishing House, 1931.

Wang Gungwu, ed. *Nation-Building: Five Southeast Asian Histories*. History of Nation-Building Series. Singapore: Institute of Southeast Asian Studies, 2005.

Webster, Anthony. *Gentlemen Capitalists: British Imperialism in South East Asia, 1770–1890*. New York: I.B. Tauris, 1998.

White, Nicholas J. *Business, Government and the End of Empire: Malaya, 1942–1957*. New York: Oxford University Press, 1996.

Wilson, Rob and Wimal Dissanayake, eds. *Global/Local: Cultural Production and Transnational Imaginary*. Durham, NC: Duke University Press, 1996.

Yadav, Surya Narain, ed. *Journey of Overseas Indians: Labour to Investor*. Vol. I. New Delhi: Global Vision Publishing House, 2005.

Yahya, Faizal bin. *Economic Cooperation between Singapore and India: An Alliance in the Making?* Routledge Studies in the Growth Economies of Asia. Abingdon, New York: Routledge, 2008.

―――. *New "Temples" of India, Singapore and India Collaboration in Information Technology Parks.* Social Sciences in Asia, vol. 21. Leidon, Boson: Koninklijke Brill NV, 2008.

Yeoh, Brenda S.A. *Contesting Space in Colonial Singapore: Power Relations and the Built Environment.* Singapore: Singapore University Press, 2003.

Yong Mun Cheong and Rao V.V. Bhanoji, eds. *Singapore-India Relations: A Primer.* Singapore: Singapore University Press, 1995.

Articles and Reports

Abraham, George. "Indians in South-East Asia and the Singapore Experience". A paper presented at the International Conference on "Contribution by People of Indian Origin (PIO) in the Development of the Countries of their Adoption". Indian Council for International Cooperation, New Delhi, 12–13 February 2000.

Asher, M.G. and S. Srivastava. "India and the Asian Economic Community". RIS Discussion Paper no. 51. New Delhi, 2003.

Awanohara, Susumu. "A Home for Genuine Effort". *Far Eastern Economic Review*, 23 November 1979, pp. 39–40.

Bell, David E. and Mary Shelman. "Olam International". Case-Study for the Harvard Business School, N9-509-002, 16 December 2008.

Chadha, Alka. "CECA Implementation: A First Look". ISAS Working Paper no. 9, Singapore, 7 February 2006.

Cohen, Robin. "Diasporas and the Nation-state: From Victims to Challengers". *International Affairs* 72, no. 3 (July 1996): 507–20.

Das, Sanchita Basu and Rahul Sen. "Singapore-India CECA: Rationale, Overview and Implications". In *Investors' Guide to India-Singapore Comprehensive Economic Cooperation Agreement*, edited by Mohan Pillay. Singapore: Reed Elsevier (Singapore), Private Limited, 2005, pp. 24–42.

Gaur, Seema. "Indian Professional Workers in Singapore". In *Mobility, Labour, Migration and Border Controls in Asia*, edited by Amarjit Kaur and Ian Metcalfe. London: Palgrave Macmillan, 2006, pp. 193–210.

Jain, Ravindra K. "Culture and Class in Indian Diaspora: India vs Bharat". *Economic and Political Weekly* 36, no. 17 (28 April– 4 May 2001): 1380–81.

Jayawardena, Chandra. "Migration and Social Change: A Survey of Indian Communities Overseas". *Geographical Review* 58, no. 3 (July 1968): 426–49.

Lamb, Helen B. "The Indian Business Communities and the Evolution of an Industrialist Class". *Pacific Affairs* 28, no. 2 (June 1955): 101–16.

Mani, A. "Indians in Jakarta". In *Indian Communities in Southeast Asia*, edited by K.S. Sandhu and A. Mani. Singapore: Institute of Southeast Asian Studies and Times Academic Press, 1993, pp. 98–130.

Mehta, Makrand. "Gujarati Business Communities in East African Diaspora: Major Historical Trends". *Economic and Political Weekly* 36, no. 20 (19–25 May 2001): 1738–47.

Mehta, Rajesh. "Economic Cooperation between India and Singapore: A Feasibility Study". RIS Discussion Paper no. 41. New Delhi, 2003.

Miller, Michael B. "The Business Trip: Maritime Networks in the Twentieth Century". Published by the President and Fellows of Harvard College. *The Business History Review* 77, no. 1 (Spring 2003): 1–32.

Mukunthan, Michael. "Rajabali Jumabhoy". NLB, <http://infopedia.nl.sg/articles/SIP_859_2004-12-27.htm>.

Palit, Amitendu. "India-Singapore Trade Relations". ISAS Working Paper no. 46, 16 June 2008.

Randhawa, Dipinder S. "Agrocorp International Pte. Ltd.". In *Best Practices, Experiences of Successful Local Enterprises*. Singapore: Productivity and Quality Research Centre, Faculty of Business Administration, National University of Singapore (NUS), 2000, pp. 97–103.

Rauch, James E. "Business and Social Networks in International Trade". *Journal of Economic Literature* 39, no. 4 (December 2001): 1177–203.

Raut, L.N. "Monsoon Wind and Maritime Trade: A Case Study of Historical Evidence from Orissa, India". *Current Science* 90, no. 6 (25 March 2006): 864–71.

Ray, Rajat Kanta. "Asian Capital in the Age of European Domination: The Rise of the Bazaar, 1800–1914". *Modern Asian Studies* 29, no. 3 (1995): 449–554.

Sandhu, K.S. "Some Aspects of Indian Settlement in Singapore, 1819–1969". *Journal of Southeast Asian History* 10, no. 2 (September 1969): 193–201.

———. "Indian Immigration and Settlement in Singapore". In *Indian Communities in Southeast Asia*, edited by K.S. Sandhu and A. Mani. Singapore: Institute of Southeast Asian Studies and Times Academic Press, 1993, pp. 774–87.

Sangaralingam, M. "The Role of Tamils in the Development of Singapore". In *Our History in Singapore* (in Tamil), edited by A. Veeramani. Tenth Singapore Tamil Youth Conference Proceedings. Singapore: The Tamil Youth's Club, 1999.

Schrader Heiko. "A Comprehensive Analysis of Chettiar Finance in Colonial Asia". Working Paper no. 208. Germany: Faculty of Sociology, University of Bielefeld, 1994.

Sen, Rahul. "The India-Singapore Comprehensive Economic Cooperation Agreement: A Good Beginning Towards an Enduring Relationship". *ASEAN Economic Bulletin*, vol. 20, no. 2 (August 2003): 179–83.

Shekhar, Vibhanshu. "India-Singapore Relations: An Overview". *IPCS Special Report* no. 41, June 2007.

Singh, Yogendra. "India-Singapore CECA Enters Second Phase". *IPCS*, Article no. 2481, 31 January 2008, <http://www.ipcs. org/printWhatsnew.jsp?action=showView&kValue=2481&s tatus=article> (accessed 29 December 2008).

Suryaprakash, Rakhee. "Singapore-India Relations: CECA and Beyond". *SAAG*, Paper no. 1493, 10 August 2005, <http:// www.southasiaanalysis.org/%5Cpapers15%5Cpaper1493. html> (accessed 5 July 2008).

Tambiah, Stanley J. "Transnational Movements, Diaspora, and Multiple Modernities". *Daedalus* 129, no. 1 (Winter 2000): 163–94.

Tan, Eugene K.B. "The Lion Engages the Dragon and the Elephant: Singapore as a Knowledge Arbitrageur in a New Asia". *Journal of Asian Business* 22/23, issue 2/3/1 (2006/07): 81–101.

Tan Wee-Liang and Siew Tong Fock. "Coping with Growth Transitions: The Case of Chinese Family Businesses in Singapore". *Family Business Review* 14, no. 2 (2001): 123–39.

Thomas, Jayan Jose. "India-Singapore CECA: A Step Towards Asian Integration?" *ISAS Insights*, no. 6, 5 September 2005.

Vertovec, Steven. "Conceiving and Researching Transnationalism". *Ethnic and Racial Studies* 22, no. 2 (March 1999): 447–62.

Yeoh, Brenda S.A. "Singapore: Hungry for Foreign Workers at all Skill Levels". Table 2, <http://www.migrationinformation. org/Profiles/display.cfm?ID=570> (accessed 2 December 2008).

Zook, Chris and James Allen. "Growth Outside the Core". *Harvard Business Review*, December 2003, pp. 1–8.

Unpublished theses and other works

Chia, Kel-li. "A Study of Ethnic Based Networking in the Singapore Indian Business Community: From Traders to Merchants".

B.A. (honours) thesis, Department of History, National University of Singapore (NUS), 2001/2002.

Fakhri, S.M. Abdul Khader. "'Mobility of Tradition' and Framework Building for the Study of Transnational Indian Communities: The Story of Tamil Migration to and the Dravidian Movement in Southeast Asia". CAS Research Paper Series no. 35. CAS, NUS, 2001.

Ibrahim, Syed Mohamed Baquir bin Md. "The Tamil Muslim Community in Singapore". Academic Exercise, Department of Social Work, University of Singapore, December 1973.

Izzuddin, Mustafa. "A Muslim Gujarati Community in Singapore: Dawoodi Bohras". Term Essay, The Civilization of India and Contemporary Indian Communities guided by Dr Gyanesh Kudaisya, South Asian Studies Programme (SASP), Faculty of Arts and Social Sciences (FASS), National University of Singapore (NUS), 5 November 2002.

Kalaivani d/o Kanagasundram. "The Indian Diaspora in Singapore: The Politics of Sameness and Difference". Academic Exercise, Department of Geography, Faculty of Arts and Social Sciences (FASS), National University of Singapore (NUS), 2003.

Kaur, Nirmaljeet. "Indians in Multiracial Singapore, 1945–1980: A History of Occupational Pattern". Academic Exercise, Department of History, Faculty of Arts and Social Sciences (FASS), National University of Singapore (NUS), 1983.

Lim Fung Ming, Kevin. "Post War Economic Recovery of Singapore, 1945–1949: The Case of Commerce". B.A. honours thesis, Department of History, National University of Singapore (NUS), 1989/90.

Loh Wen Fong. "The Singapore Houses of Agency, 1819–1900". B.A. (Hons) Academic Exercise, Department of History, University of Malaya in Singapore, 1958.

Mani, A. "The Changing Caste Structure Amongst the Singapore Indians". M.A. thesis, Department of Sociology, University of Singapore, 1977.

Mullaiselvi K. "The Singapore Indian Chamber of Commerce, 1935–1980". B.A. (Hons) Academic Exercise, National University of Singapore (NUS), 1989.

Nayagam, Francis. "'Little India': A Study of Mutual Help and Community Structure in Lower Serangoon Road Area". Academic Exercise, Department of Social Work and Social Administration, University of Singapore, 1970.

Ru Tiang Xiang. "Talking about 'Caste' in the Diaspora: Views from the Old and New Indian Diaspora in Singapore". Academic Exercise, Department of Sociology, Faculty of Arts and Social Sciences (FASS), National University of Singapore (NUS), 2007.

Singh, Neeta Devi Dharam P. "The Life of Rajabali Jumabhoy: A Pioneer Kutchee Khoja Immigrant in Singapore". B.A. honours thesis, Department of History, Faculty of Arts and Social Sciences (FASS), National University of Singapore (NUS), 1995/96.

Singh, Ravinder. "Migrants to Merchants: Dynamics of Sikh Entrepreneurship in Singapore". Unpublished thesis, Department of Sociology, National University of Singapore (NUS), 1998/99.

INDEX

taking over father's business,
102
Ranchoddas Purushottamdas
Limited, 42
Rao, Narasimha, 147
Ray, Rajat Kanta, 5
Red Sea, 3
Redington, 266, 267
Regional Headquarters Award, 170
religious and social practices,
conservatism, 30
Report of the High Level
Committee on the Indian
diaspora, 72
Report of the Straits Settlements
Trade Commission, 31
Restaurant Association of
Singapore, 232
restaurants, Race Course Road,
106
Rise of Asia, 9, 314
Robinson Road, 32
Roman Empire, maritime trade, 3
Rose & Co., 118
Rowell Road, 26
Royal Brothers Building, 111,
134
Royal Brothers Group, 110, 111
Royal Sporting House, 117
R.P. & Sons Pte. Ltd., 81
Rupee Room, 175

S
Sabeer Bhatia, 178
sago flour, sago seeds, 40

Saigon, imports from, 65
Salaries Commission, 215
Sandhu, K.S., 55, 127
Sanskritization, 177
Saravana Vilas, 105
Satyam Computers, 162, 163,
168
Savant Infocomm, 120, 167, 179
Savour, 232
Scindhia Steam Navigation Co.
Ltd., 68
Scott Holdings, 111
Scotts Shopping Centre, 111
Second World War, outbreak,
214
security guards
Punjabis, 50
Sikh, 29
Selegie Road, 26, 87
Sembawang Engineers and
Constructors Limited, 162
sepoys, East India Company, 28
Serangoon Merchant's
Association, 231, 233
Serangoon Road, 26, 32, 34, 55,
56, 57, 58, 76, 86, 87, 100,
101, 102, 103, 105, 106,
108, 121, 122, 124, 184,
230, 231, 257, 275
business structure, 56
commercial viability, 108
heart of South Indian business
community, 105
jewellery, 104
Little India, 55

ABOUT THE AUTHOR

Jayati Bhattacharya is a Visiting Research Fellow at the Nalanda-Sriwijaya Centre, Institute of Southeast Asian Studies (ISEAS) in Singapore with research interests in business history and diaspora studies in South and Southeast Asia in the modern period. She is currently the coordinator of the project on Comparative Diasporas at the Centre. Dr Bhattacharya has received her Ph.D. from the Jawaharlal Nehru University, New Delhi. She was awarded a Junior Research Fellowship by the Jawaharlal Nehru Memorial Fund, New Delhi and a scholarship by the Indian Council of Historical Research (ICHR), New Delhi to pursue doctoral studies. Dr Bhattacharya has teaching experience as Lecturer in Loreto College, Darjeeling, India and as a Guest Lecturer at Qingdao University, People's Republic of China. She has also contributed articles on business history in the colonial period of Bengal. Her forthcoming publications include Jayati Bhattacharya and Coonoor Kripalani Thadani, eds., *Indian and Chinese Immigrant Communities: Comparative Perspectives* (tentative title), (forthcoming); Oliver Pye and Jayati Bhattacharya, eds., *The Palm Oil Controversy in Transnational Perspective* (forthcoming).